Studying the Life
of Saint Clare
# of Assisi

Studying the Life of Saint Clare of Assisi

A Beginner's Workbook

By William R. Hugo, OFM Cap.
&
Joanne Schatzlein, OSF

New City Press
Hyde Park, New York

William Hugo belongs to the Midwest Capuchin Province of St. Joseph (USA). He holds an M.A. degree in Franciscan Studies from the Franciscan Institute (1983) at St. Bonaventure University. He ministered in initial formation and vocation promotion for thirty-eight years, while teaching the life and writings of Francis of Assisi. Hugo currently directs his province's International Collaboration Office and ministers in the Father Solanus Casey Center in Detroit.

Joanne Schatzlein is a member of The Sisters of St. Francis of Assisi in Milwaukee and holds an M.A. degree in Franciscan Studies from the Franciscan Institute (1984) at St. Bonaventure University. She ministered as a registered nurse and served in congregational leadership. Schatzlein currently works as liaison to congregationally sponsored ministries and leads pilgrimages to Rome and Assisi.

Unless otherwise noted, citations from the writings of Francis and Clare of Assisi come from Armstrong, Regis J., ed. and trans. *Clare of Assisi: Early Documents (The Lady)*. Second Revised Edition. New York: New City Press, 2006. Armstrong, Regis J., J. A. Wayne Hellmann, and William J. Short, eds. *Francis of Assisi: Early Documents*. Volume I: The Saint; Volume II: The Founder; Volume III: The Prophet; Index. New York: New City Press, 1999, 2000, 2001, 2002. Used with permission.

Published in the United States by New City Press
202 Comforter Blvd., Hyde Park, NY 12538
www.newcitypress.com

©2019 William R. Hugo and Joanne Schatzlein

Cover design by Leandro de Leon
Cover art by Dr. Terrence J. Riddell. Used with permission.

Library of Congress Cataloging-in-Publication Data
Hugo, William.
Studying the life of Saint Clare of Assisi: a beginner's workbook / by William Hugo and Joanne Schatzlein.
p. cm.   2019938360

Includes bibliographical references and index.
ISBN 978-1-56548-691-1 (pbk. : alk. paper)
BX3602.3.H84 2011271'.302—dc

Printed in the United States of America

Contents

Tools

Work

Abbreviations and Editions

We use abbreviations as close as possible to those used in Regis Armstrong's *Clare of Assisi: Early Documents* (CA:ED). This helps the beginning student use the workbook and that collection of primary sources with ease. Occasionally, this leads us to use abbreviations that don't match our description of a work. For example, Cardinal Ugolino can also be identified as Cardinal Hugolino, Cardinal Ugo, or Cardinal Hugo. We use Cardinal Ugolino but accept the abbreviation used in CA:ED for his *Form of Life*: FLHug. Other examples will occur.

The Writings Of Clare Of Assisi

BlCl	*The Blessing of Clare* (CA:ED 66-67)
FLCl	*The Form of Life of Clare of Assisi* a.k.a. *The Rule of Clare* (CA:ED 108-126)
1LAg	*The First Letter to Agnes of Prague* (CA:ED 43-46)
2LAg	*The Second Letter to Agnes of Prague* (CA:ED 47-49)
3LAg	*The Third Letter to Agnes of Prague* (CA:ED 50-53)
4LAg	*The Fourth Letter to Agnes of Prague* (CA:ED 54-58)
TestCl	*The Testament of Clare* (CA:ED 60-65)

The Writings of Francis of Assisi

Adm	*The Admonitions* (FA:ED I 128-137)
BlL	*A Blessing for Brother Leo* (FA:ED I 112)
CtExh	*The Canticle of Exhortation to Saint Clare and Her Sisters* (FA:ED I 115; CA:ED 394)
CtC	*The Canticle of the Creatures* (FA:ED I 113-114; CA:ED 392)
ER	*The Earlier Rule* (FA:ED I 63-86)
FLFr	*The Form of Life* given to Clare of Assisi by Francis of Assisi (FLCl VI 3; CA:ED 118)
Last Will	*Last Will Written for the Poor Ladies* (FLCl VI: 7-9; CA:ED 118)
1LCus	*The First Letter to the Custodians* (FA:ED I 56-57)
1LF	*The Letter to the Faithful* (first version) (FA:ED I 41-44)
2LF	*The Letter to the Faithful* (second version) (FA:ED I 45-51)
LMin	*A Letter to a Minister* (FA:ED I 97-98)
LOrd	*A Letter to the Entire Order* (FA:ED I 116-121)

LR	*The Later Rule* (FA:ED I 99-106)
RH	*The Rule for Hermitages* (FA:ED I 61-62)
Test	*The Testament* of Francis of Assisi (FA:ED I 124-127)

Other First Franciscan Century Sources

1C	*The Life of St. Francis* by Thomas of Celano (FA:ED I 180-308)
1.5C	*Life of Our Blessed Father Francis.* This work was recently discovered. The only English Translation is found in Jacques Dalarun's *The Rediscovered Life of St. Francis of Assisi: Thomas of Celano.* Trans. Timothy J. Johnson. St. Bonaventure NY: Franciscan Institute Publications, 2016. The text was written by Thomas of Celano between 1232-1239.
2C	*The Remembrance of the Desire of a Soul* by Thomas of Celano (FA:ED II 239-393)
2MP	*The Mirror of Perfection* (Sabatier Edition) (FA:ED II 253-372)
AC	*The Assisi Compilation* (FA:ED II 118-230)
AP	*The Anonymous of Perugia* (FA:ED II 34-58)
BC	The Bull of Clare's Canonization entitled *Clara claris praeclara* (CA:ED 263-271)
FLHug	*The Form of Life* given by Cardinal Ugolino (CA:ED 75-85)
FLInn	*The Form of Life* given by Pope Innocent IV (CA:ED 89-105)
Jordan	*The Chronicle of Brother Jordan of Giano* (Chronicles 3-77, selections)
L3C	*The Legend of the Three Companions* (FA:ED II 66-110)
LCl	*The Prose Legend of Saint Clare* by Thomas of Celano (CA:ED 277-329)
LEr	Clare's doubtful *Letter to Ermentrude of Bruges* (CA:ED 420-421)
LJS	*The Life of Saint Francis* by Julian of Speyer (FA:ED I 368-420)
LMj	*The Major Legend of St. Francis* by Bonaventure of Bagnoregio (FA:ED II 525-649)
LRay	The Letter of Cardinal Rainaldo *Matribus sororibus* (CA:ED 133-134)
PC	*The Acts of the Process of Canonization* for Clare of Assisi (CA:ED 141-196)
PrPov	*The Privilege of Poverty* by Gregory IX (CA:ED 87-88)
VL	*The Versified Legend* (CA:ED 199-261)

English Editions of Franciscan Sources and Workbook

CA:ED   Armstrong, Regis J., ed. and trans. *Clare of Assisi: Early Documents (The Lady)*. Second Revised Edition. New York: New City Press, 2006. Even though Downing provides a translation of all the writings of Clare based on the most recent critical editions, we regularly reference CA:ED in this workbook because it is a single volume that contains the majority of sources needed to do our worksheets.

Earlier editions include:

New York: Paulist, 1988. (First Edition)
Saint Bonaventure NY: Franciscan Institute Publications, 1993. (Second Edition)

Chronicles Hermann, Placid, trans. and ed. *XIIIth Century Chronicles: Jordan of Giano, Thomas of Eccleston, Salimbene degli Adami*. Chicago: Franciscan Herald Press, 1961.

Downing Downing, Frances Teresa, ed., trans. and notes. *Saint Clare of Assisi: The Original Writings*. Vol. 1. Phoenix AZ: Tau Publishing, 2012. Includes the latest reliable Latin critical editions of all Clare's writings with an English translation. Readers may prefer to use Downing's version of Clare's writings because of this. Simply note that we provide page numbers for CA:ED because it contains a greater number of sources in a single volume, which may be a more economical purchase for beginning students.

FA:ED   Armstrong, Regis J., J. A. Wayne Hellmann, and William J. Short, eds. *Francis of Assisi: Early Documents*. Volume I: The Saint; Volume II: The Founder; Volume III: The Prophet; Index. New York: New City Press, 1999, 2000, 2001, 2002. References in this workbook begin with "FA:ED" which is followed by a Roman numeral indicating the volume and then Arabic numbers indicating the pages.

Workbook I   Hugo, William R. *Studying the Life of Saint Francis of Assisi: A Beginner's Workbook*. Second edition. New York: New City Press, 2011.

Critical Editions

(A critical edition is the most authoritative version of a document in its original language. Critical editions are important because before the printing press (c. 1450 by Johannes Gutenberg) many errors and changes were introduced into texts by their copyists. While all translations vary in their value, it is always important that they be based on the best and likely the most recent critical edition.)

Becker, Marie-France, Jean-François Godet, and Thaddée Matura, eds. *Claire d'Assise, Écrits*. Paris: Les Editions du Cerf, 1985. This collection of the writings of Clare of Assisi contains the best critical editions of her *Testament* and *Blessing*, and her doubtful *Letter to Ermentrude*. Frances Teresa Downing uses these three critical editions in her translation, *Saint Clare of Assisi: The Original Writings*, 2012. This French edition contains critical editions of other documents that have more recent editions elsewhere.

Boccali, Giovanni M., ed. *Legende minores latine sancte Clare virginis Assisiensis: testi latini con traduzione italiana a fronte*. Santa Maria degli Angeli (Perugia): Edizioni Porziuncola, 2008. A critical edition of the *Versified Legend of the Virgin Clare*.

—. *Santa Chiara di Assisi. I primi documenti ufficiali: Lettera di annunzio della sua morte, Processo e Bolla di canonizzazione*. Santa Maria degli Angeli (Perugia): Edizioni Porziuncola, 2002. Includes critical editions of the *Acts of the Process of Canonization*, the papal bull of Clare's canonization (*Clara claris praeclara*), and the notification of her death.

—. *Legenda latina Sanctae Clarae Virginis Assisiensis*. Assisi: Edizioni Porziuncola, 2001. Considered the best critical edition of the *Prose Legend of St. Clare*. Contains an Italian translation by Marino Bigaroni.

Chiara de Assisi. *Lettere ad Agnese: La vision dello specchio*. Eds. Giovanni Pozzi and Beatrice Rima. Milan: Adelphi Edizioni, 1999. Considered the most recent critical edition of Clare's four known letters to Agnes of Prague. Frances Teresa Downing uses this critical edition of Clare's four letters to Agnes of Prague (c. 1211-1282) in her translation, *Saint Clare of Assisi: The Original Writings*, 2012.

Downing, Frances Teresa, ed., trans., and notes. *Saint Clare of Assisi: The Original Writings*. Vol. 1. Phoenix AZ: Tau Publishing, 2012. Includes the latest reliable Latin critical editions of Clare's writings with English translations.

Federazione S. Chiara di Assisi delle Clarisse di Umbria-Sardegna: Sinossi Cromatica. *Chiara de Assisi e le Sue Fonti Legislative*. Vol. 1. Padova: Edizioni Messaggero, 2003. Frances Teresa Downing uses this critical edition of Clare's *Form of Life* (1252) in her translation, *Saint Clare of Assisi: The Original Writings*, 2012.

Chronology

1181 or 1182	Francis of Assisi (d. 1226) was born.
1193 or 1194	Clare of Assisi (d. 1253) was born.
1198	The emerging new classes including merchants revolted in Assisi and established a commune.
1199-1205	Possible years during which Clare and others of the Offreduccio family sought refuge in Perugia.
1202	The Battle of Collestrada between Assisi and Perugia. Francis was imprisoned by Perugia.
1206	After his trial before Bishop Guido I of Assisi (c. 1195-1212), Francis began his life of penance and separated from his blood family.
1209	Pope Innocent III (1198-1216) gave verbal approval to Francis's *Form of Life* that incrementally developed into his *Rule*.
1210-1211	Clare met with Francis to discuss her vocation.
1211	Clare left her family home on Palm Sunday to begin her religious life, spending time at San Paolo Monastery and then Sant'Angelo before settling at San Damiano Monastery.
1215	Lateran Council IV
1215	Clare accepted the title of "abbess" at Francis's insistence.
1219	Cardinal Ugolino (c. 1145 or before 1170 – 1241) completed his *Form of Life* that supplemented the *Rule of St. Benedict* for a new group of female monasteries in central and northern Italy called the "Order of the Poor Ladies of the Valley of Spoleto or of Tuscany." This was the first independent order of women in the Roman Church and the first women's order directly under the papacy rather than a bishop. It spread to other parts of Europe.

1219-1220	Francis was in the Middle East.
1220	Cardinal Ugolino spent Holy Week at San Damiano Monastery in Assisi and wrote a very emotional letter to Clare describing the effect on him.
1221	Francis's *Earlier Rule*.
1223	The Franciscans' *Later Rule* was approved by Pope Honorius III (1216-1227).
1224	Clare experienced a deterioration of health.
1225	The Friars Minor arrived in Prague.
1226, Oct. 3	Francis of Assisi died.
1227, March 19	Cardinal Ugolino dei Conti di Segni was elected Pope Gregory IX (1227-1241).
1228, July 16	Gregory IX canonized Francis of Assisi.
1228	Gregory IX visited Clare at San Damiano and likely argued with her over the difficulties of sustaining a monastery practicing total and radical poverty.
1228, Aug. 18	Cardinal Rainaldo dei Conti di Segni (1199 or not before 1185 – 1261) issued *Matribus sororibus*, which announced that he had been appointed cardinal protector of 24 female monasteries in central and northern Italy. This was the first known time the order founded by Ugolino (now Pope Gregory IX) as the "Order of the Poor Ladies of the Valley of Spoleto or of Tuscany," was called the "Order of St. Damian." This is the first evidence that San Damiano Monastery in Assisi was considered part of this order. It is listed first among the other monasteries.
1228, Sept. 17	Gregory IX granted the *Privilege of Poverty* to San Damiano Monastery in Assisi in the papal bull *Sicut manifestum est*.
1230	Gregory IX issued *Quo elongati* in which he required Friars Minor to receive papal approval to enter the convents of nuns including those of the San Damiano observance. Perceiving this as a threat to her Franciscan

identity, Clare initiated what amounted to a hunger strike. Gregory relented.

1234	Agnes of Prague established St. Francis Monastery in Prague.
1234	Clare's *First Letter to Agnes of Prague*
1235-1238	Clare's *Second Letter to Agnes of Prague*
1237, April 14	With *Omnipotens Deus*, Gregory IX separated St. Francis Hospice in Prague from the monastery of the same name. This allowed St. Francis Monastery to practice the same radical poverty as that of San Damiano in Assisi.
1238	Clare's *Third Letter to Agnes of Prague*
1238, April 15	Gregory IX extended the Privilege of Poverty to St. Francis Monastery in Prague with *Pia credulitate tenentes*.
1238, May 11	Gregory IX denied the request of Agnes of Prague for her own rule with *Angelis gaudium*.
1240	Mercenaries attacked San Damiano Monastery. Clare's prayers warded them off.
1241	Assisi was freed from the imperial forces.
1241, Aug. 22	Gregory IX died, followed by the 17-day reign of Celestine IV (1241).
1243, June 25	Innocent IV (1243-1254) was elected pope.
1247, Aug. 6	Innocent IV issued his own *Form of Life* for the Order of St. Damian with his papal bull *Cum omnis vera religio*.
1252, Sept. 16	Cardinal Rainaldo approved Clare's own *Form of Life* with his letter *Quia vos*.
1253	Clare's *Fourth Letter to Agnes of Prague*
1253, Aug. 9	After visiting Clare, Innocent IV reaffirmed Rainaldo's *Quia vos* and gave Clare's own *Form of Life* papal approval with *Solet annuere*, not to be confused with the earlier papal bull of Honorius III with the same name that approved Francis's *Later Rule* in 1223.

1253, Aug. 11	Clare died.
1254, Dec. 12	Cardinal Rainaldo dei Conti di Segni was elected Pope Alexander IV (1254-1261).
1255	Alexander IV canonized Clare of Assisi at Anagni.
1260	The sisters at San Damiano Monastery moved to the new Proto-Monastery inside Assisi's walls.
1263	Pope Urban IV issued yet another *Form of Life* for the Order of St. Damian which he called for the first time the "Order of St. Clare."

PRELIMINARIES

Introductory Comments

In 1996, William Hugo published the first edition of *Studying the Life of Saint Francis of Assisi: A Beginner's Workbook* (Franciscan Press). A revised edition that harmonized the workbook with the new *Francis of Assisi: Early Documents* (FA:ED) was published in 2011 (New City Press). The goal of the workbook was to help beginning students of Francis of Assisi accomplish a guided and informed study with the critical use of primary sources. The success of the workbook is visible in its use around the English-speaking world, especially in initial formation programs of the three Franciscan Orders.

Since the publication of the first workbook, both of us have spent considerable time studying the life and writings of Clare of Assisi. This forced us to also study the wider development of female religious life in 13th-century Europe. Our combined efforts are found in this second workbook.

It is providential that early attempts to complete a workbook on Clare of Assisi failed because there has been an explosion of learning about Clare, the various female religious movements that surrounded her, other women equally inspired by Francis, and those who were not particularly attached to Francis. Some of this work began in preparation for the 800th anniversary of the birth of Clare (1993-94). In addition, many lay and secular authors rose to prominence in the study of Clare and the movements around her. Freer from typical biases associated with members of the Franciscan community, these researchers imagined new interpretations of the primary sources available to us.

These authors are responsible for a new awareness that Clare did not found what would be called the Order of St. Clare for the first time by Pope Urban IV (1263). They identified the crucial role of Cardinal Ugolino, later Pope Gregory IX, in founding a new order that he tied to San Damiano Monastery in Assisi for branding and public relations purposes. In light of their research, many old assumptions are called into question and new narratives are required.

The new state of scholarship presents new challenges for a beginners' workbook on Clare's life and writings. It's a complicated study that involves more than the expected primary sources. Thus, this workbook offers much more additional commentary than the workbook on Francis of Assisi did.

With all of this in mind, we explain a number of technical points that affect this workbook.

Many different names are used to describe the followers of Clare of Assisi or those assumed to be her followers: Sisters Minor, Poor Sisters, Poor Ladies, Minoresses, Damianites, Order of St. Damian, Clarisses, Order of St. Clare, Cloistered Women, Poor Women, Poor Enclosed Ladies, Ugolinian Sisters, Enclosed Poor of San Damiano and others. Some of these terms are more descriptions than titles. Despite the great variation of names, we are able to count Clare referring to herself and her followers as "Poor Sisters" more than sixty times in her writings (see FLCl I 1 for the official designation by Clare). In this workbook, we favor use of this name as well.

The names of men who eventually became popes can also be confusing. Cardinal Ugolino became Pope Gregory IX. Cardinal Rainaldo became Pope Alexander IV. We generally use the name of a person that was current at the moment we are describing. So, when he was the legate of Pope Honorius III we refer to Ugolino dei Conti di Segni, not Gregory IX. Referring to his *Form of Life* can be more challenging. Because it was written when he was a cardinal, we typically refer to it as Ugolino's *Form of Life*, unless the context is best served by referring to Pope Gregory IX.

We acknowledge that there is a lot of repetition in this workbook. That is because it is a workbook. Our experience teaches us that students using the workbook seldom read it from start to finish. Instead, they utilize parts of the workbook that help them complete assignments, answer questions or investigate interests. Thus, we repeat information so that individual sections or chapters can stand alone. For beginning students who do read the workbook from start to finish, we believe the repetition helps them master complex names, dates and events. It takes time to digest this enormous material.

Our intended audience is beginners who want to study the life and writings of Clare of Assisi with primary sources in a critical way. While our goal is to bring the best scholarship to the benefit of the beginner, we have striven to shape our workbook in a way that will most benefit English-speaking readers. Thus, we typically focus on English language bibliography and only mention other language sources when they represent something of great importance, e.g., a critical edition or a work containing seminal ideas. We recognize the enormous role of *Greyfriars Review*, which for twenty years provided translations of important works that otherwise would be inaccessible to English-speakers. Its translations fill our bibliographies.

The scholarly world has its own set of standards for scholarly publication. These include ample footnotes of various types. Because we aim our workbook at the beginner, we do not include footnotes. If a point is valuable to our reader, we include that information in the text itself. If reference to a source is valuable, we note it in a parenthetical note that refers to the cited or suggested reading list at the end of the chapter. Commonly accepted statements among scholars are not documented. However, we typically make parenthetical references when divergent opinions exist on a given point.

Terminology can be confusing on several fronts in this study. The first involves the use of the terms *form of life* and *rule*. Authors and readers are accustomed to using the term *rule* to describe the fundamental code governing a religious way of life. Clare typically talked about her fundamental code as her *form of life*. In an attempt to be sensitive to her own terminology, scholars have increasingly used *form of life* to describe every governing code for San Damiano Monastery beginning with the short and simple code given by Francis of Assisi. A few scholars continue to call these codes *rules*. We will use *form of life* to describe all these codes through Clare's own *Form of Life*.

However, scholars do not typically use *form of life* for a fundamental code after Clare's. Thus, we will use the term *rule* to describe the document given by Pope Urban IV (1263) and the two versions of a fundamental code written by Isabelle of France (1259 and 1263). There is nothing magical about these choices. They are simply choices.

There also can be great confusion around terms involving *San Damiano*. Let us explain.

It is historically clear that Cardinal Ugolino formed the first religious order specifically for women after he was appointed papal legate in central and northern Italy. On August 18, 1228, Cardinal Rainaldo dei Conti di Segni issued the letter *Matribus sororibus* to twenty-four female monasteries announcing that he had been appointed Ugolino's successor legate after Ugolino had been elected Pope Gregory IX. For the first time, we see in this letter the new order of Ugolino called the "Order of St. Damian" instead of the "Order of the Poor Ladies of the Valley of Spoleto or of Tuscany." The letter places San Damiano Monastery in Assisi at the top of the list of member monasteries.

This can be quite confusing because Clare and her Sisters at San Damiano Monastery were often doing things differently than the other monasteries in the Order of St. Damian. So, we have chosen to include "monastery" and the Italian version of "St. Damian" in the title of that specific foundation in Assisi led by Clare, i.e., San Damiano Monastery. When we are talking about the wider order founded by Cardinal Ugolino, we will use the saint's name in English and preface it with "Order," i.e., "Order of St. Damian."

Another decision involves how to refer to St. Francis Hospice in Prague. *Hospice, hospital, hotel,* and *hospitality* all have the same Latin root. Perhaps the English word *hospitality* best approaches that root. Thus, in its broadest meaning, a medieval hospice could provide hospitality to pilgrims and travelers (our idea of a hostel). In other uses, it meant a place caring for the dying or lepers (our idea of hospice care), or providing medical treatment to the sick (our idea of a hospital). We use *hospice* throughout this workbook to refer to St. Francis Hospice in Prague, but realize different designations are also appropriate.

There are many papal bulls that affected the Franciscan movement during the time of Clare. Various cardinals likewise issued letters of importance. While they affect many areas of study in this workbook, their greatest impact is visible in the letters of Clare to Agnes of Prague. To avoid repetition, we have created a list of such documents in chronological order with a short description in the chapter "Clare's Letters to Agnes of Prague."

The first time we mention a name of particular interest, we parenthetically indicate the time in which she or he lived. When appropriate, popes and civil rulers are marked by the span of their years in office. If a precise date is uncertain, we use the abbreviation "c." for *circa* meaning *about.* For example, "(d. c. 1270)" would mean the person died *about* 1270 and no further precision is possible.

Many users of Workbook I tell us that chapters in the preliminary section of that workbook were important in establishing helpful attitudes toward studying medieval texts. This caused us to pause when considering what to include in the preliminary section of this workbook. In the end, we chose to duplicate some of the material from Workbook I because we cannot presume that users of this workbook also have Workbook I in hand. Those who already have used Workbook I might consider skipping these chapters, though a review seldom hurts anyone.

Every enormous enterprise has many collaborators. In a special way, Capuchin novices at San Lorenzo Novitiate in Santa Ynez, California, helped by using early drafts of this workbook in their own study of Clare. Their many comments had a huge impact on the final text, and they were the guinea pigs who demonstrated that the method of this workbook could work.

Many scholars and professionals provided incalculable help in a variety of ways. They include Jean-François Godet-Calogeras of the Franciscan Institute at St. Bonaventure University; Michael Blastic, formerly of the Franciscan Institute and currently on the Franciscan novitiate staff at Old Mission Santa Barbara, California; Catherine M. Mooney of Boston

College; Frances Teresa Downing from the Poor Clare Monastery in St. Leonards on Sea, England; and Gary Brandl of New City Press. Baudry Metangmo provided translation assistance. Helmut Rakowski helped to locate German language sources.

Joanne Schatzlein and William Hugo

What Do I Need Besides This Workbook?

This is a workbook. Its purpose is to teach students to study the life and writings of Clare of Assisi with primary sources, i.e., those that come from the time and place of Clare and those around her. That implies that a student using this workbook will also need other books or sources. However, there is no definitive list of other sources that you will need. Few beginning students will have them all. So, the next question becomes, "what are the most important sources to have at hand?" We list them in order of importance, noting how important each source is. The full citations of many sources are found in the "Abbreviations and Editions" chapter of this workbook.

- *Clare of Assisi: Early Documents* (CA:ED) has gone through three editions. It was a labor of love for Regis Armstrong, its translator and editor. The third edition is the most available today. It's also the most valuable because it reflects the ongoing research of the day. However, even the third edition is a bit outdated. It was published in 2006 when so much groundbreaking research was reaching the printing press. Despite that, it is the single most important book for students to have along with this workbook. While some of the history surrounding Clare has been revised, the texts in translation are what students need close by. It is true that new critical editions of some sources are available. However, the translations in CA:ED will serve the beginning student just fine. No other single volume will contain as many sources for the study of Clare.

- *Francis of Assisi: Early Documents* (FA:ED) comes in three volumes plus an independent volume of indices. It is the next important source to have, especially volume one which contains the writings of Francis of Assisi. The writings of Francis and some of the hagiography about him have important relationships with the writings and life of Clare of Assisi. This is the second most important source to have at your side. While a study of Clare is possible without this collection, such a study would be quite limited.

- William's original workbook, *Studying the Life of St. Francis of Assisi: A Beginner's Workbook* (Workbook I), is referenced frequently in this workbook on Clare. However, having it is less important than the previous two sources.

- Frances Teresa Downing's *Saint Clare of Assisi: The Original Writings* (Downing) is the only English translation based on the best and most recent critical editions of the various writings. Her translations are elegant and nuanced. Her notes, introductions and commentaries expand our understanding of the translations. If you can have this volume close at hand, you are working with the best translations of Clare's writings. However, it is a collection of only the writings of Clare. None of the hagiography or other important documents cited in our workbook are found within it. Thus, it's not the most complete collection of sources for our students. This is why we still recommend CA:ED for the student who can afford only so many books. By the way, Downing's other three volumes in the same series are quite valuable. We will suggest them in various worksheets.

- Many of our chapters contain a section entitled, *"Cited sources and suggested reading."* These documents are too numerous to expect a beginner to have. Their primary value is to the person who has a particular interest in the topic of one of the worksheets. Most good university or college libraries will have many of them. Others are still in print or available through used bookstores.

Know *Your* Biases;
Know *Our* Biases

A hallmark of our approach to studying Clare of Assisi is to gather as much objective data about her as possible. We wish to know the historical Clare as well as we can. All other images of her (theological, spiritual, symbolic) should be based on good history.

Despite this goal, we are powerfully aware of how biased all of us are. *Bias* carries many connotations that we wish to clarify. Certainly, the word can imply a negative prejudice that might even lead to sin. Racial bias can be the unjust basis for racial discrimination. Sexism, ageism, and racism are all evils grounded upon biases.

People are also biased in favor of certain things. When watching an NFL football game that doesn't involve our favorite teams, we usually root for the underdog. That reflects a bias.

Our lives are full of biases, most of which we are unaware. They are frequently subconscious and usually unreflected upon. We don't have the mental or emotional energy to deal with all our biases. Yet at certain times it becomes critical to reflect upon them.

Biases shape perspective. Perspective helps us to recognize some realities and ignore others. Getting in touch with your biases gets you in touch with your partiality, preferences and prejudices. You become aware of your attitudes about how you think life is and, just as importantly, how you think life *should* be. What you think makes the world "go round" is partly the result of your biases. Is it love, money, power, or some other force in life?

People of faith, theologians, popes, atheists and historians are all people with biases. They and we are no different from the rest of our race. We draw out this point because many people hold the bias that some people *are not biased*. This is a difficult bias to dispel, especially if the bias involves religious belief. For example, some people believe popes are not biased because they are inspired by God's spirit. However, popes are people; they are biased. Some think saints could do no wrong. Otherwise they wouldn't be saints. Since bias is too often construed as a weakness or imperfection, they often consider saints to have been unbiased. However, saints were people; they were biased. Others view scholars as people devoted to objective truth. Since bias is not objective, scholars, at least good scholars, cannot be biased. However, scholars are people; they are biased. Teresa of Calcutta, Pope Francis, the Dalai Lama, and Aristotle all are or were biased. They are or were human beings.

That is important for our study of Clare of Assisi; she too was biased. In fact, her bias should be an object of our study of Clare.

More importantly, you are biased, and so are we. If we are to benefit from this study of Clare's life, it is critical that we are aware of our own and each other's biases. Teachers should reveal their important biases to their students. This is only fair. It's a little like truth in lending. People should know up front what they are getting into, whether the commodity is financial or intellectual. The real importance of this practice is that it leaves the students *free*. They should be free to decide for themselves, to evaluate the soundness of arguments, and to know how their teachers' biases might shape their approach to the information they share.

When teachers share their biases, students are forced to examine their own. Which biases are the important ones to reveal? The answer is different for each of us. Different biases influence each person's ideas and approaches more than others. The biases that critically shape your thinking are the important ones to become aware of, understand, examine, and reveal. It's a process that never ends.

Frankly, it's a process that excites us. This self-discovery is as important as the information we learn through study. In the end, it will help us learn about Clare of Assisi as much as reading medieval stories.

Our Lens: History

As long as we are talking about biases, we need to reveal one more. We prefer to study Clare of Assisi from a historical perspective.

Scholars study Clare using the lenses of a variety of disciplines. Church people tend to use the disciplines of theology, philosophy, spirituality, and history to study Clare. Others have studied her through art history. A surprising number of secular scholars study Clare's writings and hagiography as pieces of literature.

For our purposes, we take an unequivocally historical approach in this workbook. We have several reasons for this choice.

Our first reason lies in the nature of hagiography, which we will discuss in a few chapters. Hagiography is writing that has a heavy emphasis on *interpreting* the saints. As we will see, this image or interpretation of the saint is more important than the facts about the saint.

There is nothing wrong with simply studying these interpretations if one is willing to accept medieval interpretations as adequate for today. We don't, so, we strive to uncover as much historically reliable information about Clare as we can. Once we have done that, we need to interpret Clare again, hopefully in meaningful terms for us living 800 years after her birth.

Medieval hagiography mythologized Clare. (We use *mythologize* in a positive way.) Some describe the process of stripping away that mythology as *demythologizing*. If we want to continue with the pattern, the final step might be called *remythologizing*. All this myth-talk highlights an important factor: the myth or interpretation of Clare is just as important as the history of Clare.

We seldom know historical figures as they really were (historically). We more commonly know them through images, a few characteristics, or a solitary action for which they are famous. Actually, the same is true about modern people we know only through the media. Consider how the "handlers" of a presidential candidate work to shape our image of the candidate. Their job is to create a favorable myth or interpretation of their candidate to win votes. The truth is not as important as what people believe is true. Of course, there are limits to the handlers' abilities. Sometimes a candidate's record is so obvious that the desired image will not stick. Handlers also work to create negative images of their opponents, often with tremendous success. The frequent result is competing images in conflict. Nonetheless, the truth is that we come to know these people through their images.

Further, these myths or interpretations change with time and circumstances. When we were children, Christopher Columbus was an indisputable hero for white, middle-class America. However, by 1992, the 500th anniversary of his arrival in the Western Hemisphere, many judged his halo to be significantly tarnished. Our childhood classmates and we viewed the advent of Europeans as a blessing for America. By 1992, we were much more aware of the suffering caused to Native Americans as a result of advancing European "civilization." What happened? The myth changed. The basic facts of the story remained the same. A few newly discovered facts were added. Many known facts that were not publicized or never connected with Columbus were attached to his story.

In the end, the Columbus myth changed. We also should expect his myth to change again. We will discover a few new facts. However, more probably, we will put the known facts together in another different way. We are bound to do that as other concerns shape our perspective.

Still, unless we know the facts, adequate reinterpretations have difficulty emerging. That is why our preferred approach to Clare of Assisi is through history. In the end, our perspectives will forcefully shape our interpretations of Clare. However, our hope is that our myths or interpretations will be informed by accurate history: the facts as best we can know them. We don't need to feel sinister about this process. Many medieval people already did it for themselves. While we can learn from their interpretations, we are not obliged to accept them hook, line and sinker. In fact, we are wise to examine their interpretations closely. What was adequate for Anglo school children in the 1960's to believe about Columbus was not adequate for the children of 1992. Nor should we think what was adequate for medieval people to believe about Clare is adequate for us today.

Undoubtedly, we will experience disagreements about the historical Clare. That's okay. Professionals in every field disagree about major issues in their disciplines. However, awareness of our differences will sensitize us and make us more cautious. More importantly, we will be surprised at how much we agree upon.

There is another level for agreement and disagreement that this book will not focus on: What can we say about the shape of Franciscan life today? Still, we wrote this book to help you answer that very question. The fact is we cannot answer it for you because there is no one correct answer. Suffice it to say that unless we get our history down, it is futile to talk about the meaning of Franciscan life today.

Suggested reading

- Sheldrake, Philip. *Spirituality and History: Questions of Interpretation and Method*. New York: Crossroad, 1992. An excellent, readable summary of recent changes in approaches to history (chapter one), the history of spirituality (chapter two), the disciplinary interchange between history and spirituality (chapters three and four), case studies containing Franciscan subject matter (chapters five and six), and hermeneutics or the theory of interpreting texts (chapter seven).

Our Method:
Work with the Tools and Ask Questions

Our teaching goal is to help students discover Clare's life and writings. That's why we have written a workbook and not a historical narrative. We don't believe discovery comes easily. It usually involves a great deal of work. We give you the tools to do first-class work.

So, there are three parts to this workbook. Besides talking about various attitudes that affect a critical study of Clare in this preliminary section, we also provide information about various pre-Franciscan movements and common aspects of medieval female religious life. This is information that otherwise would be difficult for you to obtain. Thus, we provide it in summary fashion. This section gives important background information for what is to follow.

In the second section, we give you the tools to do the work presented later in this workbook. First, we help readers to understand medieval hagiography, the form or genre of most sources for Clare's life. Then, we help students learn about each of the sources for Clare's life, discovering their biases and perspectives.

In these first two sections, it's our job to impart information to you. Study it well. Read and reread each chapter. Take notes comparing one source to the others. Come back to this section even after you have begun your own work in the final section. Relearn what you have already forgotten. This is important material. If you are a group leader, you may want to learn this material beforehand and present it in lecture style. Always allow your group to ask questions and compare the various sources.

The final work section belongs to you, our students. That section systematically goes through the life of Clare. We don't tell you the story; you have to discover it. Our part is to provide you with the sources, the places where you can find your information. You must read, examine, analyze, and compare them. Use all the tools you received in the previous sections. Become critical and produce your best effort to discover something about the historical Clare.

Questions are so important to the process. That's why we believe this process is best done in groups. More minds think of more questions. No one of us can ask all the questions to get all the angles on a topic we study. The group enriches the process. Don't be afraid to have others question your assumptions or work. Furthermore, don't be afraid to question the assumptions and work of others in your group. If we don't ask questions of each other, we might as well disband as a study group. An important resource (each other's critical approach) will be squandered in our timidity. Questions make the process more valuable and interesting.

Begin with a Question:
What Don't I Like About Clare of Assisi?

We know it's an unusual place to begin. After all, we're studying the life of someone we presume you admire. Actually, that's where the problem lies.

- "Love is blind." That's why jurors have difficulty believing the testimony of the accused's spouse.

- Children frequently think they are responsible for their parents' divorce. They have difficulty understanding that their parents are responsible.

- Every four years, people in the United States of America hear campaign managers for presidential candidates tell them how their nominee slaughtered the other during a televised debate. No one expects them to be honest. Nevertheless, the country must go through the ritual of asking them.

Admiration makes it difficult for human beings to be objective and honest in their judgments. We expect objectivity and honesty in others, but find them difficult to cultivate in ourselves. Yet, we believe our study of Clare will promise valuable results only in proportion to our objectivity and honesty.

Year after year, we ask our students to think quietly for two minutes and then tell us "What don't you like about Clare of Assisi?" It frequently amazes us that about half of the students are unable to give an answer. A few announce, "Nothing!" Others are confused by the question and sheepishly confess, "I don't know." Still others answer a different question. "I couldn't live as poor as she did." "I don't understand why she fasted so severely." "It must have hurt her to abandon her family."

Why are such negative recognitions important? Because Clare of Assisi is a canonized saint of the Roman Church. Too often, people put saints on a pedestal level with God. Most will deny that is what they are doing, but that attitude seeps out in the way they talk about their saints. If anything negative can be said, it usually is about the person before conversion, when limitations and sinfulness make for a more dramatic conversion to holiness. It's the "playboy to priest" syndrome that so ably applies to Francis of Assisi.

It's also an illusion. If we want to meet the historical Clare or Francis, we have to meet their limitations. If we don't, we will preoccupy ourselves with something that is not human and of doubtful help in our own lives. It's difficult to identify with the indestructible hero, the flawless leader, or the sinless saint. We're none of those things and never will be.

Aside from the unhelpfulness of the *perfect* model, it simply isn't a historical portrayal of Clare or any human being. When we can say something negative about Clare, we have broken through a mental barrier, which allows us to be as objective and honest as we possibly can.

"I think Clare abused her body with her physical penances." "Clare's poverty was impossible to live." "I suspect Clare was part of a dysfunctional family." "Clare was not tolerant of people who opposed her."

Whether or not these judgments are true is not important at this early stage. We can test their accuracy later. However, those students who were able to say them jumped one more hurdle, which allowed them to study Clare from new perspectives. We are also happy to say that their boldness helped others to admit their own reservations about her.

Another of our biases is emerging: when saints are seen as human beings they become understandable, imitable, and, most importantly, approachable.

Take some time to answer the question for yourself: What don't you like about Clare of Assisi?

Positive Criticism

Yes, criticism can be positive. In fact, God save us from people who cannot give positive criticism of others or themselves. Without the presence of positive criticism, going to doctors, riding space shuttles, acting on investment advice from one's stock broker, and being on trial before a judge are all dangerous enterprises. We wish people in these situations good luck, because luck is all they have to lean on.

In many situations, we use *critical* to describe negative attitudes, contrary opinions, faultfinding people, or unfavorable judgments. This is not the type of criticism we propose for studying Clare. *Critical* can also mean doing the best job possible, using the finest tools and methods available, or making informed and discriminating judgments. This is the positive criticism we absolutely need for a helpful and modern study of Clare's life and writings.

Any study of Clare of Assisi must begin with some very old *medieval* sources. Medieval people typically had very different thoughts and values than we have. The rules for public writing were different from our own. If we want to understand the historical Clare, we need to understand the world and thoughts of the medieval people who wrote about her and created the first images that interpreted her importance.

The alternative is to read those medieval documents according to our assumptions for modern writing. This would be *uncritical*; we would not be using the finest tools and methods available for us to make informed judgments about what Clare was really like.

The use of positive criticism is not new to scholars in the church. Perhaps the most familiar use of positive criticism is in scripture studies. Bible scholars have used a variety of techniques aimed at understanding various aspects of the ancient writings that compose our Bible. They call these techniques criticisms, and use of the techniques helps scholars understand the various levels of interpretation going on in the text.

Form criticism seeks to understand the genre of a document. Once a genre is determined, the scholar can use its rules of composition to better understand what the author is trying to say. Sci-fi (science fiction) is a genre. One of its basic rules is that it is fiction. On the other hand, biographies are supposed to be historically accurate. Uncritical aficionados of *Star Wars* could believe the series is a "historical" biography about Luke Skywalker. That would be a gross misunderstanding. People who understand the difference in the genres are critical; those who don't understand are uncritical.

Scripture scholars identify the forms or genres of liturgical rituals, royal coronations, proverbs and creation stories in the scriptures. Identifying and understanding the genres help understand the meaning of the text. Most of the medieval writings about Clare of Assisi were hagiography. If we want to understand Clare of Assisi, we have to understand this genre through which her story and meaning are transmitted to our age. This is being critical, and we will examine this genre later in a chapter on hagiography.

There are numerous other types of criticism made famous by scripture scholars. Redaction criticism looks at the goals and biases of the person who gave a writing with a long tradition its final form. A particular book or section of the scripture may have developed over centuries, accumulating the thoughts of many authors along the way. The final editor or redactor had the advantage of selecting and rejecting the accumulated material. She or he could shape the material to reflect her or his point of view and discredit others. Stories about Clare of Assisi likewise have an organic life. They grew with time. We are lucky to possess copies of many stories at several points in their development so we can discover the biases and goals of their redactors. This is being critical.

All literature is created in a historical environment: political, social, economic, military, religious, etc. Knowledge of that environment reveals the subtleties of literature. Applying that knowledge to a piece of literature is called historical criticism. It attempts to determine what really happened.

Knowing something about ancient Egypt helps to understand the Book of Exodus. Understanding industrializing England helps one enjoy the novels of Charles Dickens. The same is true of studying Clare of Assisi. The stories all make more sense if we know something about medieval feudalism, the meaning of money, the existing forms of religious life, the inter-city wars of the Italian Peninsula, and emerging new classes.

Our first point is this: positive criticism helps us to understand the text as it was meant to be understood. It reveals the truth hidden from us by our ignorance of another time and place. Criticism prevents us from being fooled by the tricks and slyness of the time-span that separates us from the text we are reading.

Our second point follows: criticism is a friend not to be avoided. It requires us to be questioning, suspicious, and astute. However, it can also open up a world of wonder, warmth, conviction and spirit. Most importantly, it strives to understand the truth. What we do with the truth we discover is quite another question.

Don't be afraid of positive criticism. If you want to meet the historical Clare, learn the tools of criticism well and practice them. Make criticism an attitude when you pick up the stories about this remarkable woman. You will discover a lot, and what you learn will be interesting and enlightening.

Suggested reading

It is difficult to find a short yet helpful book on critical tools for studying medieval hagiography. Our best sources may be books about biblical criticism. Not all of their tools may apply, but an understanding of biblical techniques will take us a long way in developing the critical attitude that can help us discover the historical Clare. We recommend the following books.

- Bartlett, Robert. *Why Can the Dead Do Such Great Things? Saints and Worshippers from the Martyrs to the Reformation.* Princeton: Princeton University Press, 2013.

- Boadt, Lawrence. *Reading the Old Testament: An Introduction.* Revised and updated by Richard Clifford and Daniel Harrington. New York: Paulist Press, 2012. The first four chapters of this lengthy book describe tools used to understand scripture. What follows demonstrates how essential understanding a text's time and place is to understanding the text itself.

- Davies, Stevan L. *New Testament Fundamentals.* Rev. ed. Sonoma CA: Polebridge Press, 1994.

- Gillingham, Susan E. *One Bible, Many Voices: Different Approaches to Biblical Studies.* Grand Rapids MI: Eerdmans, 1998.

- Gorman, Michael J. *Elements of Biblical Exegesis: A Basic Guide for Students and Ministers.* Peabody MA: Hendrickson, 2001.

- Harrington, Daniel J. *Interpreting the New Testament: A Practical Guide.* New Testament Message 1. Wilmington: Glazier, 1979. This work focuses on New Testament issues of interpretation and uses examples from the New Testament. Its core ideas are similar to those in *Interpreting the Old Testament.*

- —. *Interpreting the Old Testament: A Practical Guide.* Old Testament Message 1. Wilmington: Glazier, 1981. This work focuses on

Old Testament issues of interpretation and uses examples from the Old Testament. Its core ideas are similar to those in *Interpreting the New Testament.*

- Sheldrake, Philip. *Spirituality and History: Questions of Interpretation and Method.* New York: Crossroads, 1992.

- Vauchez, André. *Sainthood in the Later Middle Ages.* Trans. Jean Birrell. Cambridge: Cambridge University Press, 1997.

- Weinstein, Donald and Rudolph M. Bell. *Saints and Society: The Two Worlds of Western Christendom, 1000-1700.* Chicago: University of Chicago Press, 1983.

Pre-Franciscan Movements

Introduction

Francis and Clare of Assisi lived in a church and world that were dynamic, transforming, and adjusting. This was occurring at a variety of levels, including the incorporation of new social classes, change from a feudal barter-economy to a fledgling capitalistic money economy, movement from rural areas to new cities, and new pastoral needs emerging from these situations. The changes were building on developments spanning centuries.

In the midst of these developments, new religious movements reacted to the established monastic movement in a variety of ways. Three that are important for understanding the Franciscan movement are the penitential movement, the evangelical movement, and the apostolic life movement. In fact, these were not distinct movements. The lines between them were blurry as each shared many characteristics with the others. Further, these were movements, not organizations. There were no card-carrying-members.

While the new movements shared some qualities in common, historians use these and other labels to look at the characteristics from different perspectives. Thus, historians can understand individuals like Francis and Clare of Assisi as people influenced by any number of trends or movements.

Both the Secular Franciscan Order (1978) and Third Order Regular (1982) recently wrote new rules approved by the Vatican. The preparation for these rules produced a great amount of research about the religious and spiritual movements that predated the Franciscans. The Franciscan Federation in the United States of America was particularly active in this task and published many of the documents found in the bibliography at the end of this chapter. While their work focused on the experience of the Third Order Regular, its fruit benefited all Franciscans whose manner of life grew out of the same fertile soil. We examine these three new movements after first considering the monastic status quo.

The Monastic Movement

Christian monasticism emerged primarily in the Middle East as the martyrdom of early Christians was waning. Its first practitioners were generally hermits who lived a solitary life, particularly in the desert. These were typically ascetics who left populated areas in part to flee the distractions of the world and to work on a spiritual life that promoted the values found in the Hebrew and Christian Scriptures. Some were recluses in towns. Because they typically lived alone or in seclusion, they were called monks, a word coming from the Greek *monos* meaning alone. As their numbers increased, some began to live together, frequently writing and observing a rule to guide their common lives. Famous early rules include those of Anthony the Abbot (251-356), Pachomius (c. 292–348) and Basil (330-379). It is worth mentioning Augustine of Hippo (354-430) because he wrote a rule for monks and nuns in North Africa that had tremendous influence in the medieval West.

The Life of St. Anthony by Athanasius (296-373) generated considerable interest in monastic life in the West. In France, Martin of Tours (c. 316 or 336 –397) and Honoratus of Marseilles (350-429) established important monastic traditions. However, the practice of coenobitical monasticism (living together in a monastery) was popularized in the West principally through John Cassian (c. 360 – c. 435) whose male and female monasteries in southern France boasted of over 5,000 members. Benedict of Nursia (480-547) was arguably the most important monastic founder in the West. His *Rule* enjoyed a preeminent place in western monasticism in part because Charlemagne (742-814) encouraged its use as a way to further the unification of his empire. Thus, it is not surprising that Cardinal Ugolino and Pope Innocent IV used Benedict's *Rule* as the basis for their own forms of life given to women in central and northern Italy during the time of Clare of Assisi. They also shared Charlemagne's opinion that a common monastic observance united monks and nuns, and provided for more efficient centralized oversight.

Caesarius of Arles (c. 468 – 542) is particularly important for readers of this workbook because he wrote a rule for female religious in 513 mandating strict enclosure of nuns. Its importance was visible in the fact that many bishops used his rule as a guide for religious women in their own dioceses. This spread his plan over large areas of Europe. However, the pluriformity of female religious life was also visible in the fact that Caesarius's strict cloister modified over time. This becomes important in our study of Clare because, during Clare's religious life, Pope Honorius III and Cardinal Ugolino reestablished the strict cloister for women (see Makowski for a detailed study of female enclosure). It's an element Clare accepted from monasticism without much commentary.

Moving beyond the founding figures of Christian monasticism, it is useful to briefly describe some of its perennial characteristics. Flourishing after the period of the early Christian martyrs, monasticism can be viewed as a replacement of that martyrdom. Without martyrdom, Christians searching for a radical way to express their discipleship of Jesus increasingly turned to the hermitical life in the desert or the monastic life in more populated areas. These forms of life demonstrated their total devotion to Christ and their consequent rejection of the distractions of the world. The desert was a palpable destination to this end. The remote monastery was the most available substitute in the West and other places. Intense prayer manifested the desire to be totally with Christ. Liturgy of the Hours sanctified the entire day. Manual work filled in the other moments of the day, protecting the monk or nun's imagination from worldly distractions. The Benedictine motto ably proclaimed the marriage of these two values: *ora et labora* (prayer and work).

As already mentioned, the cloister became especially important as a sign of closeness to Christ by marginalizing the outside world. For both men and women, it symbolized a pure focus on Christ. Regarding female religious, it took on the added objective to physically protect them from violent or sexual attack. In those long centuries that viewed women as the weaker sex, the female cloister also fulfilled the goal of protecting male religious from the "uncontrollable" sexual impulses of female religious. Fasting was a similar ascetical practice aimed at developing and manifesting a total focus on Christ. Its rigors were also considered proof that nuns were serious about their call to religious life. Pope Gregory IX was particularly strong on this perspective during the lifetime of Clare of Assisi.

Evangelical poverty was a more complicated characteristic of medieval religious life. Originally, it was a natural consequence of the choice to flee into the desert or remove oneself to a remote monastery. However, as time progressed, certain monasteries attracted considerable wealth. Sometimes, the wealth came through the rich families of noble men and women who joined the monasteries. In many cases, aristocratic children of rich families founded monasteries. Monasteries also grew in wealth when lay people made contributions as reparation for sin. These gifts often took the form of land, which subsequently generated considerable rents for the monastery. Though the prevalent monastic rules insisted on the individual poverty of monks and nuns, they usually allowed for corporate ownership by the monastery itself. These lines blurred when wealthy nuns brought their servants with them to the monastery (see Pennington for a short summary of monastic history and spirituality).

Many of these positive values are visible in the life of Clare of Assisi and others attracted to her style of life. These women had little choice but to include them in their lifestyle. However, their lifestyle also included innovations that manifested dissatisfaction with the shortcomings of monasticism in the 12th and 13th centuries. At the top of that list would be the inability of monasticism to address the growing spiritual desires of people in the new social classes of Europe. Traditional monastic practices like fasting, celibacy and poverty were shifting from mostly ascetical values to ways of participating in the saving work of the poor and humble Christ visible in his Incarnation and Passion. Enclosure grew less important than spiritual association with like-minded people, a development very visible in Clare's desire to have a strong relationship with the Friars Minor.

An increasing number of lay people sought tangible ways of expressing their deep spiritual aspirations. The Church of the day and the status quo of religious life were largely incapable of addressing many of their desires. This created an environment ripe for change in religious life. The variety of new experimental forms of religious life seemed endless. Sometimes, the Church ignored these new expressions, thinking they would go away. However, once their presence grew in importance, the Church frequently tried to crush them, hoping to maintain the status quo that many church leaders understood. Pope Innocent III in the early 13th century stands out as one hoping to harness the energy of these new groups by giving them papal approval and direction. His policies allowed for the appearance of Francis and Clare of Assisi.

The remainder of this chapter explores three of the new movements of the day. Like all cultural shifts, they took elements from tradition while transforming them. The sustaining viability of monasticism is clear from the fact that it remains today. The push toward reform is clear in the explosion of these new movements and especially the mendicant movement of the day.

The Penitential Movement

Both Clare and Francis of Assisi described themselves and their followers as people "doing penance." In the famous first three lines of his *Testament*, Francis described his conversion in terms of penance, "The Lord gave me, Brother Francis, thus to begin doing penance..." (Test 1). His experience with lepers was at the core of his conversion, and it turned Francis away from one way of life and toward another until he eventually "...left the world" (Test 3). Thus, Francis viewed his conversion as the beginning of a life doing penance. This is confirmed later in his *Testament* when he admonished friars who were not welcomed in a certain location to move elsewhere where they could "do penance" with the blessing of God (Test 26).

His *Earlier Rule* also understands conversion as the beginning of "doing penance." In chapter 12, Francis gave guidelines for the friars' interactions with women interested in religious life. He admonished the friars not to receive any woman into obedience. Instead, they should give sound spiritual advice, and then "...let her do penance wherever she wants" (ER XII 4). Again, Francis describes "doing penance" as a way of life flowing from conversion. This passage witnesses that Francis saw the same pattern for men and women. Thus, we can conclude that he viewed Clare's community at San Damiano Monastery in the same light.

Later in the same version of his *Rule*, Francis offered a model exhortation that any friar could deliver in public. In it, the preacher admonished the listeners to "...do penance, performing worthy fruits of penance..." (ER XXI 3). He concluded, "Blessed are those who die in penance, for they shall be in the kingdom of heaven. Woe to those who do not die in penance, for they shall be children of the devil whose works they do and they shall go into everlasting fire. Beware of and abstain from every evil and persevere in good till the end" (ER XXII 7-9). These texts do not describe "doing penance" as a succession of ascetical acts. Rather, they understand penance in an expansive way that is a manner of life. It's a life-orientation that moves one away from sin and toward the "kingdom of heaven," which is evident in the fruits flowing from such a life.

This same kind of language is used in chapter 23, which is a celebration of God's work of salvation actualized in the lives of those who do penance. In this passage, Francis equated those who "have not done penance" with those who "have not known" God the Father. Those who do know God the Father, serve him "in penance" and receive the kingdom (ER XXIII 4).

Later in the same chapter and speaking for the others, Francis noted that all the Friars Minor exhorted everyone who wished to serve the Lord to "persevere...in penance" (ER XXIII 7). It specifically mentions "penitents" in a long list of men and women comprising the Church, its various ministries and forms of life, and social categories defining people of the day. Thus, "penitents" and "doing penance" were terms Francis used to describe a way of life founded in conversion and focused on living the Gospel over a lifetime.

Moving beyond Francis's *Rule* and *Testament*, it is important to consider the two versions of his *Letter to the Faithful*, sometimes called *The Earlier Exhortation* (1LF) and *The Later Admonition and Exhortation* (2LF). The abbreviations for these documents do not indicate which came first. Scholars debate their chronological order (see Godet-Calogeras, La Lettre). 1LF is addressed specifically to penitents, and 2LF is addressed to nearly the entire world. While that includes clerics and religious, it has a focus on the experience of the laity.

Both versions contain two large sections that describe those who do penance and those who do not. 1LF lists five characteristics of those who do penance: they love the Lord; love their neighbor; hate vice and sin; receive communion; and produce the fruits of penance (1LF I 1-4). This definition describes a way of life in which one turns away from sin and toward God. 2LF contains a larger list of twenty characteristics that feature humble acts of justice and charity (2LF 18-47). Both versions then describe how the Spirit of the Lord dwells in those doing penance and puts them in relationship with Jesus as spouses, sisters/brothers, and mothers. They conclude with a proclamation of praise for these relationships (1LF I 5-19; 2LF 48-62).

The second part describes those who don't do penance as the antithesis of those who do penance. It then describes how they are in relationship with the devil and concludes with a proclamation of damnation (1LF II 1-22; 2LF 66-85; Workbook I 179-186 provides introductions and outlines of the two versions). Again, both versions of the *Letter to the Faithful* show Francis's thought about penance as a permanent lifestyle.

In Clare's relatively shorter writings, she too espoused penance as a way of life. Her own *Form of Life* states in the important sixth chapter, "After the Most High Heavenly Father saw fit by His grace to enlighten my heart to do penance according to the example and teaching of our most blessed father Saint Francis..." (FLCl VI 1).

Her *Testament* describes how God the Father moved her "to do penance according to the example and teaching of our most blessed father

Francis" (TestCl 24). She went on to link Francis's and her conversions to doing penance (25). Again, "to do penance" is described as a way of life.

Sr. Filippa was the third witness in *The Acts of the Process of Canonization* for Clare. When relating how she entered San Damiano Monastery to join Clare, she said she was moved by the saint's description of Christ's passion and death and "consented to be in the same Religion and to do penance together with her" (PC III 4). This testimony links devotion to the suffering Christ, joining religious life, and doing penance for the rest of one's life. Again, Filippa talked about doing penance as a way of life over one's lifetime that began with a conversion.

These writings of Francis and Clare of Assisi and *The Acts of the Process of Canonization* for Clare speak about penance as an ongoing lifestyle. That is a very different idea from the common ways we use the term today. We typically use "penance" to describe the Sacrament of Reconciliation, the act of repentance assigned to penitents by the priest in that sacrament, or specific ascetical practices one might practice, as during Lent. Francis and Clare also used the term in those same ways in other places, as well as to describe turning away from a particular sinful behavior (e.g., 1LCus 6; ER XII 2, XX 2; LMin 20; LR VII 2; LOrd 44; Adm XXIII 3; FLCl IX 4, 18; PC II 10:35). However, their foundational understanding of penance was a permanent lifestyle that began with a forceful conversion experience.

So far, we have discussed Clare and Francis's understanding of *penance* in order to firmly establish how resolutely they considered themselves to be members of the larger penitential movement. Next, we explain how that movement came into being. It was a development that took centuries.

Roland Faley's entire article ("Biblical Considerations of Metanoia") points out that, in both the Hebrew and Christian Scriptures, penance is associated with (1) a change of heart that (2) plays out in a new way of life in conformity with God's desires. This movement begins with a dissatisfaction about one's past and current life leading to new ways that better reflect one's genuine relationship with God. The pattern is quite visible in the four Gospels.

They portray John the Baptist and Jesus preaching repentance and conversion from the start of their ministries. The Baptist chided Pharisees and Sadducees who came for his baptism but hadn't produced the fruits of any meaningful conversion (Matt 3:10; Luke 3:9). Jesus began his ministry exhorting people to repent and believe in the Good News (Mark 1:15). John's and Jesus's ministries were geared toward people recognizing the shortcomings of their past lives, resolving to change in a moment of conversion, and carrying out that change for the rest of their lives.

Jesus tied this movement to the forgiveness of sins. While others shunned sinners, Jesus identified them as the primary objects of his ministry. His first message to a paralytic was "your sins are forgiven" (Matt 9:2). His physical paralysis was a metaphor for his spiritual paralysis overcome by repentance and concluding in forgiveness. Jesus's pastoral outreach to the sinful woman who anointed his feet during a supper hosted by a Pharisee was another defining moment of Jesus's ministry (Luke 7:36-50). His host could not understand Jesus's mission to bring sinners to repentance and forgiveness. At the very beginning of Jesus's ministry, John the Baptist called out Jesus as the "Lamb of God who takes away the sin of the world" (John 1:29).

It's amazing how few specifics the Gospels give regarding this new changed life. However, baptism is an important factor. While John baptized with water, Jesus baptized with the Holy Spirit (Mark 1:8; Matt 3:11; Luke 3:16; Acts 19:2-6). Jesus's baptism unleashed a new power in people's lives through the guidance of the Holy Spirit. It represented death to a former way of life and inclusion in a new life that was unification with Christ as Lord (Gal 2:20). Life in Christ was freedom from sin.

After biblical times, the early church had to deal with members who grievously sinned after their baptisms. Some thought a reconciliation could never happen. Others thought there could be one reconciliation after baptism. Still others thought there could be multiple reconciliations. Deciding how to deal with such sinners was a slow and gradual process.

During the first Christian centuries, the Church sometimes isolated unrepentant or grievous sinners in a manner reminiscent of Jesus's teachings to do just that (Matt 18:15-18). By the time the Church moved into the fourth century, it contained an Order of Penitents for lapsed Christians that mirrored the process for aspiring Christians belonging to the Order of Catechumens. Exclusion from Eucharist was a common practice for lapsed Christians, just as catechumens were asked to leave the Eucharistic assembly before recitation of the creed. This was not seen as punitive, but medicinal. With time, the practice of public confession of grievous sins followed by extended periods of actions symbolizing conversion became common. These included fasting and the wearing of distinctive clothing (Favazza 187-232; Stewart 98-100).

The Church's approach to lapsed Christians radically changed when Christianity became legal in the Roman Empire through various Edicts of Toleration between 311-313 CE. The change brought many converts into the faith. Many Christians who had denied Christ in the face of persecution sought to return to the faith. How to treat these *lapsi*, as they were called

(Stewart 100), became a source of tension in the Church. Some wished to emphasize forgiveness while others wanted harsh discipline as part of a process of conversion and reintegration. This latter process became known as the "canonical penance." It involved public confession, a time of exclusion from Eucharist, the performance of penitential practices, seating in special places during liturgical assemblies, and wearing distinctive clothing. Another ritual was performed when the penitential period was concluded to everyone's satisfaction.

While many of these aspects previously existed, they took on more rigor in the fourth century. The belief that such forgiveness could occur only once after baptism became widespread. In some places, the penitent never concluded his or her time of penance; instead it became a lifelong designation. Performing works of charity often became part of this permanent way of life (Stewart 101; Dallen 56-88).

The fifth century saw practices become even stricter, including the wearing of a penitential garb or "habit"; exclusion from popular gatherings; renunciation of certain ministry positions within the Church; prohibition against practicing business; mandatory celibacy; and moderation in the consumption of food and alcohol. In many cases, these were practiced for life. *Penance* no longer referred to specific practices but to a state of life. People of the day began to understand it as an *ordo* (order) that was quasi-religious and a permanent ecclesiastical status. It's generally accepted that the severity of this fifth-century development contributed to its demise. It was too strict to survive (Favazza 234-253; Stewart 101-102).

A different development occurred in Ireland in the 5th and 6th centuries. There, a pastoral practice of penance for the laity emerged out of the practice in monasteries. In so doing, reconciliation in Ireland embraced what looks more like our Sacrament of Reconciliation today. What was public, singular, harsh and life-long in the continental practice of canonical penance became private, repeatable and more pastoral (i.e., less harsh) in Ireland. It certainly did not approach a permanent state of life in the Church. These differences in Ireland also led to little focus on the power of the Spirit directing the lives of people engaged in this form of penance (Stewart 103-105; Dallen 100-128).

As the centuries continued to unfold, these two systems left a gap of unaddressed spiritual aspirations. The canonical penance was viewed as too severe. The confessional model developing in Ireland didn't seem intense enough. That left a handful of alternatives for achieving a palpable experience of forgiveness of sins. The first was monastic profession. However, joining a monastery was a radical choice with substantial consequences and obligations, and, importantly, not available to everyone, e.g., the already married. The life of a hermit presented a second possibility with similar opportunities and challenges. A third choice was to become a *conversi*, a category often over simplified. Many consider *conversi* to be unprofessed people living in a monastery. They would take on aspects of the monks' lives, but also display differences. For instance, *conversi* might not observe choral recitation of the Liturgy of the Hours as the monks did. Most often, the *conversi* vicariously participated in monastic life by offering domestic labor.

With time, the lines defining *conversi* began to blur, and they no longer were found only in monasteries. They also could live alone or as couples while practicing components of a penitential life, a fourth option. As the Middle Ages progressed, some *conversi* in this fourth category began to live together in loosely organized communities. They typically didn't live under monastic rules. Instead, they developed what would be called *proposita* (i.e., plans or schemes; *propositum* in the singular). A *propositum* was much simpler than a rule and seemed sufficient for many groups of lay *conversi* or penitents.

Because these early communal *conversi* typically lived in small groups, they generally avoided notice by bishops. Thus, there were few concerns about these arrangements. However, by the 12th and 13th centuries, the number of *conversi* living under a variety of unofficial *proposita* was exploding. By this time, they were increasingly called "penitents." Their number attracted the attention of popes and bishops, setting up many struggles.

The centuries just before Francis and Clare saw a swelling of religious interest within the laity and a desire to return to the original ideals and practices of the gospels, apostles and early martyrs. These generally included a strong witness to one's faith, sisterly and brotherly love, poverty or simple living, and joy (Chenu 219). They included an increasing interest in direct access to the scriptures. Often, penitents stood in opposition to the various scandals in the medieval church, including simony, nepotism, and the lack of clerical celibacy. Their simple common life was often seen as an antidote to these problems. They were seeking Christian perfection outside of the traditional monastic structures. In short, penitents were looking for a more palpable faith that was known through clear actions of witness. These were typically more radical actions or literal interpretations of the scriptures.

It helps us to remember that many in Francis and Clare's day did not manifest a deep faith. Many were ignorant of the Gospel, suffering from poor catechesis and frequently more influenced by superstition. Many clergy and religious lived a lifestyle that appeared centered on self and pleasure. Perhaps the fact that Christianity was part and parcel of European culture contributed to this. Everyone received a modicum of "Christian" identity just by being part of the general culture. This often led to large numbers who did not display deep belief or observance of the Gospel. In contrast, penitents wanted Christian life "intensively lived" (Horgan *Turned* 8).

The poverty of the penitential movement easily interfaced with the itinerant preaching often associated with the apostolic life movement, as any itinerant preacher would necessarily have to be poor and vulnerable in the absence of paper money. However, there was also an ideological connection in that many believed only a poor preacher could authentically preach the Gospel of the poor Christ. Asceticism was seen as a credential for authentic preaching. Alberzoni notes that, around the time of Francis and Clare of Assisi, forms of spontaneous penance were more and more assuming an apostolic model (Alberzoni, section 7).

In ways that may not be relevant to our study of Clare of Assisi, it is interesting to note that around the time of her life, pilgrims and crusaders were also increasingly considered penitents. (Recall that Clare's mother, Ortulana, made several pilgrimages.) These Christians practiced dangerous activities for the forgiveness of their sins. Their practices involved itinerancy and poverty. Their radical commitment to Christian values showed how they were led to higher levels of perfection.

The definition of a penitent is hard to ascertain during this period. Perhaps a good rule of thumb is to think of them as primarily lay people seeking Christian spiritual perfection outside of the realm of monastic life. In other words, they were creating new categories of Christian perfection. Several sources listed in the bibliography at the end of this chapter report the witness of many individuals and groups in the centuries leading up to Francis and Clare of Assisi (See especially Bolton, Davison, Grundmann, Pazzelli and Stewart). Of course, Francis of Assisi arguably became the most famous penitent. His preaching would inspire Clare of Assisi to start her own penitential life in the spirit of Francis.

We summarize the penitential movement at the time of Francis and Clare of Assisi in this way. The desire to become a penitent began with a dissatisfaction about one's previous life that led to a conversion of heart. That conversion was not an isolated event, but the beginning of a lifelong change in lifestyle motivated by a desire to advance in Christian perfection without entering a monastery. Penitents looked back to the early church for inspiration. There they found the poor and suffering Christ, who humbled himself for our salvation. They yearned to share in his sufferings as a way to identify with him. They read about the early church in *The Acts of the Apostles* which shared everything in common and took care of the physical and spiritual needs of each other regardless of social rank. They viewed the Holy Spirit as the guiding force for their lives, just as they viewed the Spirit guiding Jesus and the early church.

These penitents sought to imitate early church practices especially through living simply or poorly, caring for each other and the poor, and delving into the Scriptures as best they could. Frequently, they refused to participate in ubiquitous war and marked themselves with a Tau that had become a sign of penitence. They engaged in simple tasks that could support themselves but allow them to practice the other elements of their chosen lifestyle. Sometimes, they lived in regular homes as individuals or couples; other times, they lived together governing themselves with a very simple guide called a *propositum*. Some penitents were celibates; others remained married. Initially avoiding oversight by church leaders, these penitents eventually attracted the attention of those leaders who sought to better control them and direct their lifestyle.

Perhaps the most important characteristic was a yearning for more in the spiritual life. Some describe this as the drive toward Christian perfection for the laity, which many church leaders previously could only envision for monks and nuns. Sadly, the Church of the day did not address this yearning among laity well. Too often, the institutional church seemed threatened by the deep desires of its lay members.

Many elements of this summary probably raise thoughts about Francis and Clare of Assisi. They should, because Francis and Clare explicitly said they sought "to do penance." Return to this chapter often as you use this workbook to make even more connections between them and the penitential movement. Next, we take a brief look at the evangelical movement, which had many connections to the penitential movement.

The Evangelical Movement

Two ideas are important when considering the evangelical movement. The first was briefly mentioned in the previous section on the penitential movement, i.e., in the time just before and during the lives of Francis and Clare of Assisi there was great emphasis on returning to the vision and practices of early Christianity. That especially focused on the life of Christ as recorded in the four canonical Gospels. Since the Greek work for Gospel or Good News is εὐαγγέλιον (euangélion in English letters), we use the English word *evangelical* to describe this movement.

Like the penitential movement, the evangelical movement was a *movement* and not an organization. No one was a card-carrying-member. Thus, historians use the term to describe a collection of ideas, values and practices that help to better understand what was going on at that particular point in history. Since we have already referenced the penitential movement, it is clear that these various movements shared characteristics and help to understand each other. One cannot draw clear lines distinguishing the various movements. They overlap.

A second idea to pay attention to is *evangelical perfection*. When medieval people went to the Gospels as a source for their Christian lives, they found two passages that disclosed an important ideal. The first was Matt 5:48, "So be perfect, just as your heavenly Father is perfect." The second comes from the story of the rich young man, "If you wish to be perfect, go sell what you have and give to [the] poor, and you will have treasure in heaven. Then come, follow me" (Matt 19:21). Both passages suggest that there are more radical ways of following Jesus than simply to follow the bare minimum of the Gospel. *Perfection* is a greater than normal observance. Thus, *evangelical perfection* is a greater than normal observance of the Gospel. However, it is important to understand that "a greater than normal observance" is not the same as an observance without any imperfection. The term is about degrees, not impeccability. With these initial clarifications, we consider whether this was an important influence on Francis and Clare of Assisi.

Both surviving forms of Francis's *Rule* provide an obvious *yes* in answer to that question. His *Earlier Rule* begins with the declaration, "This is the life of the Gospel of Jesus Christ that Brother Francis petitioned the Lord Pope to grant and confirm for him…" (ER Prologue 2). The first chapter goes on to unite observance of the Gospel with the three evangelical counsels. It quotes the passage about the rich young man mentioned above and then states, "The rule and life of these brothers is this, namely: 'to live in obedience, in chastity, and without anything of their own,' and to follow the teaching and footprints of our Lord Jesus Christ, Who says: If you wish to be perfect, go sell everything you have and give it to the poor, and you will have treasure in heaven; and come, follow me" (ER I 1-3; Matt 19:21). Obviously "to follow the teaching and footprints of our Lord Jesus Christ" meant to follow the Gospel. Toward the end of that same version of his *Rule*, Francis admonished his followers to remain faithful to that initial and fundamental aspect of their way of life, "Let us, therefore, hold onto the words, the life, the teaching and the Holy Gospel of Him Who humbled Himself..." (ER XXII 41).

The final version of Francis's *Rule* reiterates what the earlier version stated, "The Rule and Life of the Lesser Brothers is this: to observe the Holy Gospel of Our Lord Jesus Christ by living in obedience, without anything of one's own, and in chastity" (LR I 1). As in the *Earlier Rule*, Francis returned to this fundamental dedication to the Gospel in the final chapter of the *Later Rule*, "I command the ministers through obedience to petition from our Lord the Pope for one of the Cardinals of the Holy Roman Church, who would be the governor, protector and corrector of this fraternity, so that, being always submissive and subject at the feet of the same Holy Church and steadfast in the Catholic Faith, we may observe poverty, humility, and the Holy Gospel of our Lord Jesus Christ as we have firmly promised" (thus ends the LR XII 4).

This witness of both surviving versions of Francis's *Rule* was confirmed in his *Testament,* "And after the Lord gave me some brothers, no one showed me what I had to do, but the Most High Himself revealed to me that I should live according to the pattern of the Holy Gospel" (Test 14).

Clare of Assisi began her own *Rule* or *Form of Life* in the same manner as Francis, "The form of life of the Order of the Poor Sisters that Blessed Francis established is this: to observe the Holy Gospel of our Lord Jesus Christ, by living in obedience, without anything of one's own, and in chastity" (FLCl I 1-2). Chapter two of her *Form of Life* invokes the same Gospel story of the rich young man when discussing new members for her community, "If she is suitable, let the words of the holy Gospel be addressed to her that she should go and sell all that she has and take care to distribute the proceeds to the poor" (FLCl II 7).

Chapter six is the central chapter of Clare's *Form of Life* and probably the chapter most influenced by her own hand. In it, she incorporates the *Form of Life* given to her many years earlier by Francis. She quotes him as saying, "Because by divine inspiration you have made yourselves daughters and handmaids of the Most High, most Exalted King, the heavenly Father, and have taken the Holy Spirit as your spouse, choosing to live according to the perfection of the holy Gospel, I resolve and promise for myself and for my brothers always to have the same loving care and special solicitude for you as for them" (FLCl VI 3-4). Francis focused on Clare's complete dedication to the service of Jesus through several metaphors involving human relationships (sister, spouse, mother), acknowledged her pursuit of evangelical perfection (doing more than the minimum), and clearly saw Clare united to his own desire to follow the Gospel. Like Francis in his *Rule*, Clare concluded her *Form of Life* by invoking the Poor Sisters' commitment to Gospel living, "... may [we] observe in perpetuity the poverty and humility of our Lord Jesus Christ and of His most holy Mother and the Holy Gospel we have firmly promised. Amen" (FLCl XII 13).

The foundation of gospel living found in the hagiography about both saints can be retrieved through a search on the website of the Franciscan Intellectual Tradition. However, it was important to establish in these brief paragraphs that both Francis and Clare's own writings contain a clear commitment to Gospel living and thus their participation in the evangelical movement. We now wish to briefly describe the content and focus of that movement.

The key concept in understanding the unique perspective of the evangelical movement was its focus on living the Gospel. Thus, it focused more on Christian lifestyle than ministry or work. This distinguished it from the apostolic life movement. This focus also distinguished it from the penitential movement, which was focused on a moment of conversion that was followed by a lifetime of penance (see the previous section of this chapter).

Jean-François Godet-Calogeras demonstrates how, in their writings, Francis and Clare of Assisi accessed some of the most radical sayings of Jesus in the Gospels. These Gospel passages draw a picture of radical evangelical life that contains the following characteristics:

- A discipleship to Jesus that is exclusive, radical, and all-consuming;

- An unconditional and inclusive love (without exception) that imitates the love of God and Jesus;

- A radical servanthood that rejects the drive for power, position and prestige; and

- A radical sharing of the earth's resources because they all really belong to God.

These four characteristics of radical evangelical life point to others as well: radical sharing through voluntary poverty, humility, unpretentiousness, obedience, submission to others, a radical sister-brotherhood, a preferential option for those on the peripheries of society (symbolized by lepers), ecological sensitivity, etc. (Godet-Calogeras's entire article—Evangelical Radicalism—is relevant to these two paragraphs, i.e., 103-121).

In its stark essentials, the evangelical movement turned people back from the status quo of medieval church practices to the renewing vision and power of the pristine Gospel itself. Different people and groups accessed that in different ways, one of them being the Franciscan movement that included a wide variety of figures. The particular characteristics of each person's appropriation would be determined by how that person understood the Gospel and what it invoked in her or him.

The Franciscan appropriation of the evangelical life focused on the goodness of God everywhere. All was a gift from God. This idea propelled Franciscans into relationships with Jesus, all of humanity and even all of creation. All this occurred under the influence and power of the Holy Spirit, expressed in simple living, reaching out to all on the peripheries, and understanding obedience as service to each other (The Sisters and Brothers of the Third Order, 289-291). No single ministry was essential because any authentic ministry or work could embody these Gospel principles.

Joseph Chinnici lists the values of the evangelical movement as purity of heart, humility, thanksgiving, courtesy, gentleness, peace, joy, patience, the blessing of persecutors, love, and fraternal-sororal living. All this was expressed in the marketplace as well as in the home (The Prophetic Heart 301). The opposing values were pride, vainglory, envy, avarice, cares and worries, detraction, complaint, anxiety, dissension, division, wrath, and insult (302).

In the end, the penitential and evangelical movements shared much in common, but could be viewed as distinct in the impulses that originated them. Both focused on a lifestyle that sought to express itself in a radical and palpable way. The penitential movement did this by focusing on the lifelong commitment to conversion and penance. The evangelical movement sought to discover its radical forms of life by going directly back to the Gospels. Both movements shared aspects with the apostolic life movement, which also had its distinctive features.

The Apostolic Life Movement

After Vatican Council II, Franciscan Third Order Regular groups began to renew themselves according to the charism of their founding period, as the council asked all religious to do (*Perfectae caritatis* 2). During that process, many members of these congregations were drawn to understand themselves as living a penitential or evangelical lifestyle rather than being defined by their work or ministry (apostolate). Joseph Chinnici argues that modern canon law does not capture this Franciscan reality through its restrictive categories of religious life as either apostolic or monastic (Chinnici, "The Prophetic Heart" 297 and "Evangelical and Apostolic Tensions" 5-6). He argues Franciscans are neither. Chinnici and others maintain that Franciscans should have their own canonical category, i.e., evangelical (Evangelical and Apostolic Tensions 6-9).

The medieval apostolic life movement had a different understanding of the term "apostolic." For its adherents, the term referred to the early life of the apostles which included a common life that was best available to them through *The Acts of the Apostles*. That idea allowed monks in the centuries before Francis and Clare to claim to be "apostolic" because their monastic communities shared everything in imitation of the apostles. Thus, modern readers have a challenge in properly understanding how Christians of the late medieval period understood "apostolic."

Since many of our readers are Third Order Regular members, we ask them not to conclude that we disagree with the insights that were incorporated into their new rule after Vatican Council II. Instead, we ask our readers to understand that the terms are used differently by these different moments in history. We believe that the apostolic life movement, as understood by many medieval people and which predated Francis and Clare by well over a century, had an impact on the lifestyles they pioneered.

This movement receives its name from the Latin phrase *vita apostolica*. People in the 11th through 13th centuries used it to refer to what they thought was the lifestyle of Jesus and his apostles. It marks a period in history when Christians sought to return to the evangelical (gospel) and historical sources of Christian life as a guarantee of authenticity (Chenu 204). There was a sense that Christianity was drifting away from authentic Christian life. The opulent and hedonistic lifestyle of many church people spawned numerous attempts to reform the Church and its ministers. Church officials masterminded some reforms as in the Gregorian Reform (1073-1085) and the four Lateran Councils (1123, 1139, 1181, and 1215). Others were grass-roots movements begun by reform-minded clergy, religious, or lay people.

The phrase gained popularity in the eleventh century when monks used the term to describe their monastic lifestyle. Abbot Rupert of Deutz (d. 1130) wrote that the apostles were the first monks. He argued that monastic life of his day modeled the internal life of early Christian communities. The core element of this similarity was the "abandonment of all private goods in favor of the common life" (Chenu 206). Monastic institutions merely formalized the pattern of the early Christians.

Those applying the term to monastic life often cited Acts 4:32-37 as a point of comparison. This passage described how the early believers were of one heart and mind, holding everything in common. Everyone was given what she or he needed. Other similar summarizing and idealized descriptions were found in Acts 2:42-47 and 5:12-16. The citation of these supporting scriptures began the collection of what we call the apostolic texts. More passages were added to the list as the notion of early Christian life developed.

It is interesting to note that those using this notion to bolster monastic life generally ignored the work and ministry of the early apostles and Christian community. Rather, they focused on the early community's lifestyle, which they compared favorably to contemporary monastic life. Thus, they equated the apostolic life with community life. Using this model, they focused on simplicity of food, clothing and shelter, modest manners, fraternal corrections, and the penitential nature of manual labor (Chenu 207). As you notice, many of these ideas and practices are also part of our description of the penitential and evangelical movements, illustrating how these movement don't have clear lines of demarcation.

Yet, as time passed, the comparison made by the monks limped in many people's estimation. While individual monks and nuns were technically poor, the grand monasteries of the day typically were centers of economic power and wealth. As the social role of the monastery expanded, it increasingly swallowed the very world it eschewed. It was difficult to live in the shadow of medieval Europe's great monasteries and imagine them to reflect the simplicity of the early Christian community (Chenu 207-208).

Furthermore, the monks were increasingly moving away from the manual labor previously encouraged in Benedict's rule. Others were brought into the monastery to perform menial and manual jobs so that the monks could devote more time to prayer, e.g., *conversi* (Chenu 208-210; see the previous penitential movement section). The use of texts that described the early Christian community at Jerusalem invited criticism of monasticism while hoping to bolster its image at the same time.

The medieval idea of the new apostolic life developed with the growth of the canons regular. Unlike monks, canons often lived in cities and ministered actively among the people. Their ministries included celebration of the sacraments with the people, preaching, teaching, and social outreach. For example, the Canons of San Rufino taught Francis at the Church of San Giorgio just outside Assisi's walls. Canons continued to live in community and, thus, seemed to embody the principles of apostolic life emphasized by the monks. However, canons wedded apostolic action to the image of that life (Chenu 214). In retrospect, it is amazing that monks felt they could invoke images of the apostles to sanctify their monastic lifestyle without also incurring the criticism that, unlike the apostles, they did not actively engage in evangelization of the people through ministry. After having accepted the teachings of Jesus, nothing was more impressive about the apostles than the way they spread that teaching.

While the canons developed the notion of the apostolic life within the confines of a clerical and celibate lifestyle, the lay apostolic movement adapted the notion to lay people open to marriage, though many did not marry. These lay people sought expressions for their religious fervor as the canons and monks had before them. Unimpeded by commitments and responsibilities to monasteries or cathedrals, many lay apostles tied itinerant (traveling) preaching with their simple lifestyle, something no monk or canon could easily do. Those who remained in one place often banded together for corporal works of mercy: caring for the sick and dying; burying the dead; feeding the hungry; providing shelter to travelers and pilgrims; etc.

These lay women and men (whether stationary or itinerant) gravitated toward cities where new classes of people gathered: merchants, artisans, manual workers, and clerks. In fact, many members of lay apostolic groups came from these new classes. They sought to provide spirituality, ministry, and religious outlets to these people too often ignored by traditional religious institutions that proved unable to adapt to the new situation.

Both the canons and lay apostles took on values that the monks derived from their reading of the early *vita apostolica*: simplicity of food, clothing and shelter; modest manners; fraternal correction; and penitential manual labor. In these ways, they shared many values with those in the penitential movement. However, they added the dimension of active ministry, which included preaching, and tending to people's social and economic needs. These new groups hungered to hear the gospel in particular and all the scriptures in general. They shared reflections on the scriptures and worked to produce vernacular editions of the scriptures. They were the antithesis of the monks by dwelling in the heart of the very "world" the monks sought to flee.

This movement, which began as a monastic renewal in the eleventh century and developed in its canonical and lay forms through the 12th, reached its pinnacle in the 13th century with the birth of the mendicant orders, including the Franciscans and Dominicans. The male mendicant orders further blended the freedom from stability of lay groups with the common life of the canons and other religious. This moment of development was more complicated for Franciscan women.

As groups began to broaden their idea of the apostolic life beyond monastic stability (people committing to live in a particular monastery for life), they also began to expand the scriptures to which they appealed to justify and support their lifestyles. We encourage you to take some time to read these scripture passages. After a while, their emphases become very clear. Once you develop an eye for these passages we call apostolic texts, you will easily identify them in the stories about and writings of Francis and Clare.

Acts 2:42-47 Acts 4:32-37 Acts 5:12-16	These passages describe the ideal early Christian community at Jerusalem. They are the foundation of the monastic renewal based on the apostolic life. The monks used the texts because they described the internal life of the early Christians in terms they could apply to monastic life. The passages emphasize common life, not ministry.
Acts 6:1-7	When people began to challenge the adequacy of monastic life exemplifying the apostolic life because it lacked a thrust toward ministry, the monks began to appeal to this passage to show that the apostles appointed others (deacons) to assist with the daily needs of the faithful, freeing the apostles up for prayer and service to the word.

Matt 10:1-42	The call and commissioning of the apostles are
Matt 28:16-20	favorite themes of the apostolic passages. The
Mark 6:7-13	commissioning passages deal with events both
Mark 16:14-18	before and after Jesus's resurrection. The canons
Luke 9:1-6	and especially lay apostles latched on to these
Luke 6:12-16	passages that portray the apostles, and in one case
Luke 10:1-12	the seventy-two disciples, as preachers of the word.
Luke 24:44-49	
John 20:19-23	

The lay dimension of this movement surmised that every Christian was called to be a preacher of God's word. Using these texts, they acquired the notions that the early apostles were poor praying pilgrims, who preached penance and peace, and resultantly experienced persecution. They expected the same to be true of themselves more than a millennium later. This description captures how their lifestyle became wedded to preaching and witness in a way that blurs the lines between the penitential, evangelical, and apostolic life movements.

Early practitioners of these movements often suffered misunderstanding and persecution from the Church. However, Pope Innocent III forged a new policy toward these groups that attempted to reconcile. His ultimate hope was to harness their religious fervor for the service of the Church. Certainly, Innocent's new and innovative policy created the environment that allowed the new mendicant orders to firmly establish and later flourish.

In the end, we believe the notion of apostolic life changed because monasticism became inexorably connected to feudalism. As feudalism fell apart, monasticism was bound to lose its appeal (see Chenu 230-231). All the things on which feudalism stood were giving way: the preeminence of land in the economy, stability of places and people, personal relationships forged by oaths between nobles and their lessers, the granting of benefices, and serfdom. The new Europe was centered in cities and towns with their markets and merchants. Money and people were in increasing circulation. Liberty from serfdom was increasingly achieved. Guilds and leagues of workers, artisans and merchants replaced feudal oaths of fealty. Medieval people were beginning to understand themselves as autonomous individuals and part of the natural world.

The monastic world was losing touch with the pulse of the changing medieval world, while other forms of life were rising up to fill in the gaps. While it should be easy to see how the apostolic life movement influenced

Francis and the Friars Minor whose rule contained significant sections about preaching and going about Arabs who were called Saracens at that time (cf. ER XVI, XVII and XXII; LR IX and XII), it may be harder to see its influence on Clare and the Poor Sisters at San Damiano Monastery. However, one example is how the sources portray Clare as a healer of both her Poor Sisters and others outside San Damiano Monastery. Healing was one of the ministries of the apostles.

Even though Clare and her sisters were not preaching in the piazzas of Assisi, they came from Assisi and other cities where they heard the preaching of others that inspired them by its content and the witness of the lives of the preachers. For sure, the women took on a lifestyle that most clearly exemplified the penitential and evangelical movements. However, it was learned in part by the preaching of those in the apostolic life movement, including their own brother, Francis of Assisi.

Conclusions

Francis, Clare and their followers were born in an era when many religious movements made forceful impressions upon European society and church. The monastic movement was the inherited status quo from which the new movements borrowed much but to which they also reacted. Three new movements stand out as important for our study: the penitential, evangelical and apostolic life movements. It is important to emphasize that they were movements, not organizations. Further, they did not contain sharp lines of distinction. Instead, they overlapped each other more often than not. With so many shared elements, perhaps what best distinguished them was their inspiring sources.

The penitential movement was characterized by a deep conversion at a particular moment in one's life, followed by a new lifestyle that lasted a lifetime and expressed a deep commitment as a disciple of Christ. The evangelical movement shared much with the penitential movement but could identify its origin in the desire for renewal based on the ancient Gospel itself. More recent humanly developed traditions in the Church did not satisfy their deep longings and were abandoned in favor of Jesus's life and message directly known through the Gospel. These two movements primarily expressed themselves as a lifestyle that those in the apostolic life movement also accessed. However, the apostolic life movement in its later manifestation also sought to express similar values through ministry, in imitation of the preaching and evangelizing apostles. At the time of Francis and Clare, pastoral care of the new classes in the new cities was a focus of this movement, and preaching was a prized form of that ministry.

Both Clare and Francis explicitly used the language of penance and evangelical living. Francis and the Friars Minor also engaged in penitential preaching and accessed the scripture passages of the apostolic texts in their rule. As a person living in enclosure, Clare could not engage in such active ministry outside San Damiano Monastery. Still, Pope Alexander IV, in his bull of canonization of Clare (*Clara claris praeclara*), could not resist including images of Clare's light bounding beyond her enclosure to the ends of the world (BC 4:17-5:26 and 23:100). The same document recounts Clare's ministry of healing both inside and outside her monastery (BC 18:78-84; also see listed cross references). These and countless other references in the papal bull portray Clare as one who "preached" by her example.

In the end, both the Friars Minor and the Poor Sisters focused more on lifestyle than on any particular ministry. When the Friars Minor did engage in ministry, there was no particular ministry that was required of everyone. No specific ministry was more important than the requirement that the ministry be compatible with the lifestyle and values of the new communities.

The blurry lines between these movements become evident when one considers that studies about them by modern historians frequently cross among them and even use the terms for multiple movements in the same sentences. For example, Robert Stewart frequently uses "apostolic life" when referring to the development of the penitential movement (see various examples within pages 109-120). Duane Lapsanski's frequently cited study, *Evangelical Perfection,* regularly switches between the terms "apostolic life," "evangelical perfection," and "evangelical life" during the first fifty pages as if they were the same thing.

Maria Pia Alberzoni exemplifies the blurriness when she combines language evoking the penitential movement and the apostolic life movement at the same time. For instance, the 4th section of her article "Agere poenitentiam" is entitled "Vita vere apostolica. Penitenza dei laici ed esaltazione della povertà" (True Apostolic Life: Penance of the Laity and Exaltation of Poverty). Here she explicitly links the apostolic life and penitential movements. Furthermore, she identifies poverty, which was typically associated with doing penance, as a required credential for doing itinerant preaching (i.e., the apostolic life). Bernard McGinn manages to reference all three movements in a single sentence: "The essential components of the evangelical understanding of the *vita apostolica* were penance, poverty and preaching (6; but see pages 5-152 for other examples).

Whether an author is talking about the penitential, evangelical or apostolic life movement, a parade of the same historical figures and groups appears:

Peter Damian (c. 1007 – c. 1073),

Rupert of Deutz (c. 1075/1080 – c. 1129),

Hugh of St. Victor (c. 1096 – 1141),

Stephen of Thiers-Muret (1045 – 1124) and the foundation at Grandmont,

Robert of Arbrissel (c. 1045 – 1116),

Norbert of Xanten (c. 1080 – 1134) who founded the Premonstratensians,

Peter Waldes (c. 1140 – c. 1205) who founded the Waldensians,

The Humiliati of Lombardy,

The Beguines of the Low Lands,

Durand of Huesca (c. 1160 – 1224) who founded the Poor Catholics in southern France, and

Bernard Prim and companions.

Many of these people seem to be considered early figures in all three movements. This only reinforces the idea that these were movements and not organizations. Their lines of demarcation were very blurry. Each of the movements shared many characteristics with the others. No student should think of any of these movements in terms that are too precise or exclusive.

These insights are important as today's Franciscans grapple with their modern identity. We need to be careful not to anachronistically read our problems, challenges and issues back into the 13th century. To correctly assert that Francis and Clare's fundamental option was to live the Gospel in lifelong penance does not mean that they were not influenced by other medieval currents in the Church. In times of flux, most choices are a mix of elements chosen from various influences.

So, while Francis and Clare made a fundamental choice for a Gospel life, they also viewed their lives as penitential, a related but slightly different inspiration. They incorporated prayer at the various times of day, even if not all could read a breviary and had to recite "the Our Fathers." They received this from monastic life, though the Friars Minor were not monks and Clare preferred the title Poor Sisters to nuns. Francis preached as did many others participating in the apostolic life movement, yet Francis would not see his mission defined by this or any other particular ministry. What is important to observe regarding Francis and Clare is how their fundamental options mediated the way they appropriated values, ideas, and behaviors from other groups and movements.

We encourage you to return to this chapter often during your study of Clare. The influence of these movements is tremendously important to understand Francis, Clare, and the entire Franciscan movement.

Sources citied and suggested reading

- Alberzoni, Maria Pia. "Agere poenitentiam: una chiave di lettura della società europea nei secoli XII-XIII." In *La Penitenza tra Gregorio VII e Bonifacio VIII: teologia, pastorale, istituzioni.* Eds. Roberto Rusconi, Alessandro Saraco, and Manlio Sodi. Cittá Del Vaticano: Libreria Editrice Vaticana, 2013. 29-60.

- Bolton, Brenda. *The Medieval Reformation.* Foundations of Medieval History. London: Edward Arnold Publishers, 1983.

- Casagrande, Giovanna. "An Order for Lay People: Penance and Penitents in the Thirteenth Century." Trans. Edward Hagman. *Greyfriars Review* 17.1 (2003) 39-54.

- Celaschi, Nancy. "The Biblical Language of Penance." *The Cord* 33.9 (1983) 259-270. Reprinted in *Resources for the Study of the Third Order Regular Rule.* Ed. Kathleen Moffatt. Washington D.C.: Franciscan Federation, 1994. 259-270.

- Chenu, M.-D. *Nature, Man, and Society in the Twelfth Century: Essays on New Theological Perspectives in the Latin West.* Trans. Jerome Taylor and Lester K. Little. Chicago: University of Chicago Press, 1968. Pay special attention to chapter six, "Monks, Canons, and Laymen in Search of the Apostolic Life" (202-238), and chapter seven, "The Evangelical Awakening" (270-309). Chenu is a highly-respected authority on this period of European history. This collection of essays in translation includes many articles considered classics in the field.

- Chinnici, Joseph. "Evangelical and Apostolic Tensions." In *Franciscan Charism Today.* New Jersey: Fame, 1987. 1-32.

- —. "The Prophetic Heart: The Evangelical Form of Religious Life in the Contemporary United States." *The Cord* 44.11 (1994) 292-306. A transcription of Chinnici's keynote at the 29th Annual Franciscan Federation Conference on August 31, 1994. This presentation has a more contemporary focus than Chinnici's article above.

- Constable, Giles. *The Reformation of the Twelfth Century.* Cambridge: The University Press, 1996. Constable offers a broad description of the need for reform and resulting movements slightly before the time of Francis and Clare of Assisi.

- Cusato, Michael F. "To Do Penance/*Facere poenitentiam.*" *The Cord* 57.1 (2007) 3-24. Also published in *The Early Franciscan Movement (1205-1239): History, Sources and Hermeneutics.* Medioevo francescano. Saggi 14. Spoleto: Centro Italiano di Studi sull'Alto Medioevo, 2009. 49-68.

- Cusato, Michael and Jean-François Godet-Calogeras, eds. *Vita Evangelica: Essays in Honor of Margaret Carney. Franciscan Studies* 64 (2006) 22 articles contained in 537 pages.

- Dallen, James. *The Reconciling Community: The Rite of Penance.* New York: Pueblo Publishing, 1986. A detailed description of the development of the penitential movement.

- D'Auria, Clare Andrew. "Franciscan Evangelical Life and the Third Order Regular Charism." *The Cord* 44.11 (1994) 307-316.

- Davison, Ellen Scott. *Forerunners of Saint Francis and Other Studies.* Ed. Gertrude R. B. Richards. Boston: Houghton Mifflin Co., 1927. Part One (3-284) provides an extensive discussion of pre-Franciscan reform movements.

- Devlin, Dennis. "Feminine Lay Piety in the High Middle Ages: The Beguines." In *Distant Echoes.* Eds. John A. Nichols and Lillian Thomas Shank. Medieval Religious Women 1. Kalamazoo MI: Cistercian Publications, 1984. 183-196.

- Faley, Roland. "A Biblical-Theological View of Penance and Its Present Day Expression." In *Resources for the Study of the Third Order Regular Rule.* Ed. Kathleen Moffatt. Washington D.C.: Franciscan Federation, 1994. 85-97.

- —. "Biblical Considerations on Metanoia." *Analecta Tertii Ordinis Regularis Sancti Francisci* XIII/123 (1974) 1-16. Reprinted in *Resources for the Study of the Third Order Regular Rule.* Ed. Kathleen Moffatt. Washington DC: Franciscan Federation, 1994. 13-33.

- Favazza, Joseph A. *The Order of Penitents: Historical Roots and Pastoral Future.* Collegeville MN: Liturgical Press, 1988.

- Franciscan Intellectual Tradition at https://franciscantradition.org. Click on Early Sources and then do a search on the words "penance," "evangelical," "Gospel," etc.

- Gill, Katherine Jane. *Penitents,* Pinzochere *and* Mantellate*: Varieties of Women's Religious Communities in Central Italy, c. 1300-1520.* Ph.D. diss., Princeton University, 1994.

- Godet-Calogeras, Jean-François. "Evangelical Radicalism in the Writings of Francis and Clare of Assisi." In *Vita Evangelica: Essays in Honor of Margaret Carney.* Eds. Michael Cusato and Jean-François Godet-Calogeras. *Franciscan Studies* 64 (2006) 103-121.

- —. "La Lettre aux Fidèles de François d'Assise et le document de Volterra: une généalogie discutée." In *Una strana gioia di vivere a Grado Giovanni Merlo.* Eds. Marina Benedetti and Maria Luisa Betri. Milano: Edizioni Biblioteca Francescana, 2010. 265-281.

- Grundmann, Herbert. *Religious Movements in the Middle Ages.* Trans. Steven Rowan. Notre Dame IN: University of Notre Dame Press, 1995. This is a translation of Grundmann's 1935 classic that was revised in German in 1961. Newer research corrects many of Grundmann's positions. However, it remains an important source.

- Guarnieri, Romana. "Beguines beyond the Alps and Italian *Bizzoche.*" Trans. Roberta Agnes McKelvie. *Greyfriars Review* 5.1 (1991) 91-104.

- Horgan, Thaddeus. "Life according to the Holy Gospel." *The Cord* 32.9 (1982) 273-278.

- —. *Turned to the Lord.* Pittsburgh PA: Franciscan Federation, 1987. A summary of Horgan's ideas about the core Franciscan charism as it specifically applies to *The Rule and Life of the Brothers and Sisters of the Third Order Regular of St. Francis* (1982). The opening chapters reflect on the focus of Francis of Assisi on conversion, Gospel living and penance. They include information applicable to all Franciscans and pertinent to this chapter of our workbook. The remainder is an interesting reflection on how to appropriately live out core Franciscan values.

- Hutchison, Patricia. "Apostolic Life." *The Cord* 57.4 (2007) 439-448. Hutchison reflects on being apostolic and evangelical after 25 years of experience living with the new *Third Order Regular Rule.*

- Iriarte, Lazaro. "Francis of Assisi and the Evangelical Movements of His Time." Trans. Edward Hagman. *Greyfriars Review* 12.2 (1998) 169-191. Iriarte explains how Francis of Assisi envisioned his life as living the Gospel.

• —. "The Friar Minor as Penitent and Prophet." Trans. Paul Barrett. *Greyfriars Review* 2.1 (1988) 1-47. Iriarte's article demonstrates how the Friars Minor are in the line of penitents that preceded them. In the process, he gives good descriptions of what it meant to be a penitent before and during the time of Francis and Clare of Assisi.

• Lambert, Malcolm. *Medieval Heresy: Popular Movements from the Gregorian Reform to the Reformation.* Rev. ed. London: Blackwell, 1992. This work focuses on heretical groups but discusses underlying currents that also influenced orthodox lay movements.

• Lapsanski, Duane V. *Evangelical Perfection: An Historical Examination of the Concept in the Early Franciscan Sources.* Theology Series 7. St. Bonaventure NY: Franciscan Institute Publications, 1977.

• —. *The First Franciscans and the Gospel.* Chicago: Franciscan Herald Press, 1976.

• Lawrence, C. H. *Medieval Monasticism: Forms of Religious Life in Western Europe in the Middle Ages.* Second Edition. New York and London: Longman, 1989. Focused on the development of monasticism, this work explains the changes in Cistercian life that prepared ground for the novel mendicant movement, including the Franciscans.

• Leclercq, Jean. "Woman's Monasticism in the 12th and 13th Centuries." Trans. Edward Hagman. *Greyfriars Review* 7 (1993) 167-192.

• —. *The Friars: The Impact of the Early Mendicant Movement on Western Society.* London and New York: Longman, 1994. This book is a small treasure chest of information about the social and church environment spawning the Franciscans. The first two chapters are particularly relevant about causes of the apostolic life movement and its expression in the Franciscans.

• Little, Lester. *Religious Poverty and the Profit Economy in Medieval Europe.* Ithaca: Cornell University Press, 1978.

• Makowski, Elizabeth. *Canon Law and Cloistered Women:* Periculoso *and Its Commentators, 1298-1545.* Studies in Medieval and Early Modern Canon Law 5. Washington DC: The Catholic University of America Press, 1997.

- Marini, Alfonso. "'*Vestigia Christi Sequi*' or '*Imitatio Christi*': Two Different Ways of Understanding Francis of Assisi's Gospel Life." Trans. Cyprian Rosen. *Greyfriars Review* 11.3 (1997) 331-358.

- McGinn, Bernard. *The Flowering of Mysticism: Men and Women in the New Mysticism—1200-1350.* The Presence of God: A History of Western Christian Mysticism 3. New York: Crossroad, 1998. Especially pages 1-69.

- Pazzelli, Raffaele. *St. Francis and the Third Order: The Franciscan and Pre-Franciscan Penitential Movement.* Chicago: Franciscan Herald Press, 1989.

- Pennington, M. Basil. "Monasticism, Monastic Spirituality." In *The New Dictionary of Catholic Spirituality.* Ed. Michael Downey. Collegeville MN: The Liturgical Press, 1993. 665-670. A short treatment of the history of monasticism with additional bibliography.

- Preparatory Commission of the 2006 General Chapter of the Order of Friars Minor. "*Vivere secundum formam sancti Evangelii:* A Time of Grace to Re-situate Our Vocation and Mission." *The Cord* 57.2 (2007) 160-165.

- Rivi, Prospero. "Francis of Assisi and the Laity of His Time." Trans. Heather Tolfree. *Greyfriars Review* 15.Supplement (2001) v-vii, 1-108. Chapter one succinctly describes the laity's reawakening from the eleventh century until the time of Francis and Clare of Assisi.

- The Sisters and Brothers of the Third Order Regular of Saint Francis. "Response to the *Lineamenta* in Light of the 1994 Synod of Bishops on Consecrated Life in the Church." *The Cord* 44.11 (1994) 289-291.

- Southern, R. W. *Western Society and the Church in the Middle Ages.* New York: Penguin, 1970. The chapters on religious orders provide background to the apostolic life movement.

- Stewart, Robert M. "*De illis qui faciunt penitentiam*" *The Rule of the Secular Franciscan Order: Origins, Development, Interpretations.* Rome: Istituto Storico dei Cappuccini, 1991. Distributed in the USA by the Franciscan Institute at St. Bonaventure University. Pages 91-133 discuss the historical context leading up to the penitential movement. Pages 135-179 provide a detailed analysis of 1LF and 2LF as well as a good summary of recent scholarly writing about them. We recommend this readable resource.

- Van Leeuwen, Bertulf. "Clare, Abbess of Penitents." Trans. Joseph Oudeman. *Greyfriars Review* 4.2 (1990) 73-81.

- Vatican Council II. *Perfectae caritatis* (October 28, 1965). In *Documents of Vatican II: The Conciliar and Post Conciliar Documents*. Volume 1. Ed. Austin Flannery. Northport NY: Costello Publishing Co., 1984. 611-623.

- Vauchez, André. *The Spirituality of the Medieval West: The Eighth to the Twelfth Century*. Trans. Colette Friedlander. Kalamazoo MI: Cistercian Publications, 1993. Succinctly describes the changing spirituality that helped create and then embrace the Franciscans.

- Vicaire, M. H. *The Apostolic Life*. Chicago: The Priory Press, 1966. Focuses on the Dominicans. However, much of this book is applicable to the Franciscan movement.

Medieval Religious Women

Introduction

To understand the life and writings of Clare of Assisi, we must understand the beliefs, values, and practices that surrounded women who practiced religious life before and during her lifetime. Clare's choices are raised in relief when viewed against this backdrop, helping us to better appreciate how her choices might be viewed as Franciscan or not. Doing so also helps us understand how she was similar and different from Francis of Assisi.

In this chapter, we discuss seven such factors that we consider important for our study of the life and writings of Clare. It is intended to be read causally from start to finish. Later, you may benefit by coming back to one of the sections for review.

Parenthetical reference in this chapter refer to documents listed at the end of each section.

Medieval Religious Women

"Distant Echoes"

Nearly every study of medieval women's religious life starts with a remark about how few sources there are for the study; how few women are found as sources; and how most knowledge about women comes indirectly from writings by men, about men, and for men. John Nichols and Lillian Thomas Shank edited an important book highlighting this reality and appropriately entitled it *Distant Echoes*. An article embodying the same observation in its title is "Muffled Voices" by Jo Ann McNamara.

Philip Sheldrake observes the dearth of women's voices in the surviving documentation of female spirituality in general and religious life in particular. He places this within the general context of how remembered history develops. Sheldrake distinguishes between the *universal historical process*, which includes all that has occurred, and *recorded history*, which by its nature must be selective (57). This selection process naturally reflects the interests, concerns, and situations of the powerful and those who prevailed in the situation being documented.

Thus, the lives of those who lost the struggle for political, cultural, economic, military, or religious dominance were seldom documented in the recorded history of the victors. The testimonies about them, which may be few to begin with, were often destroyed or kept from general circulation by those who controlled the development of the record (58-67). Sheldrake includes women as major victims in this suppression of minority voices in the historical record (67-72). Thus, we learn about medieval religious women primarily through the writings of men who were either their supporters or critics.

This phenomenon is visible in Franciscan studies by comparing the collected primary sources about Clare and Francis of Assisi. FA:ED about Francis contains three volumes of documents. CA:ED about Clare is a single volume.

Cited sources and suggested reading

- Abrahamse, Dorothy de F. "Byzantine Asceticism and Women's Monasteries in Early Medieval Italy." In *Distant Echoes.* Eds. John A. Nichols and Lillian Thomas Shank. Medieval Religious Women 1. Kalamazoo MI: Cistercian Publications, 1984. 31-49.

- Clark, Elizabeth A. "Women, Gender, and the Study of Christian History." *Church History* 70 (2001) 395-426.

- Labarge, Margaret Wade. *A Small Sound of the Trumpet: Women in Medieval Life.* Boston: Beacon Press, 1986.

- McNamara, Jo Ann. "Muffled Voices: The Lives of Consecrated Women in the Fourth Century." In *Distant Echoes.* Eds. John A. Nichols and Lillian Thomas Shank. Medieval Religious Women 1. Kalamazoo MI: Cistercian Publications, 1984. 11-29.

- Nichols, John A. and Lillian Thomas Shank, eds. *Distant Echoes.* Medieval Religious Women 1. Kalamazoo MI: Cistercian Publications, 1984.

- Schulenburg, Jane Tibbets. "Strict Active Enclosure and Its Effect on the Female Monastic Experience (ca. 500-1100)." In *Distant Echoes.* Eds. John A. Nichols and Lillian Thomas Shank. Medieval Religious Women 1. Kalamazoo MI: Cistercian Publications, 1984. 51-86.

- Sheldrake, Philip. *Spirituality and History: Questions of Interpretation and Method.* New York: Crossroad, 1992.

- Thompson, Sally. "Why English Nunneries Had no History: A Study of the Problems of the English Nunneries Founded after the Conquest." In *Distant Echoes.* Eds. John A Nichols and Lillian Thomas Shank. Medieval Religious Women 1. Kalamazoo MI: Cistercian Publications, 1984. 131-149.

Nuptial Spirituality

The four known letters of Clare of Assisi to Agnes of Prague are replete with references to a spousal or nuptial relationship with Jesus. This type of spirituality has a long history; Clare did not invent it. Malatesta reports that, as long ago as in ancient Greece and through Judaism and Christianity, this type of symbolism was used to describe the relationship of a people or individuals with God, and especially "the most profound communion with God that a devout person can experience" (631).

Spousal imagery describes Israel's relationship with God in Hosea 2, Isaiah 54:5-6; 62:4-5, Ezekiel 16:8, and Jeremiah 2:2; 3:20. The Christian Scriptures portray the church as the bride of Christ in Ephesians 5:25-27, 2 Corinthians 11:2, and Revelations 19:7-9; 21:2; 22:17. Among the fathers of the church, Tertullian of Carthage (c. 155 – c. 240), Origen of Alexandria (c. 184 – c. 253), John Chrysostom (c. 349 – 407), and Theodoret of Cyrus (c. 393 – c. 458/466) used this imagery to describe the effects of Christians' sacramental life. Origen is credited with being one of the first to tie the *Song of Songs* to spousal spirituality and to apply it to the loving relationship of individuals with God.

The portrayal of Agnes of Rome (d. c. 304) as the bride of Christ in the *Legend of Saint Agnes of Rome* resonated in the Church throughout the Middle Ages. The legend was very popular around the time of Clare of Assisi. Clare in her letters and Pope Alexander IV in his bull of canonization of Clare amply quoted it (See our chapters "Clare's Letters to Agnes of Prague: The Example of Agnes of Rome, Martyr," and "*Clara claris praeclara*"). Finally, just before the time of Francis and Clare of Assisi, Bernard of Clairvaux (1090-1153) became famous for describing an individual's union with God by using the images of human love, sexual experiences, and marriage from the *Song of Songs* (Malatesta 631; McGinn *Growth* 193-224).

McGinn describes Bernard's understanding of bridal love as uniquely pure, single-minded, disinterested in self, and total. He considered bridal love even more true than that of a child, who might be interested in a future inheritance, be distracted by other goals, have mixed interests, be self-interested, or be imperfect in love. In contrast, the love of spouses is simply for the other, according to Bernard. Thus, it isn't hard to imagine why he chose spousal love to describe the heights of a person's relationship with God (McGinn *Growth* 198).

Bernard's ideas generated considerable excitement almost immediately. However, his nuptial images were not immediately applied to female religious. McGinn notes that one of the first witnesses to a female application is a Middle High German poetic translation and commentary of *A Teaching of the Loving Knowledge of God,* which was addressed to cloistered women and appeared shortly after 1160 (McGinn *Growth* 347 and 350). That was only 74 years before Clare wrote her first letter to Agnes.

It is not surprising that Clare of Assisi would express her own spiritual quest in spousal symbolism, as was increasingly common in her day. Since Clare is not considered to have written a great deal compared to other medieval religious women, we are lucky to have her use of this symbolism in her letters to Agnes of Prague. It is interesting that neither her *Form of Life* nor *Testament* utilize it, perhaps because they show the influence of other collaborators more than Clare's letters do.

McGinn makes a very important statement that we believe is especially relevant to Clare of Assisi: "The love relation of which Bernard [of Clairvaux] speaks is a marriage, not a love affair..." (McGinn *Growth* 204). This statement cautions us from over sexualizing our understanding of nuptial spirituality. That's important because medieval marriages frequently did not contain many of the sexually romantic ideas we have of marriage today. Marriages among nobles were arranged. Women were often bargaining chips for fathers, uncles and brothers to achieve political, military or economic goals. Wives were expected to totally serve the projects of their husbands. In part, their mutual love was visible in their shared mission, i.e., women subject to their husbands' missions, purposes, and desires.

This subjugation is visible in the letters of Clare to Agnes of Prague in which Clare's nuptial spirituality was essentially an imitation of the mission and methods of Jesus, their spouse. Thus, Clare emphasized that their marriage was to the poor and humble Christ. By imitating Christ through the same attributes, the Poor Sisters took part in the mission and means of Christ or, as we like to express it, the project of Christ. Jean Leclercq notes the uniqueness of Clare in this regard (St. Clare and Nuptial Spirituality 173-174). While she used romantic language to convey the close personal experience of being one with Christ, she employed the words *poor* and *humble* about the Poor Sisters to express their closeness to Christ's mission and means.

Francis of Assisi already announced the same understanding when, in his two versions of *The Letter to the Faithful,* he declared that penitents were sisters and brothers of Christ because like Christ they do the will or work of the same heavenly Father. He declared them spouses of Christ because all these faithfully obedient children of the Father were united with Christ by the same Holy Spirit (1LF I 7-9 ; 2LF 49-53; repeated in 1LAg 12). In these letters, Francis's imagery is much more focused on participating in the project of the Father accepted by Christ than on romantic sexual union.

Bernard of Clairvaux also discussed contemplation and visions in the context of nuptial spirituality (McGinn *Growth* 207-217). The contemplative vision of Jesus goes hand-in-hand with the experience of being a bride because it makes union with him possible. It is interesting that Clare also talks about contemplation in a similar way. Again, avoiding sexualized language, Clare essentially believed that by gazing, considering, and contemplating the poor and humble Christ, the Poor Sisters were led into imitation, which ultimately was Clare's way of supporting Christ's project (2LAg 20; 3LAg 13 and 4LAg 15-26).

The use of sexual, marital, and unitive images to describe a deep relationship with God requires some consideration. It is important to realize that these images are metaphors that compare things we know to lesser known things. To interpret the metaphor literally is to distort the truth. Thus, it is incorrect to suggest that nuptial spirituality implies mystics were having sex with Jesus. Instead, the truth being described was a deep relationship with God.

That relationship is disclosed in nuptial love's exclusiveness, permanence, longevity and intimacy. The exclusiveness highlights the single-mindedness of a deep spiritual relationship. The permanence and longevity have an eschatological quality that leads the mystic into the end times and the everlasting nature of the relationship. The intimacy of human marriage helps appreciate the indescribable euphoric joy of a deep contemplative relationship with Christ.

Bernard of Clairvaux's teaching on these matters is found in many of his writings. It is best that readers wanting more information go to a secondary source. We recommend McGinn's *Growth*, pages 193-224. Our subsequent chapter on Clare's letters to Agnes will offer a more in-depth opportunity to explore this theme in Clare's thought.

Cited sources and suggested reading

- Goodich, Michael. *"Ancilla Dei*: The Servant as Saint in the Late Middle Ages," in *Women of the Medieval World: Essays in Honor of John H. Mundy*. Eds. Julius Kirshner and Suzanne F Wemple. Oxford: Basil Blackwell, 1985. 119-136.

- Hames, Susan. "Bridal Mysticism." In *The New Dictionary of Christian Spirituality*. Ed. Michael Downey. Collegeville MN: The Liturgical Press, 1993. 106.

- Leclercq, Jean. "St. Clare and Nuptial Spirituality." Trans. Edward Hagman. *Greyfriars Review* 10.2 (1996) 171-178.

- Malatesta, Edward J. "Marriage, Mystical." In *The New Dictionary of Christian Spirituality*. Ed. Michael Downey. Collegeville MN: The Liturgical Press, 1993. 631.

- McGinn, Bernard. *The Flowering of Mysticism: Men and Women in the New Mysticism—1200-1350*. The Presence of God: A History of Western Christian Mysticism 3. New York: Crossroad, 1998. Pages 1-69 are relevant to the emergence of the male and female Franciscan movement. Pages 64-69 focus on Clare of Assisi.

- —. *The Growth of Mysticism: Gregory the Great through the 12th Century*. The Presence of God: A History of Western Christian Mysticism 2. New York: Crossroad, 1994. Pages 193-224 and 347-352 are particularly pertinent.

- Vauchez, André. "Between Virginity and Spiritual Espousals: Models of Feminine Sainthood in the Christian West during the Middle Ages." *Medieval History Journal* 2 (1999) 349-359.

Celibacy and Enclosure

Celibacy is a multifaceted religious choice at any time in history. Many accept or choose it for the freedom it provides to minister. Others view it as an eschatological witness to the end times. Still others use their celibacy as a way to show their total devotion and service to God. We also know that some choose it for psychological reasons that are not always healthy.

Medieval people were no different in having a variety of motivations to choose celibacy. The religious or spiritual reasons are more easily discoverable because they are openly discussed in the religious literature of the day. Other reasons can be discovered with the help of general histories of medieval sexuality and marriage.

Most of the medieval attitudes toward evangelical celibacy had something to do with practices and ideas about the medieval marriages of nobility. An important reality was that marriages were typically arranged by fathers, uncles and brothers to advance their own political, military, and economic interests. The bride's new life totally focused on the affairs of her new husband. Those affairs included homemaking, physically caring for her husband, entertaining his guests, child bearing, and child rearing. She seldom had much of a life of her own. In other words, the bride's purpose was to serve the men in her life and ultimately the goals, interests, and mission of her husband.

When noble women became nuns and viewed themselves as the brides of Christ, they understood that their purpose was to serve the goals, interests, and mission of Christ. In the early applications of this nuptial spirituality, that service was primarily expressed through the time spent in prayer with the Lord. Clare and the Poor Sisters who followed her way adjusted that understanding through their appreciation of Jesus as the poor and humble Christ. Since Christ's mission was tied up in his poverty and humility, Clare's followers saw their service as literally imitating the same characteristics. To be poor and humble was to share in the ministry of the poor and humble Christ.

A second idea regarding medieval marriage of nobles that impacted female religious life was the importance of female virginity before marriage. The medieval period did not particularly value male virginity before marriage. However, that of females was paramount in achieving the most desired marriage arrangement.

This manifested itself in a variety of practices that protected virginity through female seclusion and constant chaperoning. Noble women typically lived in a separate part of the noble property. Their general seclusion was such that it was considered improper for them to even appear at a window where others could see them. Outings from the family complex were rare and usually reserved for church events. Whenever they did occur, the women were typically at least in pairs if not larger groups and frequently accompanied by a man of the family or servant staff. These practices were common for both unmarried daughters and long-married wives.

The translation of these ideas and practices to the female monastery was not difficult. The enclosure protected nuns' virginity for Christ just as the medieval noble home protected its women. This involved protection from violent attach as much as the danger of casual acquaintance with visitors. The noble home was a place where wives devoted themselves to the service of their husbands and girls learned how to serve their future husbands. The monastic enclosure was a place where nuns served Christ alone. In both places, distractions were kept at a distance.

A third related medieval concern was for the physical safety of women. Medieval war was ubiquitous. The spoils of war included the sexual exploitation of the losers. General lawlessness was also a concern. Our later worksheet on the invasion of San Damiano Monastery by mercenaries illustrates the threat. The physical safety of female religious was always part of the reason for the enclosure, even when higher theological reasons were proposed.

If many medieval people feared for the safety of female religious in the face of harm from the outside, they also feared that harm could come from within the monastery. This fourth concern addressed the fear that women might enter religious life for inappropriate reasons. At different times in this diverse history, church figures addressed this by making sure religious life was difficult enough that slackers would not be attracted. Pope Gregory IX was always concerned about this possibility which caused him, in part, to enforce a strict enclosure and require sever fasting regulations.

In those long centuries that viewed women as the weaker sex, the female enclosure also addressed this threat from within by protecting male religious from the "uncontrollable" sexual impulses of female religious. In other words, the enclosure of female religious was thought to protect male religious on the outside as much as female religious on the inside.

Our final point is that female religious celibacy could also be a means to highly desired freedom for women. The powerful goals of arranged marriages too frequently led to unhappy and dismal marriages. The task of serving the projects of one's husband was not appealing to every woman. Despite the limitations of religious life, it could be a much desired alternative. Of course, this reality also caused church leaders to be sure religious life was strenuous enough to discourage undesirable applicants. Further, this option expected a medieval woman to transfer her commitment from the service of a husband to the service of Jesus in a monastery.

A parade of important people figures into the long history of these ideas, issues, and concerns. Certainly, the enclosure was always part of monastic life in the West for men and women. Perhaps the desert itself served as a type of enclosure for the early hermits. However, for our purposes, it is most useful to start with Caesarius of Arles, who in 513 wrote a rule for nuns that mandated a very strict cloister. His motivations were likely mixed, striving to assure the physical safety of the nuns and to promote a spirituality free from outside distractions. His *Rule* was important because other religious founders, bishops, and diocesan councils used it as a model for other female monasteries. This disseminated Caesarius's ideas about and regulations for female religious life.

It was probably inevitable that such a strict approach to enclosure would not last forever. Over time, observance of the cloister loosened. There is considerable evidence that in subsequent centuries some abbesses and other nuns conducted business outside the enclosure and made occasional trips for various reasons.

Just before and at the time Clare was beginning her religious life at San Damiano Monastery (1211), numerous new ways of religious life for women were emerging. Groups of women sought to live an unenclosed form of evangelical or penitential life much like the new mendicant male orders did, e.g., the Friars Minor (Franciscans), Friars Preachers (Dominicans), and Servites. Many women hoped to actually be members of those and other preexisting orders that included double monasteries, i.e., adjacent foundations, one for each gender. The Premonstratensians, Cistercians, the Fontevrault Abbey founded in 1100 by Robert of Arbrissel and others already had a history of doing this.

Increasingly, historians believe there were unenclosed groups of female religious living under the inspiration of Francis of Assisi already by 1216 (see the next section of this chapter). Other groups lived an enclosed life, but with very flexible rules, allowing for occasional interaction with outsiders and the ability to conduct regular business affecting the monastery. Romagnoli shows that there were times, including that leading up to the advent of Franciscanism, when rules in general and specifically about enclosure weren't that important to the average religious (Romagnoli 98).

Before and through the papacy of Innocent III (1198-1216), fluidity around these issues was common. While previous popes seemed intent on crushing a great deal of the innovation going on in the Church regarding religious life, Innocent sought ways of reconciling these groups and harnessing their energy for service to the Church. However, beginning with Pope Honorius III (1216-1227) and especially through his papal legate for religious in central and northern Italy, Cardinal Ugolino dei Conti di Segni, the Roman Church continuously moved with determination toward a more strictly enforced enclosure for religious women. (See Makowski for a detailed study.)

Ugolino considered the enclosure the premier characteristic of female religious life. A strict enclosure and stringent fasting regulations assured that women entering religious life were not undesirable candidates who might cause scandal to the rest of the Church. Agnes of Prague experienced some confusion about these fasting rules, and Clare would address them in her third letter to Agnes. However, never did the two abbesses ever question the enclosure. They simply assumed that it was part of their life and focused on other issues of more concern to them.

It is clear from various church documents and the letters of Clare of Assisi to Agnes of Prague that few people had as strict a view of the enclosure as Gregory IX. Clare and Agnes always desired to keep their ties to the Friars Minor strong. This was a large part of their Franciscan identity. Allowing Franciscan men to enter areas of the enclosure with greater ease than Gregory desired was always important to these two Franciscan abbesses. In the end, Gregory would capitulate to the abbesses' desires.

This mixture of issues and motivations was sanctified by the image of female religious as brides of Christ, whose virginity needed to be protected. Indeed, strict enclosure for female religious seemed to have become an end in itself under Pope Gregory IX (see Schulenburg 78-79 and Makowski 126). The next section of this chapter addresses how Clare responded to expectations for enclosure in her own monastery.

Cited sources and suggested reading

- Caesarius of Arles. *Rule for Nuns.* Trans. Mary Caritas McCarthy. Washington DC: Catholic University of America Press, 1960.

- Hunt, Noreen. "Enclosure." *Cistercian Studies* 21 (1986) 51-63 and 22 (1987) 126-151.

- Makowski, Elizabeth. *Canon Law and Cloistered Women:* Periculo-so *and Its Commentators, 1298-1545.* Studies in Medieval and Early Modern Canon Law 5. Washington DC: The Catholic University of America Press, 1997.

- Romagnoli, Alessandra Bartolomei. "Women's Franciscanism from Its Beginnings Until the Council of Trent." Trans. Edward Hagman. *Greyfriars Review* 19.2 (2005) 91-168. A lengthy article that spectac-ularly places Clare of Assisi within the larger world of 13th-century female religious life and papal policy.

- Sensi, Mario. "Women's Recluse Movement in Umbria During the 13th and 14th Centuries." Trans. Edward Hagman. *Greyfriars Review* 8.3 (1994) 319-345.

- Schulenburg, Jane Tibbets. *Forgetful of Their Sex: Female Sanc-tity and Society, ca. 500-1100.* Chicago: University of Chicago Press, 1998.

- —. "Strict Active Enclosure and Its Effect on the Female Monastic Experience (ca. 500-1100)." In *Distant Echoes.* Eds. John A. Nichols and Lillian Thomas Shank. Medieval Religious Women 1. Kalama-zoo MI: Cistercian Publications, 1984. 51-86.

Enclosure and Clare of Assisi

We have no evidence that Clare of Assisi ever left San Damiano Monastery after moving there in 1211. Her religious life was shaped in profound ways by the all-encompassing structure of the enclosure. From time to time, scholars have argued over whether or not Clare would have chosen the limits of the enclosure if the Church had not required it. Few believe Clare considered it among the major issues affecting her chosen form of religious life. A radical poverty and a close relationship with the Friars Minor were clearly her two primary issues. Elizabeth Makowski succinctly summarized Clare's situation by writing, "While St. Clare waged a decades-long struggle for a form of life that would confirm the privilege of poverty, she clearly accepted the life of the cloistered contemplative. In every version of the rule, including the one formulated by Clare herself in 1252, strict enclosure remained a constant" (35). However, was it always that way?

For some recent decades, authors have become more aware of Jacques de Vitry's description of the early Franciscans in a document he wrote in 1216 (CA:ED 427-428). In it, he referred to the "brothers and sisters minor" in the Umbrian area of Italy, which many understood to be the Friars Minor and the Poor Sisters at San Damiano Monastery. He described both sexes as living in radical poverty and without an enclosure. This led some to conclude that, in the beginning, Clare and the women at San Damiano did not observe the enclosure. There always have been others who disputed this claim, noting that no reference by Clare supports this interpretation. Regardless of one's opinion, it is clear that in 1211 when Clare and her blood-sister Agnes of Assisi first arrived at San Damiano, a tightly controlled enclosure was impossible simply because the building was nothing more than a small chapel with a cramped attached residence that once served a resident priest.

Recent research has given more attention to various letters by Popes Gregory IX and Innocent IV criticizing a group of "religious" women in central and northern Italy called the "Sisters Minor." These women did not observe the enclosure, which was the premier element of female religious life for the popes. They engaged in apostolic activity and wore a habit similar to Clare's sisters at San Damiano Monastery. These papal bulls were issued from 1241 through 1257 (see our chapter entitled "Clare's Letters to Agnes of Prague: Papal Bulls Affecting Clare of Assisi, Agnes of Prague and Other Monasteries of the Order of St. Damian"; cf. *Ad audientiam nostrum* issued in 1241*)*.

The letters demonstrate that there were unenclosed women following a Franciscan inspiration when we certainly know that Clare and her Poor Sisters were observing a strict enclosure under the *Form of Life* given by Cardinal Ugolino. So, scholars increasingly doubt that De Vitry was referring to the sisters at San Damiano specifically, but probably to a more general movement of apostolic women in 1216.

However puzzling or disconcerting the expectation to be enclosed may appear to some readers, it did not appear so for Clare. While she demonstrated a desire for a more flexible approach to enclosure than the popes, we have no record that she resisted the enclosure entirely. Perhaps this is because so much of her attention was drawn to her real concern: absolute and radical personal and corporate poverty and close ties with the Friars Minor.

Some, as in Bartoli's biography of St. Clare (94), assume that Clare included the enclosure in her own *Form of Life* because, without such a reference, her document would not have been approved by the papacy. Peruse our chapter "Clare's Letters to Agnes of Prague: Papal Bulls" to see how various popes sought to impose the enclosure.

Cited sources and suggested reading

- Bartoli, Marco. *Clare of Assisi.* Trans. Sister Frances Teresa, OSC. Quincy IL: Franciscan Press, 1993.

- —. *Saint Clare: Beyond the Legend.* Trans. Frances Teresa Downing. Cincinnati OH: St. Anthony Messenger Press, 2010. Chapter eight on "Damianites, Poor Sisters or Poor Ladies Enclosed?" contrasts Pope Gregory IX's insistence on enclosure for nuns with Clare's focus on absolute poverty, which was itself at odds with Gregory's program to stabilize female monasteries through a sufficient permanent endowment.

- Beha, Marie. "'Go Forth Swiftly.'" *The Cord* 40.7 (1990) 211-221.

- Bruzelius, Caroline. "Nuns in Space: Strict Enclosure and the Architecture of the Clarisses in the Thirteenth Century." In *Clare of Assisi: A Medieval and Modern Woman.* Ed. Ingrid Peterson. Clare Centenary Series 8. St. Bonaventure NY: The Franciscan Institute, 1996. 53-74.

- Makowski, Elizabeth. *Canon Law and Cloistered Women: Periculoso and Its Commentators, 1298-1545.* Studies in Medieval and Early

Modern Canon Law 5. Washington DC: The Catholic University of America Press, 1997.

• Romagnoli, Alessandra Bartolomei. "Women's Franciscanism from Its Beginnings Until the Council of Trent." Trans. Edward Hagman. *Greyfriars Review* 19.2 (2005) 91-168. A lengthy article that spectacularly places Clare of Assisi within the larger world of 13th-century female religious life and papal policy.

Financial (In)dependence

Medieval women were quite dependent on men for their financial sustenance. Even widowhood could impoverish a woman once married to a prosperous husband. With few exceptions, men controlled the money and property of families. If a husband died, it was common for the widow's brother-in-law or son to take things over. Women had a hard time becoming in charge of many important things. However, religious practice was one area where women could exert some independence. For example, Clare's mother was quite a pilgrim, travelling to many of the major pilgrimage destinations of medieval Christians. Others fasted to manifest their independence (See Bynum, *Holy Feast and Holy Fast* 219-244 for an in-depth explanation).

In medieval Europe, mostly noble women entered female monasteries. They were able to bring their dowries with them to help support their monasteries. Often, noble women brought servants with them into religious life. In the days before the penitential, evangelical and apostolic life movements, poverty was not as important to women entering a monastery.

However, the papacy remained concerned that too many monasteries did not have the financial resources to sustain themselves. Nuns in some monasteries were close to starving to death. Working for Pope Honorius III, Cardinal Ugolino quickly realized a better solution was needed. He devised a plan where he grouped various monasteries in central and northern Italy into a new order that followed the *Rule of St. Benedict* as supplemented by Ugolino's own *Form of Life.* The monasteries had ample endowments, often in the form of land, that would support the women indefinitely. Ugolino himself bought the property needed for some of these monasteries.

This would have worked in earlier times when the corporate poverty of a monastery was not so important, However, some of the new female monasteries had a deep desire to live poorly as they believed Jesus, the apostles, and the Virgin Mary did while they lived on earth. For many, corporate poverty was a way to share in the mission of Jesus by sharing in his suffering. Clare of Assisi was an example of this desire.

After Clare left her family home to become a religious and was invested at the Portiuncula, she first landed in San Paolo delle Abbadesse in Bastia. This was a monastery of noble women with a few servants. Interestingly, Clare would have been entering as a servant since she had already disposed of her dowry. However, after only a short time, she left San Paolo most likely because it was not the type of religious life she was seeking. Most historians believe Clare wanted a more radical personal and corporate poverty than the nuns at San Paolo practiced.

However, an endowed monastery became even more important as the Church, under the influence of Cardinal Ugolino, increasingly imposed a strict enclosure. Religious women's economic affairs were complicated by the expectation that, unlike male religious, they never or rarely leave their enclosure. Male monks seemed to always have the freedom to leave their enclosure, even if rarely, to conduct business, sell their wares, beg for support, provide occasional ministries of various sorts, or engage in the church debates of the day. The new mendicant orders prized itinerancy as a fundamental value; without an enclosure they were free to do many different ministries. On the other hand, poor female religious often were dependent on male religious to share a portion of their financial support or to beg specifically for the benefit of the female religious.

The scant financial resources to support female monasteries necessarily limited the number of women able to enter religious life. Further, female religious life would favor wealthy women over the poor because of their ability to bring support in various forms to the enclosure. McNamara states that in medieval times, "social status, dowry and family influence were the major qualifications for entry" into female religious life (Muffled Voices 23).

This was a point that drove a wedge between Gregory IX and Clare of Assisi for the duration of his life. Clare was one of those women attracted to the penitential and evangelical movements' values, including poverty. It is important to understand the more general economic situation of female religious in medieval Europe to better appreciate the tension between these two religious figures.

Cited sources and suggested reading

- Bynum, Caroline Walker. *Holy Feast and Holy Fast: The Religious Significance of Food to Medieval Women.* Berkeley and Los Angeles: University of California Press, 1987.

- McNamara, Jo Ann. "Muffled Voices: The Lives of Consecrated Women in the Fourth Century." In *Distant Echoes.* Eds. John A. Nichols and Lillian Thomas Shank. Medieval Religious Women 1. Kalamazoo MI: Cistercian Publications, 1984. 11-29.

Medieval Religious Women

The Connection to Male Religious

Several medieval male orders were willing to cooperate with and support female "members" or divisions until the end of the 12th century. Well known examples were the Cistercians and Premonstratensians (Norbertines in the USA). Gilbert of Sempringham's Gilbertines (an order less known today) closely supervised and provided for women religious in late 12th-century England. Robert of Arbrissel established the famous double monastery of Fontevrault in western France along the Loire River. Robert organized the community so that the abbess governed both men and women. The legal and organizational structure of this community seemed to provide for greater stability. Other male orders were less stringently connected to female religious by simply providing pastoral care to them. This was called the *cura monialium*.

However, there was a big change at the end of the 12th century and continuing through the 13th. The new mendicant orders seemed reticent about engaging with female religious even of their own tradition. Some of these new orders developed female divisions, e.g., the Franciscans, Dominicans, and Carmelites. However, the men were often not as enthused about the connection as the women would have hoped for. Sometimes, these male orders became involved because of papal pressure to do so. At other times, they enlisted the support of the papacy to free them from any responsibility toward female foundations of their own or other traditions.

Just as the mendicant orders were appearing on the scene, even those monastic male orders that previously had a strong relationship with female counterparts were pulling back from their commitments. The Premonstratensians discontinued associations with female monasteries in 1198. The Cistercians stopped affiliating new female communities in 1228 and tried to limit their responsibilities to those already affiliated.

This dynamic appeared in the relationships among Clare and Francis of Assisi, the Friars Minor in general, and the papacy. Francis was willing to help a woman discern her vocation, but then sent her off to execute her own plans alone. This is reflected in his *Earlier Rule* that forbade the friars from receiving a woman into obedience and his *Later Rule* that forbade friars from entering a female monastery without permission from the Holy See (ER XII 4; LR XI). Francis's legislation reflected the requirements of Cardinal Ugolino's *Form of Life* (10). In *Quo elongati* (1230), Pope Gregory IX made it difficult for male Franciscans to be significantly present at San

Damiano. The tension was visible in Clare's laments that Francis did not visit her at San Damiano Monastery as frequently as she hoped.

Why did the sentiments change? One reason was the increasingly enforced strict enclosure for female religious. This was a way for the Holy See to control who was influencing nuns, including their visitators. However, religious men in general were growing weary of the burden of caring for female religious. As the number of female monasteries expanded, the male orders were forced to devote more men to their care. They often didn't have the men to do this or didn't want to offer them.

The male mendicant orders had additional reasons compared to the monastic orders. Increasingly, the male mendicant orders were involved in the pastoral care of the laity, especially as preachers. The care of female religious seemed to compete for the same competent friars who could be excellent preachers or ministers in other venues.

Both reasons might already be visible in the reticence of Francis of Assisi to associate with the Poor Sisters at San Damiano Monastery (2C 204). Bartoli counts thirty-two references to Francis by Clare in her writings. There are none about Clare in the writings of Francis (*Beyond the Legend* 97). The lack of symmetry in their relationship is stunning. Dalarun cautions us from assuming the relationship between Francis and Clare was more than it was (73). Still, Godet-Calogeras points out that Francis wrote numerous missives to the Poor Sisters at San Damiano Monastery. Those that survive demonstrate a warm and supportive relationship (61-81). After Francis's death, the leaders and educated among the Friars Minor increasingly resisted pastoral care of women because of their desire for more ministry to the laity.

Cited sources and suggested reading

- Bartoli, Marco. *Saint Clare: Beyond the Legend*. Trans. Frances Teresa Downing. Cincinnati: St. Anthony Messenger Press, 2010.

- Bolton, Brenda. "Mulieres Sanctae." In *Women in Medieval Society*. Ed. Susan Mosher Stuard. Philadelphia: University of Pennsylvania Press, 1976. 141-158.

- Dalarun, Jacques. "Francis and Clare of Assisi: Differing Perspectives on Gender and Power." *Franciscan Studies* 63 (2005) 11-25.

- —. *Francis of Assisi and the Feminine*. St. Bonaventure NY: Franciscan Institute Publications, 2006.

- Godet-Calogeras, Jean-François. "From Brother Francis to the Poor Sisters of San Damiano: What Is Left of Their Correspondence?" In *Her Bright Merits: Essays Honoring Ingrid J. Peterson, OSF."* Eds. Mary Walsh Meany and Felicity Dorsett. Spirit and Life 17. St. Bonaventure NY: Franciscan Institute Publications, 2012. 61-81.

- Gold, Penny Shine. "Male/Female Cooperation: The Example of Fontevrault." In *Distant Echoes*. Eds. John A Nichols and Lillian Thomas Shank. Medieval Religious Women 1. Kalamazoo MI: Cistercian Publications, 1984. 151-168.

- Knox, Lezlie. "Audacious Nuns: Conflict Between the Franciscan Friars and the Order of Saint Clare. " *Church History* 41 (2000) 41-62.

- McLaughlin, Eleanor C. "Equality of Souls, Inequality of Sexes: Women in Medieval Theology." In *Religion and Sexism: Images of Woman in the Jewish and Christian Traditions*. Ed. Rosemary Radford Ruether. New York: Simon & Schuster, 1974. 233-251.

- Southern, R.W. *Western Society and the Church in the Middle Ages*. Baltimore: Penguin, 1978. 309-331.

Medieval Food Practices

Many people today are confused or dubious about the frequently extreme or even bizarre food practices of medieval female saints. Thus, it should not be surprising that these practices have been the subject of many scholarly studies. The hagiography including such stories needs to be understood within its own rules and tendencies at the time. These studies show us how the available models of holiness shaped the behavior of medieval female religious.

Caroline Walker Bynum is one of the premier English-speaking scholars in this field. While we mention many of her works in various bibliographies throughout this workbook, her book, *Holy Feast and Holy Fast: The Religious Significance of Food to Medieval Women* in 1987 was a groundbreaking best-seller in the field. It is the best book to read first on this theme. Our comments here are largely dependent on her work. Page citations here refer to this book unless otherwise cited.

Studies about medieval female hagiography show that the legends of female candidates for sainthood were expected to display extraordinary eating behaviors. Such behaviors fulfilled expectations for saints found in the available models of holiness or stock incidences common in hagiography (see our chapter entitled "Hagiography"). Many times, this led to exaggeration, even in eyewitness reports. Of course, that was always the reason such reports were included in hagiography; when a report was superhuman, the obvious conclusion for the reader was that it was miraculous, confirming the sanctity of the subject.

Bynum writes that canonization proceedings regularly included testimony about fasting, in part, because that was expected of a holy person, especially women. Sometimes, Bynum reports, the testimony was contradicted by other information gathered during the processes for canonization. Thus, extraordinary and ordinary eating patterns could be reported about the same people. After citing several examples, Bynum concludes that, "'eating nothing' in hagiographic accounts often means 'not eating normally'" (82-83). This can mean the subject had inconsistent eating or fasting practices, or was not as extreme as the hagiography indicated. Often, she adds, fasting practices were connected with Eucharistic devotion, including living by consumption of the Eucharist alone (82).

How did this affect the hagiography that survives down to our own age? Bynum notes, "Hagiographers were thus expected to include at least passing references to food abstention and Eucharistic piety in their accounts of pious people. There is, moreover, some reason to think that women's *vitae* in the later Middle Ages were even more stereotypical than male *vitae*. In part, this may be because women's lives were in fact less diverse and because women often learned patterns of piety from one another" (83).

In our study of Clare, we want to be careful to understand that meditation, fasting and Eucharistic devotion were all considered preparation for contemplation in the Middle Ages. Further, these same things helped especially women to share in the sufferings of Christ which was their goal and obligation as "spouses" of Christ. Admirers of the saints looked on the same practices as signs of supernatural power and confirmation of their sanctity. Thus, Bynum cautions that accounts of such behavior actually tell us more reliably about the stereotypes of holiness of the day than the actual practices of the saints themselves (84).

Bynum points out that while the popular forces of hagiography were emphasizing extreme asceticism in the 12th and 13th centuries, monastic leaders and popes were encouraging moderation (84-85). This was true in Clare's case as the bishop of Assisi and Francis of Assisi counseled her to greater moderation (PC I 8:25; II 8:27; IV 5:14; VL 30-33; LCl XII 19). The fact that church officials did this might suggest some credibility to the excesses. It is also important to understand that the reading public considered these practices more important as signals of holiness than the saint's obedience to authority. This fact clearly communicates the power of these stock incidences about dietary practices to shape the public's expectations for their saints.

Bynum notes that while hagiography exalted these physical penances, it didn't expect the readers to imitate them. In part that is because these practices are obviously beyond the abilities of ordinary people since they are super-human. On another level, they achieve their goal because they bring the reader to the admiration that causes them to consider their subjects to be saints (85).

One final point is worth mentioning. In a world in which women had so little control or power, food (especially what a woman ate herself) was a vehicle of independence. Others could not force a woman to eat. Thus, through fasting and abstinence, women were able to take some facet of their lives into their own hands and make decisions. In this way, their familial, social and ecclesial relationships were altered by eating habits that strove to express a spirituality. Caroline Walker Bynum offers perhaps the best explanation of this phenomenon in a chapter entitled "Food as Control of Circumstance" from her informative book, *Holy Feast and Holy Fast* (219-244).

Cited sources and suggested reading

Caroline Walker Bynum's writings show interesting connections among spirituality, fasting, the body, and the Eucharist for medieval women. *Holy Feast and Holy Fast: The Religious Significance of Food to Medieval Women* is a good book to read first on this topic.

- Bartoli, Marco. *Saint Clare: Beyond the Legend*. Trans. Frances Teresa Downing. Cincinnati OH: St. Anthony Messenger Press, 2010. Chapter five on "Penitence" clarifies medieval ideas about penance as a change of lifestyle. It goes on to situate Clare's penitential practices within the practices of others at the time, including St. Francis. It focuses on sharing in the sufferings of Christ and being with Jesus.

- Bynum, Caroline Walker. "…And Woman His Humanity: Female Imagery in the Religious Writing of the Later Middle Ages." In *Gender and Religion: The Complexity of Symbols*. Eds. Caroline Walker Bynum, Stevan Harrell, and Paula Richman. Boston: Beacon Press, 1986. 257-288.

- —. *Fragmentation and Redemption: Essays on Gender and the Human Body in Medieval Religion*. New York: Zone Books, 1991.

- —. *Holy Feast and Holy Fast: The Religious Significance of Food to Medieval Women*. Berkeley and Los Angeles: University of California Press, 1987.

- —. *Jesus as Mother: Studies in the Spirituality of the High Middle Ages*. Berkeley and Los Angeles: University of California Press, 1982. Four of this book's five essays focus on 12th-century religious life.

- —. "Religious Women in the Later Middle Ages." In *Christian Spirituality: High Middle Ages and Reformation*. Ed. Jill Raitt. New York: Crossroad, 1987. 121-139.

- —. "The Veneration of the Eucharist among Women in the Middle Ages." In *The Word Becomes Flesh: Radical Physicality in Religious Sculpture in the Later Middle Ages*. Symposium. Holy Cross College, Worcester MA, 1985.

- —. "Women Mystics and Eucharistic Devotion in the Thirteenth Century." *Women Studies* 11 (1984) 179-214.

Assisi's Revolution

Context is important for understanding historical events. Historians are constantly trying to better understand the world in which Clare of Assisi lived. Often, when learning about context, a big and flashy event captures our attention. However, it frequently turns out to be only the tip of an iceberg that leads us to deeper, subtler, and more complicated causes. Such is the case with what we call Assisi's Revolution. It traumatized both Clare and Francis of Assisi. It also leads us to more important changes that were the root causes of conflict in the early 13th century.

We begin by relating the flashy events that were involved. In 1198, when Clare was four or five, the citizenry of Assisi overtook and destroyed the local castle (Rocca Maggiore). Today, the ruins of this later rebuilt castle are prominently visible on the hill above Assisi. It was the strong hold of the recently deceased Holy Roman Emperor, Henry IV (1191 – 1197), who was the political ally of the nobility in Assisi. Mostly members of the new merchant class orchestrated the event.

That doesn't mean that the merchant class was an ally of the papacy, which was the other major power in northern Italy at the time. In fact, the thrones of both the papacy and the Holy Roman Empire had been empty at the same time and for a while. The merchant class sensed a power vacuum and an exciting opportunity to expel both powers from city politics. They might have hoped to build a commune that would be somewhat like an antecedent to the forthcoming city-states. As the rebellion expanded, other buildings and homes of local nobles were also destroyed.

On the local level, the violent uprising represented growing competition between the traditional landed nobility and the fledgling merchant class. The nobility was in decline, though still very powerful. The merchants were on the rise, but still insufficiently established. The nobility was jealous of the merchants' new wealth. The merchants were jealous of the nobles' status. The old order was just beginning to weaken and pass away. The traditional barter system associated with land-based economies was moribund and giving way to nascent capitalism based on more fluid currency, the basis of trade.

The thrilling exploit of the new classes populating Assisi struck at the previously invincible landed nobility. Clare's noble family, the Offreducci-os, was among the defeated. It's very probable that Clare's family, like others, fled to nearby Perugia in 1202 as hostilities intensified. Some believe it could have fled as early as 1198. Noble women and children seemed more certain to have fled. While we can imagine the impact of the conquest and exile on the young and impressionable Clare and her family, there are no records to inform us of their precise experiences. However, the old order was not yet defeated. The tide turned when Assisi grimly fell to Perugia at the Battle of Collestrada in 1202.

Italian cities were at constant war among themselves at this time. What were the causes of this moment? Perugia had welcomed the Assisian nobility for a variety of reasons that all suggested a future war with Assisi. First, Perugian nobility probably wanted to prevent a similar uprising by its own merchant class. Second, while Perugia was used to the constant power struggle between pope and emperor, it was likely uncertain how a third power base in the valley, i.e., an independent Assisi, would play out in the long run. Finally, Perugia certainly did not want the Assisian nobility to become permanent refugees in Perugia. They had to be returned to Assisi and stability restored.

As with all medieval war, the Battle of Collestrada was brutal. Francis of Assisi fought for Assisi. He was taken prisoner probably for his value as a hostage. He was imprisoned for about a year in the normally deplorable conditions of medieval prisons. Within that time, Assisi worked out terms for peace that would require it to restore and rebuild the property of nobles. That included the Rocca on top of the hill. With the terms in place, Francis's father, Pietro Bernardone, paid the ransom that led to Francis's release. Clare and many Assisian nobles would remain in Perugia for a time, slowly trickling back to Assisi as the time seemed right.

Francis came home sick, and it seems to have taken about another year for him to restore his health. In the meantime, the buildings of nobles were slowly rebuilt. Francis would be healthy enough by 1205 to think of joining Walter of Brienne on a ruinous military campaign toward southern Italy. That same year, Clare's family may have thought conditions safe enough for the children and women to return to Assisi. Both sides wondered when the two movements in history, feudalism and the nascent money economy, would crash into each other again. However, for the moment, the truce reunited two citizens, Francis and Clare, one from each of the warring classes.

Francis did not fight with Walter of Brienne. Instead, he began his own religious way of life. Clare noticed him, but it's also important to realize that not only Francis influenced Clare's religious choices. The bigger monastic, penitential, evangelical and apostolic life movements were also working on her imagination. Francis and Clare met secretly until both had abandoned the promises and obligations of their respective social ranks. They would attempt to forge lifestyles unimaginable to each of their originating lineages.

Both were turning trauma and struggle into conversion and new forms of religious life.

That's the part of the iceberg that everyone could see easily, even 800 years later. However, submerged below the surface were deep causes that few people understood. The 12th century and the beginning of the 13th saw many economic changes which were tied to two connected events: the crusades and economic exchange with the East. These events certainly encouraged the development of the merchant class in Italy, which was also developing ties to various parts of France and the Lowlands.

New social groups created new social stress. Money began to replace land as the primary source of wealth, undermining the privileged position of the nobility. The growth of trade routes and money resulted in new industries. Principle among them were textiles and metallurgy. A host of smaller cottage industries began to spring up as well, and these helped support many of the new religious groups popping up across Western Europe (e.g., Beguines made lace, and Humiliati made cloth).

Thus, besides merchants, Western Europe saw the development of another new class, the laborer, who, unlike the serf, exchanged his labor for money, not a share of the agricultural product he raised. This changed the ethic of Western Europe; work and wealth became increasingly connected and valued, often at the expense of what church people of the day considered proper Christian living. Many viewed this fledgling capitalism as the root of late medieval selfishness and individualism.

Some in the Church responded by participating in a variety of linked movements that fall under numerous names: the penitential movement, the poverty movement, the evangelical movement, the lay apostolic life movement, the clerical apostolic life movement (epitomized by the growth of canons regular), the mendicant movement, and others.

For many of the participants in these movements, poverty became a key element of reform. This was because poverty was viewed as altering what was most reprehensible about the changing medieval person: greed, selfishness, and individuality. Poverty functioned within these movements to change the individual, and, thus, more effectively reform the entire church and society. It seemed to eliminate the causes of conflict at the time.

The poor and humble Christ became the image of this transformation. The imitation of Christ focused on the way to transform the self. In many ways, the surge of reform movements in the Church, popular and official in origin, traced its origin to the religious and ethical presuppositions many were making about the changing Western European church and society.

Francis and Clare involved themselves in these movements without any plans to change anyone else. Their only goal seemed to have been to change themselves and those who decided to join them. They chose to become poor not to heal the breach between the poor and the rich, but to imitate Christ who was poor as they understood him. Grau identifies *insecurity* as the determining characteristic that fed Francis and Clare's desire to live without property (St. Clare's *Privilegium* 333-334). Insecurity signified trust in God, not in money. Undoubtedly, their choice was a response to the growing desire for security achieved through work and money. They rejected this drive for wealth and chose to imitate the poor and humble Christ.

Cited sources and suggested reading

- Bartoli, Marco. *Saint Clare: Beyond the Legend.* Trans. Frances Teresa Downing. Cincinnati OH: St. Anthony Messenger Press, 2010. Chapter nine on "War and Peace" begins with a good thumbnail description of political and military tensions between the noble and new merchant classes in Assisi, and then the war between neighboring Perugia and Assisi.

- Fortini, Arnaldo. "New Information about Saint Clare of Assisi." Trans. M. Jane Frances. *Greyfriars Review* 7.1 (1993) 27-69. This is a translation of an article first published in 1953. So, "new" information is a relative term.

- Grau, Engelbert. "Saint Clare's *Privilegium Paupertatis*: Its History and Significance." Trans. M. Jane Frances. *Greyfriars Review* 6.3 (1992) 327-336.

Who Founded the Order of St. Clare?
Setting the Stage with a Narrative

This is obviously a question that gets your attention, and there are other questions that do the same. For instance, are Clare of Assisi and the Poor Sisters of San Damiano Monastery the normative medieval experience of "Franciscan Second Order" monasteries? Did Pope Gregory IX and Clare get along? Did Francis of Assisi warn Clare about the plans of Pope Gregory, and did Clare do the same for Agnes of Prague? Other provocative questions could also be asked.

These are serious questions that aren't asked just to get your attention. They are questions receiving new answers. However, more importantly, they lead to a narrative that lays the groundwork for much of the work to be done with this workbook. This was not a narrative commonly told even 25 years ago. The biases of those telling the story then shaped it in ways that are now being abandoned. Earlier, mostly Franciscans of one type or another were telling the story. Today, lay and secular scholars without Franciscan vested interests are shaping the narrative. It is a complex story that has many parts. Every beginning student wants to familiarize her or himself with the new narrative before beginning a study of the life and writings of Clare from primary sources. It begins in this way.

Before Clare of Assisi left her family home and began living religious life, other women had done similar things. Central and northern Italy were dotted with new female monasteries. Quite a few were inspired by the penitential, evangelical and apostolic life movements of which Francis was a part, but which also predated him (See our previous chapter on these movements). There were new female foundations north of the Alps as well.

The movements had numerous values that included a return to the Gospel as the primary source of Christian living, preaching, a simple life style, care of the poor, an intense prayer life, working for peace, and penance. The imitation of the historical Jesus was becoming a central characteristic. However, different monasteries and groups did that to varying degrees of radicalism. Some, like Clare, insisted on total personal and corporate poverty in imitation of Christ as she understood him. Others emphasized different values from the movements.

These groups operated under relative freedom from overt church control. Few observed an established religious rule. Some may have had their own *propositum* for life, simple as it may have been. Others may have followed the *Benedictine Rule*, a well-known rule at the time. However, the

primary characteristic of these new groups was that they were founded on
a lived experience that was shared and passed on by the group. Initially,
there was little interest in writing a rule or founding a religious order. Participants simply wanted to live their own spiritual inspirations in a free and
unobstructed manner.

Clare of Assisi was not much different. After her departure from her
family home, Francis of Assisi participated in her "investiture" at the Portiuncula in the valley below Assisi. Needing to find a socially suitable
place for a young religious woman, Clare settled into San Paolo delle Abbadesse in Bastia. This was a monastery of noble women with a few servants. It was a prestigious monastery near Assisi and definitely not what
Clare had in mind.

Clare quickly departed San Paolo and settled at Sant'Angelo di Panzo,
a more "modern" establishment of religious women, perhaps in the Beguine style. More than San Paolo, Sant'Angelo di Panzo would have been
influenced by the penitential, evangelical and apostolic life movements. Yet
for some reason, Clare was not content there either. Before long, she left
and permanently settled into the simple chapel of San Damiano just below a
gate of Assisi. It originally contained a small living quarters for priests who
no longer lived there. There, Clare began a life without a formal rule. She
does not seem to have intended to found an order, but simply a monastery
where she and others with the same intention could live out their vocation.
They did not have an official name. They simply were the Poor Sisters who
lived at San Damiano Monastery.

Later, in her own *Form of Life* and *Testament*, Clare considered Francis of Assisi her inspiration and the person to whom she repeatedly went
back for clarification, even when he was not very responsive. She and those
attracted to her simply wanted to live the life that inspired them, through
Francis's influence, without interference.

Two things dominated Clare and her early companions: an absolute
and radical personal and corporate poverty in imitation of Jesus and a tight
relationship with the Friars Minor. Francis of Assisi had given Clare a short
Form of Life (FLCl *VI 3-4*) that, for the sisters, was enough to guide their
entire life at San Damiano Monastery. However, it hardly described a comprehensive way of religious life. Clare considered Francis the founder of her
group and relied on a tight connection with the Friars Minor to maintain her
Franciscan identity.

At this early time, the Poor Sisters, as they called themselves, lived in
what looked like an enclosure, but with great flexibility. They were tied to
a place that was so small it was impossible to go outdoors without leaving

what might have been considered the enclosure. Friars Minor were frequent visitors who preached to the sisters and celebrated sacraments with them. Various Friars Minor begged on behalf of the sisters, and, after some time, a few friars lived in huts surrounding the small San Damiano complex.

This was how things went for six to seven years, as other monasteries, each with its unique origin, continued to spring up in central and northern Italy. That was until Pope Honorius III appointed Cardinal Ugolino dei Conti di Segni as his legate or representative to religious women in central and northern Italy in 1218. That year, Honorius issued the papal bull *Litterae tuae nobis* giving Ugolino authority to establish female monasteries subject to the Bishop of Rome.

Cardinal Ugolino had not seemed engaged with the Franciscan movement before the death of his uncle, Pope Innocent III, who appointed him a cardinal in 1206. Records suggest that others in the hierarchy mediated Franciscan relationships with the papacy in those years. With Innocent's death in 1216, Pope Honorius III kept Ugolino as a close advisor. This was when Ugolino's relationship with Franciscans began or changed. After an initial trip through the region, Ugolino quickly diagnosed problems plaguing the new female establishments.

First, the lack of juridical unity among the monasteries made it difficult for the Holy See to have an administrative impact on them. Each monastery needed to be dealt with individually as long as they had no unifying rule. Second, while some of these foundations may have been financially stable at first due to wealthy and/or noble women being part of the foundation, over time, many female monasteries became financially unsustainable. There were even reports of the nuns in some foundations nearly starving to death for lack of financial support. Ugolino immediately saw the problems and just as quickly devised solutions.

In 1219, Ugolino composed his own *Constitutions* or as we will call them in this workbook, his *Form of Life*. It henceforth defined his relationship with female religious, including Franciscan women. From then on, Ugolino would relentlessly work to achieve the following papal policy goals in relationship to women.

1. This female religious life was based on the traditional and trustworthy *Rule of St. Benedict*. Ugolino's own *Form of Life* added how to live that in the early 13th century. In some ways, this responded to the declaration of the Fourth Lateran Council that no new religious rules be approved. In reality, his *Form of Life* had more impact on the female monasteries than the *Rule of St. Benedict*.

2.   Each monastery was to be adequately endowed so it could support itself into the foreseen future.

3.   Strict enclosure was to be the premier characteristic of this way of life. This provision avoided any possibility of scandal and enhanced the spirituality of these women as brides of Christ (see our earlier chapter "Medieval Religious Women: Nuptial Spirituality").

4.   Rather significant fasting regulations were imposed in this *Form of Life* as Ugolino saw this as a clear sign that his nuns were serious about their vocation and not offering any scandal. Some nuns might have seen this as a way to participate in the sufferings of Jesus whom they strove to imitate.

5.   Unique features of individual monasteries were handled through papal exemptions, sometimes called privileges. There were many exemptions granted for many monasteries. So, such exemptions were not unusual. Monasteries focusing on poverty utilized exemptions to achieve their desired way of life since Ugolino's *Form of Life* only mentioned poverty once.

6.   Local episcopal control of female monasteries increasingly transferred to the papacy. Local bishops only oversaw liturgical practices, the pastoral care of the women, and the installation of the abbesses. Real control was placed in the hands of the pope or his legate. A pound of wax became the symbolic annual payment from female monasteries to local bishops for rent or diocesan taxes.

Surprisingly, this was the first order in the history of the Western Church to be founded specifically and exclusively for women. Previous forms of female religious life were tied to male foundations.

With his new *Form of Life* in hand, Ugolino began to travel through central and northern Italy inducing as many female monasteries as possible to embrace it. Few escaped his plan. Shortly thereafter, this group of female monasteries became known as the Order of the Poor Ladies of the Valley of Spoleto or of Tuscany.

With these developments in mind, many today consider Ugolino the founder of this group since he was most responsible for grouping the various monasteries together in the first place. Second, he imposed the *Benedictine Rule* and his own *Form of Life* on these monasteries, giving them their legal framework. Finally, he defined the charismatic identity of the order in that he gave them the founding principles or gifts (religious charism) of strict enclosure and severe dietary regulation.

However, Clare of Assisi was not attracted to this new order founded by Cardinal Ugolino. She saw the founder of her monastery as Francis of Assisi. The idea of forming an endowment to secure the financial future of San Damiano Monastery opposed Clare's desire to live in total and radical personal and corporate poverty, as Francis himself did and intended for the Poor Sisters of San Damiano Monastery. Finally, the strict enclosure that Ugolino envisioned threatened San Damiano Monastery's close ties with the Friars Minor who were frequent visitors to San Damiano and pastoral agents for the sisters. They also begged on behalf of the sisters for what they could not provide for themselves.

Ugolino's transition was quite successful within only two years and was an enormous shift in the relationship between female religious and the papacy. Ugolino was the vehicle of the relationship. He wasted no time bringing monastery after monastery into the new order, and it would seem that in 1220 he had clearly intended to bring Clare's San Damiano Monastery in Assisi into it as well.

While Francis of Assisi was travelling in the Middle East and encountering Sultan Al-Malik al-Kamil (c. 1177 – 1238) at Damietta, Cardinal Ugolino visited Clare at San Damiano Monastery during Holy Week of 1220. It is widely believed that he attempted to bring Clare's monastery into his new order. Regardless of his level of success, Ugolino had a moving experience with the Poor Sisters as is seen in his subsequent letter to Clare (CA:ED 129-130) in which he lamented his necessary departure and confessed a heightened sense of his own sinfulness. The letter suggests a close relationship between the two. However, future correspondence and actions indicate two sets of values in conflict for the remainder of their relationship.

A few monasteries were particularly taken by Clare of Assisi's manner of life at San Damiano Monastery and chose to live in its lifestyle. Her radical personal and communal poverty struck an important cord among them. Some also strove for a similar close relationship with the Friars Minor. These included Monticelli near Florence, Monteluce near Perugia, San Salvatore di Colpersito in San Severino, and monasteries in Foligno, Spello, and Arezzo (Alberzoni, *Clare of Assisi and the Poor Sisters,* 35).

North of the Alps, we would have to include St. Francis Monastery in Prague founded by Agnes of Prague in 1234. Her desire to imitate the plan of Clare as closely as possible was the foundation for the four known letters from Clare to Agnes of Prague studied in this workbook. Monticelli and Monteluce were particularly remarkable because they were early monasteries founded with Ugolino's direct help. The conversion of all these monasteries to Clare's form of life witnessed to the attractiveness of Clare' form of life and constituted a challenge to the papal policies implemented by Ugolino.

It would seem that Ugolino and Clare proceeded for the next eight years without being sure what the other would do. Ugolino continued to cajole the female monasteries in central and northern Italy to join his new order and follow his *Form of Life*. Clare found it difficult to resist the pressure of the cardinal, but continued to live in total and radical poverty in apparent opposition to Ugolino's *Form of Life*. The two seemed headed toward a collision course.

It's reasonable to believe Clare didn't worry about compromising her values earlier because most female religious houses had simple or unwritten forms of life, and essentially based their lives on the experience and desires of its members. However, for Clare, it had to be unsettling to learn that Francis had died on October 3, 1226. Even though he frustratingly kept his distance from Clare after he helped her establish her own way of life, she always considered him the inspiration and founder of her community.

Francis was her reference point, not Ugolino. Her commitment to total and radical poverty flowed out of the same commitment in Francis. Even though Francis was scarce around San Damiano, other friars lived in huts around the monastery, provided spiritual care, and begged on behalf of the sisters as needed. As long as he was alive, her dream of Franciscan life for the Poor Sisters seemed safe and secure. With his death, Clare felt more vulnerable. Yet, she remained committed to the values she assumed after that Palm Sunday when she left her parental home.

A decisive and clarifying moment occurred after Cardinal Ugolino was elected Pope Gregory IX in 1227. Early in 1228, he wrote *Deus Pater* to Clare and the Sisters at San Damiano Monastery. At first glance, it can be read as an emotional and personal appeal for their prayerful support of his fledgling papacy. In this way, it can seem similar to his 1220 letter to Clare after his Holy Week visit to San Damiano Monastery. However, *Deus Pater* adds more. It also encouraged the sisters to transform what had been bitter into something sweet and to forget difficult past experiences. Could these admonitions acknowledge resistance from Clare and her Poor Sisters to his way of life? The truth might never be discovered.

On August 18, 1228, Cardinal Rainaldo dei Conti di Segni issued the letter *Matribus sororibus* announcing to twenty-four female monasteries in northern and central Italy that he had been appointed their new cardinal protector. For the first time, we see the new order of Ugolino called the Order of St. Damian instead of the Order of the Poor Ladies of the Valley of Spoleto or of Tuscany. The letter lists San Damiano Monastery in Assisi at the top of the list of member monasteries.

The timing of the letter suggests that once Ugolino gained supreme authority in the Church as Pope Gregory, he intended to unrelentingly drive forward with his plans to force women religious in Italy to follow his *Form of Life*. Modern historians are also quite united in believing that the letter discloses additional goals of Gregory. Not only did he desire San Damiano Monastery to be part of his new order; he also wanted to capitalize on the superb and widespread reputation Clare of Assisi enjoyed, first in Italy and eventually through all of Christian Europe. By bringing San Damiano Monastery into the order and renaming the order after San Damiano itself, Gregory achieved an incredible branding and public relations accomplishment that could appear as a coup or takeover of Clare's vision for the Poor Sisters of San Damiano Monastery.

The suddenness of the change, its radical implications, and the subsequent struggles of Clare with the papacy suggest that little was copacetic about the arrangement. Clare and Pope Gregory no longer seemed to hold the mutual admiration that was visible in his letter of 1220. The relationship was likely strained already for some time. Could things have changed when Francis died in 1226? Could the strain have emerged even earlier?

A clue emerged a month after Cardinal Rainaldo issued his letter including San Damiano Monastery in the new order of Ugolino and renaming it the Order of St. Damian. On September 17, 1228, Pope Gregory IX issued his much-celebrated papal bull *Sicut manifestum est* which grants to Clare and the sisters at San Damiano Monastery what is called the *Privilege of Poverty*. It only applied to that single monastery.

It is important to understand what the *Privilege* granted and how it functioned within Gregory's vision for female religious life. The *Benedictine Rule* and Ugolino's *Form of Life* allowed the observing nuns to corporately own property and have endowments of various kinds to assure the monastery's financial viability into the future. Clare always understood this principle as an option, not a requirement. She and the sisters at San Damiano Monastery steadfastly chose to never own anything personally or corporately. However, they worried that at some point church officials might force ownership on them. This was not an unreasonable worry since Ugolino as cardinal and pope was pressuring monastery after monastery to accept and establish endowments of many kinds. Agnes of Prague would also be concerned about this possibility after founding St. Francis Monastery in Prague in 1234.

This 1228 *Privilege of Poverty* granted, only to the sisters of San Damiano Monastery, the exemption or privilege that no one could force them to accept property. Note that the *Privilege* did not require that San Damiano refrain from accepting or establishing an endowment. Clearly, Pope Gregory was hoping that the sisters at San Damiano Monastery someday would change their minds and conform to the pattern of ownership and endowment that he believed best assured the future survival of the monastery.

At some level, this *exemption* might not seem unusual. From the beginning, Ugolino, with the blessing of then-Pope Honorius III, thrust the *Rule of St. Benedict* and his own *Form of Life* onto female nuns, expecting individual monasteries to request exemptions that allowed for their individuality and uniqueness. Was this not exactly what Clare was asking on behalf of San Damiano Monastery? An exemption?

It would seem not. While the *Privilege* used the form of exemption to secure the lifestyle of San Damiano Monastery, Gregory hadn't envisioned that such a fundamental exemption would be granted. The content of the *Privilege* was totally at odds with the core of his program to stabilize female religious life in Italy. He saw poverty as a threat to survival and stability. His solution was to endow each monastery. The *Privilege* granted San Damiano Monastery the right to reject such endowments. It all makes very little sense and can only be explained by suggesting that Clare somehow was able to muster an incredible amount of influence to achieve her goal.

Other testimonies present a mixed appraisal of what went on between Clare and Gregory at this time. The first three witnesses in the *Acts of the Process of Canonization* (Pacifica, PC I 13; Benvenuta, II 22; and Filippa, III 14) all describe how Clare resisted the attempts of Gregory to bring Clare and the sisters at San Damiano Monastery to own property. They described ownership as the Pope's "desire" to which Clare would "not consent." Filippa alone added that the *Privilege of Poverty* was granted to her, indicating a possible compromise.

On the other hand, the *Prose Legend of St. Clare* (IX 14) recounted the great admiration Gregory had for Clare and the sisters as he was granting the *Privilege of Poverty*. In this rendition, Gregory "congratulated" Clare and "with great joy" wrote out the *Privilege* in his own hand. However, it goes on to portray the pope as trying to persuade Clare to accept possessions only to be rebuffed. It is possible to have different opinions and still respect each other, but it is difficult not to read between these lines and see great tension and positioning.

In the end, Gregory would have to be satisfied with a diminished number of accomplishments regarding San Damiano Monastery: (1) he successfully incorporated San Damiano Monastery into his new order; (2) he established the principle that even San Damiano Monastery would live under *the Rule of St. Benedict* and Gregory's own *Form of Life*; and (3) he was able to pull off a branding and public relations coup by renaming the new order the Order of St. Damian and enlisting the prestige of Clare for the order. Gregory took what he could get. Finally, since the *Privilege of Poverty* was an exemption, not a requirement, Gregory could always hope that at some future time, San Damiano Monastery would not exercise the exemption and accept property.

Ambiguity about the developing relationship evaporated when Clare learned of Gregory's rulings in *Quo elongati* of 1230. This bull was Gregory's response to numerous questions that a General Chapter of the Friars Minor forwarded to him when the friars themselves could not resolve the questions. Gregory appeared more than happy to answer their questions; they provided another opportunity for Gregory to shape both the Friars Minor and the Order of St. Damian as he desired.

Among the clarifications, Gregory ruled that Friars Minor needed papal permission to visit monasteries associated with Clare of Assisi's lifestyle at San Damiano Monastery. Most monasteries did not follow Clare's radical poverty, and Gregory had already placed restrictions on friars visiting those monasteries. The question was whether those restrictions also applied to monasteries associated with Clare's rigorous poverty, i.e., San Damiano in Assisi, Monticelli near Florence, Monteluce near Perugia, San Salvatore di Colpersito in San Severino and monasteries in Foligno, Spello, Arezzo (Alberzoni, *Clare of Assisi and the Poor Sisters,* 35). *Quo Elongati* clarified that the restriction did extend to those monasteries with a stronger Franciscan connection.

This crushed Clare who considered regular contact with Friars Minor essential to her Franciscan identity, and she responded in acute terms. In protest, she dismissed not only Friars Minor who offered pastoral care (as *Quo elongati* prescribed), but also the friars who begged for the benefit of the Poor Ladies in San Damiano Monastery, a decision that amounted to a hunger strike involving all the sisters (LCl XXIV 37:7-10). Gregory was backed into a corner by a very determined, feisty, and famous woman. He backed off this plank of *Quo Elongati* and allowed the Friars Minor to continue their presence at San Damiano as before. Interestingly, this reversal is only reported in the *Prose Legend of St. Clare* and not confirmed in any extant papal document. There is no record of any personal correspondence between Clare and Gregory after *Quo elongati.*

It would be a mistake to understand this issue simply as a struggle between Gregory and successor popes, and sisters living in the radical style of Clare at San Damiano Monastery. The conflict was multi-facetted. In some ways, Gregory's interpretation in *Quo elongati* (1230), that the Friars Minor could not enter the monasteries with close ties to Clare, can be seen as a blunder on his part. As his efforts to enforce the strict enclosure continued, he realized that the sisters in his new order needed to be connected to some already-existing men's order for pastoral and financial support. After all, the strict enclosure made it impossible for them to beg, which also necessitated the acceptance of an endowment. Gregory's first choice was the Friars Minor.

However, the Friars Minor were increasingly involved in the pastoral care of the laity. The care of so many female monasteries was experienced as a burden and distraction from what they really wanted to do. This pattern was already visible in the Cistercians and Premonstratensians who were trying to extricate themselves from responsibilities toward the female branches of their orders that had been forged in previous decades.

So, while *Quo elongati* appeared to side with the Friars Minor for freedom from care of the women, the apparent papal backdown and subsequent papal documents kept the Friars Minor involved with the women in Gregory's new order. This especially satisfied those following the more radical way of Clare at San Damiano Monastery. Gregory's *Vestris piis supplicationibus* of 1241 and Innocent IV's bull of October 21, 1245 with the same name reinforced the permission for Friars Minor to enter female monasteries for a variety of reasons. The permission applied to both the Poor Sisters living in the style of San Damiano Monastery and any monastery in Gregory's Order of St. Damian. On this front, the Poor Sisters desiring a tighter relationship with the Friars Minor achieved a temporary victory.

Many readers may think the arrival of Agnes of Prague in the story simply replicated the same issues in a northern city. While that's partially true, the arrival of Agnes on stage changed the political equation that altered the conclusion of the story.

On Aug. 30, 1234, Gregory issued *Sincerum animi* in which he acknowledged the entrance of Agnes of Prague into religious life at St. Francis Monastery, which she founded. Copies of the bull with the same name were sent to various officials over the next days. While the purpose of the letter was to appoint Agnes as abbess of the new foundation, an important detail was the letter's affirmation that Agnes's brother Vaclav, the king of Bohemia (1230-1253), had donated the land on which the monastery and a hospice named after St Francis were to be built.

Perhaps Gregory did not fully appreciate that major inspirations for Agnes were the examples of Francis and Clare of Assisi. Agnes heard about Clare's lifestyle at San Damiano Monastery, including its total and radical poverty in imitation of Christ, from the Friars Minor who had brought their order to Prague in 1225. Agnes wanted to live the same life, even though she was unsure of all its details.

Later this would be the reason for Agnes to write various letters to Clare asking questions about life at San Damiano Monastery. However, at this early moment, Clare also must have heard about Agnes of Prague. In 1234, Clare wrote the first of four known letters to Agnes. Using formal address, Clare's letter was an exuberant welcome of Agnes to religious life in the style of San Damiano Monastery.

More importantly, this moment introduced a powerful new actor into the struggle between Gregory's pragmatism and the idealism about total and radical poverty that Clare increasingly had to defend after Francis's death. She now had a powerful ally who just happened to be the daughter and sister of Bohemian kings: daughter of King Premysl Ottokar I (1198-1230) and sister of King Vaclav. Of particular interest was the fact that her father and brother were key players in the power struggle between Pope Gregory and the Holy Roman Emperor, Frederick II.

Gregory, perhaps unaware of a pending conflict with Agnes, made his normal move to financially secure St. Francis Monastery with a reliable endowment by issuing *Cum relicta saeculi* on May 18, 1235. In it, he instructed that the Hospice of St Francis give a regular income to the Monastery of St. Francis. It even gave St. Francis Monastery permission to increase its assets. On July 25, 1235, Gregory issued *Prudentibus virginibus religiosam* in which he affirmed many aspects of *Cum relicta saeculi* but went further by listing the specific and numerous endowed properties of the hospice.

This had to be alarming and confusing to Agnes. If she had assumed that Clare and Gregory were on the same page, she was mistaken. One thing was very obvious: Agnes became very active between 1234 and 1238 to clarify her desired way of life at St. Francis Monastery and to seek papal approval of that way.

Perhaps the clearest manifestation of Agnes's drive was Clare's second letter to Agnes. It seemed to respond to a previous letter from Agnes that we do not have, but its questions are visible in Clare's response. In this second known letter, Clare admonished Agnes to stick to her original commitment to total and radical poverty in imitation of Christ. She specifically mentioned Brother Elias of Cortona (c. 1180 – 1253), who was the minister general of the Friars Minor, as a trusted ally and source of reliable advice. She further instructed Agnes to ignore those who might give her contrary advice.

This would seem to have included Pope Gregory IX who already had laid the foundation to mitigate total and radical poverty. He favored the pragmatism of placing St. Francis Monastery on a firm financial footing through endowment from St. Francis Hospice. Thus, Clare was struggling with Gregory IX on at least two venues: San Damiano Monastery in Assisi and St. Francis Monastery in Prague. We can't be entirely sure that she also wasn't engaged in the same battle involving other monasteries in the Order of St. Damian that chose to live in the radically poor way of San Damiano Monastery in Assisi.

To understand the political importance of Agnes entering this struggle, we need to briefly describe Pope Gregory IX's political and military struggle with Frederick II. Frederick, whose political and military center was in northern Europe, was constantly on the doorstep of Gregory in Rome. He was particularly strong in the Spoleto Valley, which included Assisi. The famous Rocca Castle on the hill above Assisi signified Frederick's military presence in the area.

What makes the story more interesting is that the father of Agnes of Prague had once contracted for Agnes to marry Frederick II's son Henry VII (1211 – 1242). That marriage was discarded by Frederick to arrange a marriage with the daughter of a different king whose alliance would be more useful. Later, the widowed Frederick himself would ask for the hand of Agnes, a request that was not accepted. Further, it seemed to be in King Vaclav's interests to be an ally of Pope Gregory. However, rather than just throw his support behind the pope, Vaclav cleverly used his support as a bargaining chip to achieve his sister Agnes's desire to live in total and radical poverty in imitation of Christ.

The ploy worked, as on April 14, 1237, Gregory IX issued *Omnipotens Deus* in which he established the independence of the sisters in Prague from St. Francis Hospice. Control of the hospice was given to the Knights of the Cross with the Red Star, an order also founded through Agnes that followed the *Rule of St. Augustine*.

This essentially removed the endowment from St. Francis Monastery, making it truly poor as an institution and dependent on the support of others. However, it placed Agnes of Prague in a similarly awkward position as that of Clare. Agnes was freed from the unwanted endowment of the Hospice of St. Francis but still required to follow the *Rule of St. Benedict* and Gregory's *Form of Life*.

To many, it might seem that both Clare and Agnes had achieved victories in their respective struggles. However, it is clear that neither felt secure in her arrangement nor pleased by the seeming contradiction of her situation. We also know that the two women continued to make requests of the papacy that would place their dreams on a firmer foundation. Agnes achieved another victory when Gregory IX extended the *Privilege of Poverty* to St. Francis Monastery in Prague through the papal bull *Pia credulitate tenentes* issued on April 15, 1238. Then, both women increasingly turned their energy toward approval of their own rules having a Franciscan orientation that would specifically enshrine their close relationship with the Friars Minor, and a total and radical poverty in imitation of Christ.

This was evident from *Angelis gaudium* issued by Gregory IX on May 11, 1238, just a month after granting the *Privilege of Poverty* to Agnes. In this bull, Gregory denied Agnes's request for her own form of life or rule, documenting that she had asked for it. In making this denial, Gregory pointed out that San Damiano Monastery observed the *Rule of St. Benedict* and his own *Form of Life*. He commented on the maturity and superiority of this arrangement over what Francis gave to Clare in her early days of religious life. Gregory emphasized obedience over poverty as an evangelical value and reminded Agnes that she and Clare had vowed obedience to the *Rule of St. Benedict* and his own *Form of Life*. The perceived momentum since granting the *Privilege of Poverty* had stopped. Still, Agnes had to at least be grateful that she had been granted a papal exemption from ownership and endowments that so many other female monasteries were pressured to accept.

Gregory was also pursuing other issues during these same years, notably enforcement of a strict enclosure and rigorous fasting rules. Clare even discussed these issues in her letters to Agnes. However, they were never as important to Clare or Agnes as were poverty and the sisters' relationship to the Friars Minor through which they received their identity. Agnes must have been confused by discrepancies between papally promulgated fasting rules and those observed at San Damiano Monastery in Assisi. However, Clare's response to the questions in her third letter to Agnes treated them as a side issue to Clare's real concern, i.e., how Christ was a mirror that reflected to them the manner of their lives and how their own lives should reflect the life of Christ to others.

The strict observance of the enclosure was perhaps the most important aspect of female religious life for Pope Gregory IX. A hint of this emphasis is visible in a side comment in Gregory's *De conditoris omnium* issued on May 9, 1238, which was intended to encourage Agnes. This aside is the first official mention of Francis as the founder of three orders: The Order of Friars Minor, the Enclosed Sisters and the Community of Penitents. Notice that Gregory doesn't use either of his previous names for what would become known as the Franciscan Second Order (i.e., Poor Ladies of the Valley of Spoleto or of Tuscany, or the Order of St. Damian). Instead he uses a descriptive phrase that highlights the women's enclosure.

Three years later, Gregory went on a full-throated attack against unenclosed women in central and northern Italy living a penitential and evangelical life while serving especially the poor. They clearly associated themselves with Francis of Assisi by calling themselves the Sisters Minor (Sorores Minores). In *Ad audientiam nostrum* dated December 21, 1241, Gregory called for the suppression of this group, noting that they weren't even enclosed, as if that was the essential characteristic of female religious life. He went on to be sure that no one confused women in this group with those *enclosed* at San Damiano Monastery in Assisi.

The failure of *Ad audientiam nostrum* might be due in part to the long interregnum after Gregory IX's death and before Innocent IV's election, punctuated by the brief papacy of Celestine IV. Regardless, the persistent "problem" of the Sorores Minores became evident when Innocent IV issued multiple versions of *Cum harum rector* that likewise criticized them, with the first known copy dated October 2, 1246. His different editions occurred in 1246, 1250 and 1251. Pope Alexander IV reissued the same bull in 1257. Copies with different dates were sent to places throughout central and northern Italy, France and England.

With so much papal attention to the enclosure, it's amazing that Clare and Agnes of Prague talked so little about it. They seemed to simply accept the enclosure without ascribing to it all of the importance Gregory IX heaped upon it. Thus, many scholars assume that when Clare finally did successfully propose her own rule at the end of her life, it would include provision for an enclosure. Certainly, without such a provision, no rule or form of life could win papal approval. However, the important point here is that the enclosure was never an issue worth struggling over with the papacy. Absolute poverty and close ties with the Friars Minor were.

In considering the relationship of Ugolino/Gregory IX with Franciscan women, it is impossible for us to think that Francis was not thinking about him in part when he told Clare, "...live always in this most holy life and poverty. And keep careful watch that you never depart from this by reason of the teaching or advice of anyone" (FLCl VI 8-9). Interestingly, Clare gave the same advice to Agnes of Prague in her second letter, "If anyone has said anything else to you or suggested any other thing to you that might hinder your perfection or that would seem contrary to your divine vocation, even though you must respect him, do not follow his counsel" (2LAg 17).

Within seven years of the first visible failure to achieve a uniquely Franciscan form of life enshrining radical poverty and close ties to the Friars Minor, the pressure for such a form of life for women was building again. Beginning on November 13, 1245, Innocent IV issued a series of bulls all named *Solet annuere* in which he reaffirmed that all monasteries of the Order of St. Damian were to follow the *Rule of St. Benedict* and Ugolino's *Form of Life*.

Clearly, there had been agitation for a new solution, and the restlessness of the "Franciscan" women was unrelenting. In an attempt to solve the problems, Innocent IV issued his own *Form of Life* on August 6, 1247 in his bull *Cum omnis vera religio.* It never mentioned the *Rule of St. Benedict* and assumed that it was based on the *Later Rule* of the Friars Minor. However, his own *Form of Life* was based on that of Ugolino and continued to require endowments for female monasteries.

Innocent must have thought the problem was purely symbolic and that by eliminating reference to the *Rule of St. Benedict* all would become calm. He was wrong. His *Form of Life* was accepted by few female monasteries. He tried one more time by reminding the monasteries of the Order of St. Damian to observe his *Form of Life* in *Quoties a nobis* issued on August 23, 1247. By 1250, Innocent IV had given up trying to impose it.

Success for Clare seemed at hand when, on September 16, 1252, Cardinal Rainaldo dei Conti di Segni issued a letter approving Clare's own *Form of Life,* which was written with the help of collaborators and a compilation of various important documents to Clare. Still, Clare, who was quite sick and apparently dying, was not satisfied until she achieved papal approval for her own *Form of Life.* This was granted two days before she died by Innocent IV on August 9, 1253 through yet another bull entitled *Solet annuere.* The bull only approved Clare's *Form of Life* for the Monastery of San Damiano in Assisi. With time Agnes of Prague would receive permission to follow it at St. Francis Monastery in Prague, as would a handful of other monasteries in Italy.

Clare was buried at San Giorgio in the crypt that formerly held St. Francis's body until it was moved to the new Basilica of St. Francis. Eventually, the new Basilica of St. Clare and the Proto-Monastery were built over the place of San Giorgio, and Clare's body was moved under the high altar of that basilica.

Ten years after Clare received papal approval for her own *Form of Life* on her deathbed, Pope Urban IV promulgated his own rule in 1263, which for the first time called the order Ugolino had created "The Order of St. Clare." There were many attempts to coax the Poor Sisters, then living at the Proto-Monastery, to abandon Clare's *Form of Life* and adopt Urban's, but they resisted for a time. Their temporary success was visible in yet another bull named *Solet annuere* received on December 31, 1266 from Pope Clement IV (1265 – 1268) that reaffirmed their observance of Clare's *Form of Life*. This technically removed them from the Order of St. Clare since they didn't observe its rule. The same could have been said in 1252 when Clare received approval of her own *Form of Life*. However, the Holy See continued to treat San Damiano Monastery as if it were part of the Order of St. Damian, now called The Order of St. Clare.

Eventually, even the Proto-Monastery would abandon Clare's *Form of Life* in favor of Urban's *Rule*. An early copy of Clare's *Form of Life* had been buried with her, and that remains a metaphor for what happened later. Though people knew of Clare's *Form of Life*, they increasingly ignored it. Colette of Corbie (1381 – 1447) could not find a copy in all of France when she founded her reform of the "Poor Clares" (later called the Colettines) in the 15th century. She had to write to Italy to secure a copy.

Interestingly, Urban's rule was not the only one composed after Clare's death in 1253. Though she never became a member, Isabelle of France, the sister of the famous King St. Louis IX of France (1226 - 1270), founded a female Franciscan monastery at Longchamps outside Paris and wrote two versions of a rule for it (1259 and 1263). Isabelle's *Rule* is instructive because it documents that women other than Clare garnered a different vision of female Franciscan life from Francis of Assisi.

Like Clare and Agnes, Isabelle obtained her Franciscan identity from Francis through an association with the Friars Minor. However, Isabelle focused much more on minority and less on poverty in contrast to Clare of Assisi. In fact, Isabelle called her sisters the "Sisters Minor," a term that not even Clare used for her sisters, possibly to avoid confusion with the unenclosed women in central and northern Italy so harshly condemned by Popes Gregory IX and Innocent IV (see above). Recalling Isabelle's use of this name is reason to offer a flashback reviewing its use.

Before papal concern about groups with this name, Jacques De Vitry first used the name in a letter written in 1216. Not long ago, most scholars thought this was a reference to the Poor Sisters at San Damiano Monastery in Assisi and other monasteries that would become the Order of St. Damian. More recently, scholars believe De Vitry was referencing a wide swath of female religious inspired by Francis of Assisi and living a great variety of lifestyles. Some of these early groups embraced the enclosure and others did not. In the view of these scholars, De Vitry didn't intend to specifically identify Clare's group at San Damiano Monastery. Alberzoni believes the group condemned by Gregory IX and Innocent IV was already visible in De Vitry's letter and other documents of the 1220s (*Clare of Assisi*, 174).

After the struggle between various popes and the unenclosed Sisters Minor in Italy, Isabelle of France was the first to use the term "Sisters Minor" for her sisters, this time without embarrassment, concern, or hesitation. Perhaps she was unaware of the earlier problems in Italy. Perhaps the earlier Italian groups had been successfully suppressed and forgotten. However, without doubt, the restored name clearly aligned her Sisters Minor with the Friars Minor, affirming their Franciscan connection and identity. Secondly, it clearly identified sorority and minority as the defining charisms of her group. Poverty, so important to Clare of Assisi and Agnes of Prague, was present, but in the back seat.

For Isabelle, this name clearly established her foundation as a Franciscan monastery and focused on the Franciscan humility that was typical of minority. The same humility was emphasized by her chosen name for the Longchamps abbey: The Abbey of the Humility of the Blessed Virgin Mary. Isabelle was not concerned with being exempt from property ownership or endowment at Longchamps. In fact, her rule required only personal poverty, not corporate poverty by the religious foundation itself. This would have conformed with both forms of life given by Gregory IX (1219) and Innocent IV (1247). Isabelle had a different reason for wanting her own rule or form of life at Longchamps. She wanted her nuns to be known as the *Sisters Minor (Sorores minores)*.

Isabelle and Clare of Assisi were drawing on different fonts within Francis of Assisi. Yet both wanted close ties to the Friars Minor, a desire not reciprocally shared by the men who increasingly felt burdened by the care of so many enclosed Franciscan women. The men repeatedly sought assurances from Rome that they would not be responsible for the spiritual or economic care of the female Franciscans.

The case of Isabelle of France presents an important testimony about the diversity of female Franciscan origins. This diversity is visible in their different rules and the lack of references to each other. Both women's rules mention Francis of Assisi, but neither mentions the other woman. Clare would not have known of Isabelle's foundation because she had already died. However, Clare was well known in Europe at her death, and Isabelle apparently saw no reason to connect her enterprise with that of Clare.

In the same year he approved Isabelle's second version of a rule (1263), Pope Urban IV himself wrote a rule for the Order of St. Damian that he called for the first time "The Order of St. Clare." He clearly took advantage of the renown of Clare of Assisi in ways that former popes could not. Still, Urban had to massage Clare's message, as his *Rule* continued to envision corporate ownership and endowments. The papal policy that was by then forty-four years in the making continued. It is interesting that, in her day, Isabelle's *Rule* seemed more pitted against Urban's rule than against Clare's *Form of Life* (Field 115-116).

This raises questions about which rules or forms of life were the most popular or utilized. Field hints at an answer by describing the 1266 letter from Pope Clement IV (successor to Urban IV) to Cardinal Orsini. In it, he expressed dismay at a large group of Franciscan women from many lands who visited him in Viterbo asking to be exempt from Urban's recent *Rule* and able to live by either a rule of their own or another, like the *Rule* given by Isabelle in 1263 (Field 109-110).

Further, during the lifetime of Isabelle, we know her rule was also used at Sainte-Catherine of Provins. In the decades after her death, it was used by more female monasteries associated with the Capetian royal family than those using Clare's *Form of Life* in the immediate years after her death (Field 116-118). The use of Isabelle's *Rule* was great in England beginning around 1293 (Field 118-119). Even in Italy, the home of Clare of Assisi, female monasteries took Isabelle's *Rule*. Spain had at least one (Field 119-120).

So, by the middle of the 14th century, there were at least twelve and as many as fifteen Franciscan female monasteries in Europe following Isabelle's *Rule*, while only a handful are known to have followed Clare's. Even the Poor Sisters in Assisi, who had moved from San Damiano Monastery to their more impressive Proto-Monastery inside Assisi's walls, eventually accepted the *Rule* given by Urban IV (Field 119-120).

When all these observations are taken together, a picture very different from the traditional one of unified women following Clare as the founder of the Franciscan Second Order emerges. It is clear that the organic development of these various strands was quite independent.

This chapter starts with questions. They are asked simply to alert us to the complex history that is involved in the answers. Perhaps attempting to answer the lead question helps to complete that goal: Who founded the Order of St. Clare? The answers to this single question depend on what one means by the "Order of St. Clare" and by "founder."

The most obvious answer might be Clare of Assisi. However, in truth, she really only founded San Damiano Monastery. The existence of a network of monasteries observing the lifestyle of San Damiano Monastery might suggest Clare as a foundress. Clare did send her blood-sister Agnes of Assisi to Monticelli near Florence and other monasteries to teach them the ways of San Damiano Monastery. However, it is important to remember that Monticelli predated Agnes's assignment and began with a land-grant from none other than Cardinal Ugolino who did the same for the monastery of Monteluce near Perugia. St. Francis Monastery in Prague followed a lifestyle patterned after San Damiano Monastery in Assisi, but Agnes of Prague obviously founded that monastery. Oddly, even Clare does not consider herself to be the founder of her way of life. She attributes that to Francis (see FLCl VI). Clare was an inspiration to many and in that sense we might consider her a foundress. However, she lacked many other characteristics we typically assign to founders and foundresses.

Cardinal Ugolino seems to be the most reasonable answer if the question is aimed at who originally brought these monasteries together in the first place. He also could be the founder in the sense of establishing the norms for this group of monasteries, i.e., the *Rule of St. Benedict* and his own *Form of Life*, promoting endowments and strict enclosure, and expressing uniqueness through exemptions. He brought San Damiano Monastery in Assisi into the fold.

There also are arguments for considering St. Francis of Assisi as the founder. Clare always considered Francis the founder of her monastery. Further, the sources tell of Francis influencing the foundation at San Severino in the Marches of Ancona (1C 78 and 2C 106). Various popes and hagiography about St. Francis note that he founded three orders. However, Francis clearly did not have a direct role in the foundation of the majority of female monasteries involved in the process described here. Obviously, once Rainaldo linked Ugolino's new order to San Damiano Monastery in 1228, some sort of public relations link was also made to Francis who was associated with Clare's conversion. Gregory IX made that link concrete in *De conditoris omnium* to Agnes of Prague, issued on May 9, 1238. In a side comment, Gregory IX contended that Francis founded three orders. Later, Innocent IV, in various editions of *Cum harum rector,* identified Francis as the founder of the Order of St. Damian. Still, the sources portray Francis as quite distant from the Poor Sisters after Clare's initial conversion. That doesn't make him a very convincing founder.

If the question asks who founded the majority of monasteries, the answer would be very complicated indeed. Different women who had their own specific visions initially founded most of the monasteries. Clare, at San Damiano in Assisi, was only one of them. Through the years, different monasteries followed different forms of life or rules. In many ways, each monastery had its own founder.

If the question asks who gave the name "Order of St. Clare," the answer would be Pope Urban IV. His *Rule* of 1263 officially named the order that

Ugolino began, "The Order of St. Clare." However, this was only possible in 1263 after the incremental developments related above. Before that, the Roman curia had failed to give the group a compelling name that would stick in the imagination. Urban IV gave the group identity and cohesiveness by uniting it around a single figure as the Order of St. Clare, as erroneous as the title was.

The truth is that Clare, while an important figure among these stories, was not the foundress. It might be more accurate to say that the federation of monasteries was a movement in search of a founder that discovered Clare of Assisi. That being so, they were given her name, The Order of St. Clare.

For centuries, Franciscans of all kinds would henceforth presume that Clare was the founder of the Second Franciscan Order. Not until more recent research does the more complicated picture of the Second Order come to light. Scholars like Roberto Rusconi and Maria Pia Alberzoni in Italian, and then Lezlie Knox, Joan Mueller and Catherine Mooney in English have helped to better appreciate that picture.

Add to this complex matter the list of forms of life or rules that various sisters lived with. We observe that never did all of the sisters live under any single rule:

The Form of Life given by Francis of Assisi
The Rule of St. Benedict
The Form of Life given by Cardinal Ugolino/Pope Gregory IX
The Form of Life given by Pope Innocent IV
The Later Rule of St. Francis of Assisi
The Form of Life of Clare of Assisi
The Rule given by Pope Urban IV
The Rule given by Isabelle of France for Longchamps (two versions)

Can a single order be living under so many different forms of life or rules at the same time? The complications boggle the mind.

In the end, it may not be necessary to answer these questions as much as be able to explain the complex situation. Certainly, knowing about the struggles and the specific developments involved helps us to better understand some of Clare's writings studied in this workbook. It will be useful to return to this thumbnail sketch of the history often.

Finally, it is necessary at the end of this chapter to explain why we wrote it in the first place. To begin with, knowing this history helps understand the context of Clare's four known letters to Agnes of Prague and the genesis of her own *Form of Life*. However, more importantly, recounting this history can free us from the bias that Clare's vision of life for San Damiano Monastery was the obvious and correct path for female Franciscans. The history helps us understand that the tensions in female Franciscan life weren't just between Clare and various popes, but also between Clare and the Friars Minor, and between Clare and other women who felt inspired by Francis of Assisi. This history helps users of this workbook understand why the earlier chapters on bias, positive criticism, and likes and dislikes are so important in general and when studying Clare of Assisi in particular.

Cited sources and suggested reading

Maria Pia Alberzoni was one of the first scholars to read the primary documents involving this history in a new way. She wrote in Italian, and *Clare of Assisi and the Poor Sisters in the Thirteenth Century* translates four of her important essays into English.

Joan Mueller, Lezlie Knox, and Catherine Mooney have built on Alberzoni's work in English. Much of Mueller's reinterpretation of this history is found in works dedicated to studying Clare's four known letters to Agnes of Prague. These three authors are arguably the most important English-speaking scholars currently reinterpreting this history.

Sean Field has published the most in English about Isabelle of France. While his books don't detail the struggles of Clare and Agnes in the same way as the scholars previously identified, his research helps us to see that not all women inspired by Francis of Assisi were interpreting him like Clare of Assisi and some of her close imitators were. There was diversity from the beginning.

- Alberzoni, Maria Pia. "Clare and San Damiano Between the Order of Friars Minor and the Papal Curia." Trans. Edward Hagman. *Greyfriars Review* 20.1 (2006) 1-46.

- —. *Clare of Assisi and the Poor Sisters in the Thirteenth Century*. Ed. Jean-François Godet-Calogeras. St. Bonaventure NY: The Franciscan Institute, 2004. Alberzoni is a principle author for understanding that Clare of Assisi cannot be considered the foundress of the entire Second Franciscan Order.

- —. "Clare of Assisi and Women's Franciscanism." *Greyfriars Review* 17.1 (2003) 5-38.

- —. "'Nequaquam a Christi sequela in perpetuum absolve desidero' [I will Never Desire in anyway to be Absolved from the Following of Christ]: Clare between Charism and Institution." Trans. Nancy Celaschi. *Greyfriars Review* 12 (1998) 81-121.

- —. "San Damiano in 1228: A Contribution to the 'Clare Question.'" Trans. Edward Hagman. *Greyfriars Review* 13 (1999) 105-123.

- Carney, Margaret. *The First Franciscan Woman: Clare of Assisi and Her Form of Life*. Quincy IL: Franciscan Press, 1993.

- Constable, Giles. *Monastic Tithes: From their Origins to the Twelfth Century*. Cambridge: Cambridge University Press, 1964.

- Downing, Frances Teresa. *Saint Clare of Assisi: The Context of Her Life*. Vol. 2. Phoenix AZ: Tau Publishing, 2012. Pages 5-8 briefly recount the relationship between various popes and the holy Roman emperors, including how it influenced politics in Assisi. Later chapters refer to Clare's relationships with specific popes.

- Falskau, Christian-Frederik. "*Hoc est quod cupio*: Approaching the Religious Goals of Clare of Assisi, Agnes of Bohemia, and Isabelle of France." *Magistra* 12 (2006) 3-28.

- Field, Sean L. *Isabelle of France: Capetian Sanctity and Franciscan Identity in the Thirteenth Century*. Notre Dame IN: University of Notre Dame Press, 2006. Perhaps the best English-language source about Isabelle, her Franciscan foundation at Longchamps, her forms of life, and her differences from Clare of Assisi. Field's very helpful work gives the English-only reader access to a great amount of information otherwise available only in other languages. While the entire book is a valuable read, this short summary relies heavily on chapter three about Isabelle's *Rule* of 1259 (pp. 61-94) and chapter four on her *Rule* of 1263 and its spread (pp. 95-120). Field's notes are extensive and contain references to many primary and secondary sources. Highly recommended for anyone interested in female Franciscan life that was not connected to Clare of Assisi.

- —. "Franciscan Ideals and the Royal Family of France (1226-1328)." In *The Cambridge Companion to Francis of Assisi*. Ed. Michael J. P. Robson. Cambridge: Cambridge University Press, 2012. 208-223.

- —. *The Rules of Isabelle of Francis: An English Translation with Introductory Study*. Studies in Early Franciscan Sources 4. St. Bonaventure NY: Franciscan Institute Publications, 2013.

- Flood, David. "Cardinal Ugolino on Legation." *Haversack* 11.2 (1987) 3-9, 24.

- Godet-Calogeras, Jean-François. "Francis and Clare and the Emergence of the Second Order." In *The Cambridge Companion to Francis of Assisi*. Ed. Michael J. P. Robson. Cambridge: Cambridge University Press, 2012. 115-126.

- Knox, Lezlie. "Audacious Nuns: Conflict Between the Franciscan Friars and the Order of Saint Clare. " *Church History* 41 (2000) 41-62.

- ——. "Clare of Assisi: Foundress of an Order?" In *An Unencumbered Heart: A Tribute to Clare of Assisi 1253-2003*. Eds. Jean-François Godet-Calogeras and Roberta McKelvie. Spirit and Life 11. St. Bonaventure NY: Franciscan Institute Publications, 2004. 11-29. A shorter and earlier publication than *Creating Clare of Assisi* on the same topic.

- ——. *Creating Clare of Assisi: Female Franciscan Identities in Later Medieval Italy*. The Medieval Franciscans 5. Leiden: Brill, 2008.

- Makowski, Elizabeth. *Canon Law and Cloistered Women:* Periculoso *and Its Commentators, 1298-1545*. Studies in Medieval and Early Modern Canon Law 5. Washington DC: The Catholic University of America Press, 1997.

- Mooney, Catherine. *Clare of Assisi and the Thirteenth-Century Church: Religious Women, Rules, and Resistance*. Philadelphia: University of Pennsylvania Press, 2016. An excellent summary of current research on the history of the "Order of St. Clare" through the 1260s. Mooney breaks new ground in suggesting that the commonly discounted *Privilege of Poverty* once thought to be issued by Innocent III may actually have been issued by Innocent IV (161-167); that Cardinal Rainaldo (later Alexander IV) was the main force behind the failure of Innocent IV's *Form of Life* (1247) and not Clare of Assisi's resistance (135-160); and that Cardinal Rainaldo may have had a more substantial and definitive role in the final redaction of Clare's *Form of Life* than previously thought (161-196).

- Mueller, Joan. *Clare of Assisi: The Letters to Agnes*. Collegeville MN: Glazier, 2003. A terrific popular treatment of the letters without the scholarly aspects of the Franciscan Institute text.

- —. *Clare's Letters to Agnes: Texts and Sources.* St. Bonaventure NY: Franciscan Institute Publications, 2001. Mueller provides (1) an original translation of the four letters of Clare of Assisi to Agnes of Prague, (2) introductions to all the letters and each individual letter, (3) copious notes on the text, (4) the original Latin text facing the translation, (5) a list of sources for Clare's texts, (6) cross-references, (7) analyses of the sources for Clare's letters including those about Agnes of Rome, and (8) an English translation of *The Legend of Saint Agnes of Rome.* Highly recommended.

- —. *A Companion to Clare of Assisi: Life, Writings, and Spirituality.* Leiden: Brill, 2010. Chapter four, entitled "The *Ordo* that Gregory IX founded: Clare Among Other Ugolinian Sisters" is among the best summaries of this theme. 91-115.

- —. *The Privilege of Poverty: Clare of Assisi, Agnes of Prague, and the Struggle for a Franciscan Rule for Women.* University Park PA: The Pennsylvania State University Press, 2006.

- Pásztor, Edith. "The Popes of the Thirteenth Century and Women Religious." Trans. Ignatius McCormick. *Greyfriars Review* 7.3 (1993) 381-405.

- Roest, Bert. *Order and Disorder: The Poor Clares between Foundation and Reform.* The Medieval Franciscans 8. Leiden: Brill, 2013. The first 74 pages are a succinct summary of the various relationships among Clare, various popes, the Friars Minor, and other female monasteries that constituted the Order of St. Damian. These pages are very relevant to the treatment in this workbook about the organization of female religious life at the time of Clare. The remainder of Roest's book shows how these seminal relationships played out in the Observant Reform of Poor Clares, the Colettines, and other lesser known groups through the 16th century.

- Romagnoli, Alessandra Bartolomei. "Women's Franciscanism from Its Beginnings Until the Council of Trent." Trans. Edward Hagman. *Greyfriars Review* 19.2 (2005) 91-168. A lengthy article that spectacularly places Clare of Assisi within the larger world of 13th-century female religious life and papal policy.

- Rusconi, Roberto. "The Spread of Women's Franciscanism in the Thirteenth Century." Trans. Edward Hagman. *Greyfriars Review* 12.1 (1998) 35-75.

- Verheij, Sigismund. "Personal Awareness of Vocation and Ecclesiastical Authority as Exemplified in St. Clare of Assisi." Trans. Ignatius McCormick. *Greyfriars Review* 3.1 (1989) 35-42.

TOOLS

Hagiography

The worst part of mastering this chapter is learning how to pronounce the word, especially the first "g." *Webster's* indicates four acceptable ways to pronounce the first syllable. We prefer to pronounce the first "g" like the "j" in *John* and the first "a" long as in *day*. Consult your dictionary for other acceptable pronunciations.

Enough about pronunciation; on to the meaning of the word. Most people think hagiography is biography of saints. The most accurate part of that definition is that the object of hagiography is a saint—or someone an author hopes will be considered a saint. *Biography* is a more complicated matter.

Modern Westerners expect biographies to be objectively true. Well, maybe we hedge a bit. Richard Nixon's autobiography might contain subjective interpretations from Nixon's perspective, but we still expect his *facts* to be reliable. If they are not, critics, colleagues, and historians will trash it as *untrue*.

Hagiography technically carries a meaning that does not presuppose *truth* in the same way. Hippolyte Delehaye wrote what we still consider the best easy-to-read book on hagiography available in English. He defines it as "writings inspired by devotion to the saints and intended to increase that devotion" (3 in Fordham edition).

The motive of the hagiographer is the key to understanding the difference between hagiography and modern biography. Delehaye says it is to "increase . . . devotion" to the subject, the saint. He breaks that down to five elements: to *edify* the reader, to *verify* the subject's sanctity, to *increase* the reader's devotion to the saint, to *move* the reader to moral change, and to *please* the reader by the writer's description and style.

Edification is a curious activity. The word's basic meaning is *to build up*. In religious circles, it typically means *to build up the soul*. This involves spiritual improvement, instruction, and enlightenment. We usually reserve the word for those times when basic values are at stake. Through their writings about saints, hagiographers hope to teach readers what it means to be a Christian. The focus of attention is the ideal Christian life.

Moderns generally want to verify facts; medieval people typically wanted to verify holiness. Relating events involving the saint is the undisputed way many medieval hagiographers did that. However, they did not hesitate to fudge on the facts to achieve their final goal, i.e., to convince the reader that the subject was a saint.

Devotion begins with holding someone in high esteem. It expresses itself by talking about the person, fussing over her or him, and trying to extend the devotion to others. When involving saints, devotees read the life and writings of their saints, try to live out the saints' values, and often pray privately or publicly to them. This prayer and devotion are called the cult of the saint.

The religious salvation of readers was the goal of every good medieval hagiographer. Gospel living was the means of receiving that salvation. Unless readers learned from the saint's story and changed their behaviors accordingly, the medieval hagiographer was a failure.

Modern people enjoy a well-crafted story. So did medieval people. Boredom is the curse of education in all ages and situations. Without an interesting writing style, a hagiographer's work might not be read or circulated in the medieval world. If people don't read the saint's story, they cannot be built up by it, believe the saint was holy, become a saint's devotee, or change their lives. Don't be fooled by hagiographers' declarations of humble writing ability. They knew their goals depended on interesting writing, and not a few of them were proud of their literary accomplishments.

Edification, verification of holiness, increasing devotion, moral change, and interesting writing styles were the goals of good hagiographers. None of these goals demand that a hagiographer hedge on the truth, much less out-and-out lie. However, objective truth about historical facts in a person's life was not a medieval value, even though hagiographers go out of their way to claim objectivity and trustworthiness. They were products of an era with different values and notions of truth. When we fully understand their goals, it is easier to understand their techniques, which often offend modern readers. Let's explore some of the more common techniques.

Plagiarism

Medieval writers typically felt no shame when incorporating the work of a previous author into his or her own work. In a sense, "borrowing" was a form of flattery. No one considered it immoral, and certainly there were no laws making it illegal. Verbatim transfers of texts were not uncommon. Use of similar organization was routine. Often, a story was reproduced in a later work with subtle changes that served the new author's particular purposes. In all these cases, don't expect a footnote from the medieval writer citing the source. If the reader could figure out the source, the author was thought to be well read. If not, the reader would be all the more amazed by the story in hand.

Saintly models and replacements

Saintly models were burned into the medieval mind. Medieval people typically measured new saints against the models depicted in older and better-known saints. Hagiographers used the established models of holiness to convince their readers that the subjects of their current works were also saints. Through the centuries, these models included the heroic martyr, the missionary founding bishop, the founder of a religious order, and the sainted person who appeared like an angel, unencumbered by a human body.

Pressure to portray a holy person within a predefined model or role also created strings of saints whose lives seemed strikingly similar. Sometimes, two saints might only have shared a particular event in common; at other times, their entire lives may have appeared as reruns. Through this phenomenon, saints tended to replace one another in the history of hagiography.

The early Roman martyr Agnes frequently figures into the hagiography about Clare, Clare's letters to Agnes of Prague, and papal letters to Agnes of Prague. Agnes of Rome was a medieval model of the sainted virgin. Medieval people knew that Clare and Agnes of Prague were also holy because they followed the pattern visible in Agnes of Rome.

Stock incidences and exaggeration

While hagiographers often employed models to portray holiness, they also used stock incidences to make their points. Stock incidences are different from models in that they are special stories which can be cut-and-pasted from any saint's story to another's, even if the two saints follow different models. Stock incidences abound in hagiographic material. If one saint is portrayed by a stock incidence, a thousand others are as well, and that's the point. If so many proven saints did a particular action, what better way to prove your saint's holiness than to portray her or him with the same behaviors.

In Clare's case, stories about her fasting and Eucharistic devotions might be considered stock incidents. Late medieval female holiness was strongly tied to both practices. Super human stories abound about medieval women eating nothing, except perhaps the host at Mass. Through Eucharistic devotion and shared suffering manifested through extreme fasting, they demonstrated total attention to serving Christ.

This exaggeration in hagiography is like salt in a stew; it spices things up and brings out the flavors that are already there. We, in our century, criticize exaggeration in historical writing. From our perspective, it distorts the truth. However, from the medieval hagiographer's perspective, exaggeration promoted the truth. It helped them illustrate the saint's holiness and moved readers to astonishment and the desire to change their lives. Many medieval people would think of exaggeration in hagiography more as embellishment than deception.

Exaggeration can shape hagiography in many ways. It can simply take a historical story and build upon that truth, making it more dramatic. It can take a story from one saint's life and embellish it for use in another's story. It also can use exaggeration to so change a story that moderns would find it unbelievable. The medieval person accepted that embellishment as a reliable testimony to a subject's holiness.

Hearsay

Hearsay is inadmissible as proof in today's courtrooms. In medieval days, it could be as good as eyewitness testimony. Hagiographers used any material that supported their cause, even hearsay. Many examples are visible in the *Acts of the Process of Canonization* for Clare. There were twenty witnesses questioned for this investigation. When asked how they knew what they were reporting, many said they heard others talking about it. That's hearsay. Most modern courts would want to hear from the person who witnessed an event, not someone who heard about it.

Miracles

Miracles were indispensable in the portrayal of a person as a saint in medieval times. Many people today continue to look for miracles or at least extraordinary phenomena in their saints.

No period in history has a completely unanimous idea of holiness. There are always critics in a society or church that oppose the exultation of certain people as heroes or saints. Relating miracles involving the person attempts to put the debate to rest. Once God demonstrates favor toward humans by performing super-human feats through them, opponents are left at a loss for a credible argument. This was and is especially true in cultures or periods that lend easy acceptance to unexplained events as miracles. The more scientific person who suspends judgment until more data can be gathered to explain the unexplainable is usually discounted. Many people of faith live somewhere in the middle, i.e., believing in miracles, but not necessarily seeing them everywhere.

The medieval period was intensely taken up by the miraculous. Its pre-scientific mentality not only easily accepted alleged miracles, but also sought to see them wherever possible. In its worldview, God was constantly sending messages through incredible signs and wonders.

It is no wonder that most medieval people could not conceive as saints people who apparently never performed miracles. After all, if they were indeed saints, God would have made that clear through miraculous events during and after their lives. Few medieval people could be canonized or develop a serious cult without being portrayed as a miracle worker. The most important technique of medieval hagiographers was a generous dose of miracles. Nothing else could take their place. However, the necessity to include so many miracles in hagiography causes historians to question whether all of them are true. Even supposed eyewitness accounts can be questioned. When people are looking for something so intensely, they often find it.

That's enough techniques for the moment. We hope you are getting the idea that hagiography is not the same as biography and operates under a different set of goals, presumptions, and rules. We now need to examine how this difference affects our study of Clare.

Our assumption is that spirituality changes from place to place and time to time. Modern Christians share a great deal with medieval Christians. We also are very different. We know a lot more than they did and have very different values. Our notions of truth are unique to our periods. Our worldviews are far apart. What we take for granted, they could not conceive, and vice versa.

Medieval hagiographers constructed images of Clare that met the spiritual needs of their day. Frankly, they were very successful; they accomplished their goals. However, if we continue to read the same medieval stories with the same medieval eyes of understanding, we will not end up with an adequate Franciscan spirituality for the vigorous demands of our own day. We will become anachronistic: living in a time and place other than our own. We need to access the stories of Clare and appropriate from them what will help us today.

How can we do this? Certainly not by applying our modern notions of historical accuracy to medieval hagiographic texts. Those living around Clare's time started with the historical Clare they experienced and built up an interpretation with their hagiography. We have to do something similar. Our difficulty is that we cannot experience the historical Clare. She is dead. So how do we do it?

We are left to ask our historical questions of documents which never intended to provide historical answers. Historians have had to deal with this limitation for centuries. Our goal is to help readers learn from those historians and to develop a new attitude about and approach to hagiography. The attitude is suspicion; the approach is to question, question, and question. Once we know the goals and techniques of many medieval hagiographers we can use that knowledge to peel off the layers of hagiography that cover the historical Clare. In the end, we will be left with very little knowledge about Clare. However, what little we have will be more reliable for our modern minds.

That part of the process is the primary goal of this book and the easier of the two parts. The second part is more difficult and beyond the scope of this book: reconstructing an image of Clare that interprets her importance for today. Her meaning for today must be ferreted out in a group process that often will not be conscious. Many individuals will have to share their ideas. Groups of religious will need to make decisions about their common life. In the end, a consensus will emerge that will adequately interpret Clare for our time and place.

Suggested reading

Much more is written about the hagiography of Francis of Assisi than that of Clare. Still, many of those sources help us understand how the techniques of hagiography affect the sources about Clare.

- A more extensive version of this chapter is found in William Hugo's Workbook I, 36-46.

- Bartlett, Robert. *Why Can the Dead Do Such Great Things? Saints and Worshippers from the Martyrs to the Reformation.* Princeton: Princeton University Press, 2013.

- Delehaye, Hippolyte. *The Legends of the Saints.* Trans. V. M. Crawford. Notre Dame: University of Notre Dame Press, 1961.

- —. *The Legends of the Saints.* Trans. Donald Attwater. New York: Fordham University Press, 1962. (This is the version we quote in this chapter.)

- Dalarun, Jacques. "The Death of Holy Founders from Martin to Francis." Trans. Edward Hagman. *Greyfriars Review* 14.1 (2000) 1-19. Dalarun shows how the hagiographic descriptions of Francis's death demonstrate Francis's holiness by following the established patterns of saints' deaths.

- Dolciami, Francesco. "Francis of Assisi in Devotion, Cult and Liturgy." Trans. Edward Hagman. *Greyfriars Review* 18.1 (2004) 75-115. While Dolciami's interest is the devotion to St. Francis and how that expressed itself in his cult, especially his liturgy, he spends considerable time explaining a new model of holiness emerging through Francis's canonization process and subsequent hagiography.

- Paciocco, Roberto. "Miracles and Canonized Sanctity in the 'First Life of St. Francis.'" Trans. Patrick Colbourne and Edward Hagman. *Greyfriars Review* 5.2 (1991) 251-274. A discussion of the role of miracles in establishing the sanctity of saints in the early 13th century.

- Paul, Jacques. "The Image of St. Francis in the *Treatise on the Miracles* by Thomas of Celano." Trans. Edward Hagman. *Greyfriars Review* 14.3 (2000) 257-276. Paul argues that miracles had a limited appeal in the cult and hagiography of Francis of Assisi and that Francis's virtues were considered of greater value. Still, certain sectors demanded that miracles be included more abundantly and explicitly in the written record.

- Prinzivalli, Emanuela. "A Saint to be Read: Francis of Assisi in the Hagiographic Sources." Trans. Edward Hagman. *Greyfriars Review* 15.3 (2001) 253-298. Prinzivalli's study illustrates how many techniques of hagiography influenced the medieval literature about Francis of Assisi.

- Short, William. "Hagiographical Method in Reading Franciscan Sources: Stories of Francis and Creatures in Thomas of Celano's *First Life* (58-61)." *Greyfriars Review* 4.3 (1990) 63-89. Short illustrates many of the techniques studied in this chapter through a very focused topic.

- Vauchez, André. *Sainthood in the Later Middle Ages.* Trans. Jean Birrell. Cambridge: Cambridge University Press, 1997.

- Ward, Benedicta. *Miracles and the Medieval Mind: Theory, Record, and Event, 1000-1215.* Philadelphia: University of Pennsylvania Press, 1982.

- Weinstein, Donald and Rudolph M. Bell. *Saints and Society: The Two Worlds of Western Christendom, 1000-1700.* Chicago: University of Chicago Press, 1983.

Who Wrote Clare's Writings?

Francis's use of secretaries is documented in the sources for his life and writings. They include Leo of Assisi (d. c. 1270) (AC 113), Bonizzo of Bologna (AC 113), and Benedict of Piaroco (AC 17). We also know that Caesar of Speyer (d. 1239) was asked to embellish the *Earlier Rule* with scripture passages (Jordan 15). William Hugo described at length how we then might consider Francis the "author" of the works ascribed to him in Workbook I (51-53).

It is important to remember that many illiterate and highly literate people in the Middle Ages used secretaries of one sort or another to commit their thoughts to parchment. Since the ideas are theirs, we consider them the authors. In other cases, when expressions seem foreign to an attributed author or there are many different styles within a single work suggesting ongoing editing of the text, scholars might conclude that the person in question did not author a given work. This could be a question regarding Francis's *Earlier Rule* and *Later Rule*. However, despite the collaborative nature of those compositions, no one doubts that they should be included among the writings of Francis of Assisi. Yes, they were a collaborative effort, but principally express Francis of Assisi's thought.

There are no such testimonies to secretaries in Clare's case. However, the texts themselves suggest her use of secretaries. As with Francis's *Later Rule*, Clare's *Form of Life* or *Rule* displays a legal awareness unseen in her other writings and unexpected from a person with her background. We know Clare would have received an education similar to our home-schooling system. This would suggest that Clare had assistance in writing her *Form of Life*. Still, scholars consider her the author. For other examples, see our subsequent chapters on *The Blessing of Clare* and *The Testament of Clare,* summarized in our citation of Bartoli Langeli below.

Though Clare's four known letters to Agnes of Prague appear consistent in style to the casual reader, suggesting Clare herself wrote them, some scholars see the influence of others. Ingrid Peterson has listed numerous studies affirming that some accomplished writer had to have helped Clare write her letters (37). Timothy Johnson provides compelling evidence that her fourth letter was dictated and has explored the possibility that Leo of Assisi was involved, which is consistent with studies listed by Peterson. Despite this collaboration, no one concludes that Clare should not be considered the author of these letters.

Regis Armstrong notes that Clare's *Testament* was the most difficult of her writings to translate (CA:ED 29). This is due to the changing styles, suggesting that different people were involved in its composition at different times. Some have wondered whether it was composed well after Clare's death to support the ideals of the more rigorous friars of the primitive observance (see Bartoli Langeli and Maleczek). Today, the authenticity of Clare's *Testament* is more generally accepted. Some understand it as a collection of Clare's sayings from various moments in her life which might explain the differences in style based on the report of those recalling her sayings. Clare's *Blessing* uses scriptural references not found in her other writings, leading some to doubt Clare's authorship (see CA:ED 29). Others accept its authenticity.

Thus, we need to understand that many of the techniques visible in Clare's writings are not unusual for the Middles Ages, and even considered normal. Her use of secretaries, who sometimes even polished her dictation, does not discredit her as the author. Nor does her inclusion of other's writings (e.g., two pieces by Francis of Assisi in her own *Form of Life*) or the fact that some of her writings (e.g., *The Testament*) may be sayings of Clare compiled by one or more editors later, even after her death. In all these situations, scholars consider Clare the author, and so should we.

Cited sources and suggested reading

- Bartoli Langeli, Attilio. *Gli Autografi di Frate Francesco e di Frate Leone.* Turnhout: Brepols, 2000. Clare's *Testament* and *Blessing* contain many hints that they were compilations or recollections of Clare's sayings, perhaps even after her death. Werner Maleczek argued that the Messina Manuscript containing them was a 15th-century forgery, probably written to support the Observant Reform of the Friars Minor. Thus, he disputed Clare's authorship. This work by Bartoli Langeli matched the handwriting in the Messina manuscript to that of Leo of Assisi in his other known works, thus changing the date of the Messina Manuscript to no later than 1270, the death date of Leo of Assisi. This has supported those who believe Clare can legitimately be considered their author as they recalled her thoughts by those who knew her.

- Blastic, Michael W., Jay M. Hammond, and J. A. Wayne Hellmann, eds. *The Writings of Clare of Assisi: Letters, Form of Life, Testament and Blessing.* Studies in Early Franciscan Sources 3. St. Bonaventure NY: Franciscan Institute Publications, 2011. This publication provides valuable information about the authorship of all writings attributed to Clare of Assisi. Highly Recommended.

- Johnson, Timothy. "Clare, Leo, and the Authorship of the Fourth Letter to Agnes of Prague." *Franciscan Studies* 62 (2004) 91-100.

- Lynn, Beth. "Early Friars and the Poor Ladies in Conversation: *Scripta Leonis* and the Writings of Clare: A Common Matrix of Evangelical Contemplative Life for both Men and Women." *The Cord* 45.1 (1995) 21-30.

- Maleczek, Werner, "Questions about the Authenticity of the Privilege of Poverty of Innocent III and of the Testament of Clare of Assisi." *Greyfriars Review* 12.Supplement (1998) 1-80. Maleczek's article offered strong arguments against Clare's *Testament* and *Blessing* being authentically written by her. He argued that the Messina Manuscript containing them was a 15th-century forgery, probably written to support the Observant Reform of the Friars Minor. Bartoli Langeli dealt Maleczek's argument a serious blow when he convincingly dated the Messina Manuscript containing Clare's *Testament* and *Blessing* no later than 1270 when Leo of Assisi died. He argues that Leo wrote the manuscript, restoring the authenticity of the writings.

- Peterson, Ingrid. "Letters to Agnes of Prague." In *The Writings of Clare of Assisi: Letters, Form of Life, Testament and Blessing*. Eds. Michael W Blastic, Jay M Hammond, and J. A. Wayne Hellmann. Studies in Early Franciscan Sources 3. St. Bonaventure NY: Franciscan Institute Publications, 2011. 19-59.

The Notification of Clare's Death
1253
(CA:ED 135-138)

With this chapter, we begin an exploration of various medieval primary sources for the life of Clare of Assisi. It is important to learn this information well, as it allows us to evaluate the data coming from these sources for each of the stories about Clare's life.

Date

It is clear from the context of this text that it was written shortly after Clare died on August 11, 1253. It is an announcement of death, which would have little purpose too many days after the death. Toward the end, the text states that Pope Innocent IV stayed in Assisi to attend Clare's funeral, so it must have been written after the funeral. However, the exact date is uncertain. This document ends abruptly in the middle of a sentence, indicating that there likely was more to the document than is preserved. That also means we may be missing an exact date of composition that was included at the end of the original copy.

Authorship

No single person is identified as the author of this notification. The opening line of many medieval documents indicated the recipient and sender. Here, we are told that the senders are simply the sisters living in Assisi, which would be at San Damiano Monastery. This document could have a collaborative authorship by all or various sisters there. A single sister on behalf of them all could have written it. Perhaps the entire monastery was allowed to comment on the text or approve it. However, all of this is conjecture.

Scholars note that there is only one manuscript copy of the notification. This leads some to suspect that the document was never circulated. If that were true, we next have to ask why. Why would someone or some group compose this and not distribute it? The manuscript that contains the one copy we have also contains other documents that were considered models for writing letters for various occasions. Such a collection would be of interest to people working for some official in the Church, perhaps even the

138

Holy See. If that were the case, the author could be a curial official who knew enough details about Clare's life and death to compose it.

However, the emotionalism, and scattered and erratic writing style doesn't fit well with that theory. A cool and disciplined curial official would not likely write a model document in such a way. In the end, little can be said for sure about the authorship of the notification.

Origin and purpose

The event causing the composition of this document would seem to simply be the death of Clare. Its purpose was to announce the death to other members of the Order of St. Damian. In the process, the sisters of San Damiano Monastery also shared their grief and simply expressed her meaning for them.

Two interesting aspects of this purpose are important. First, the sisters did not intend this as an announcement to the whole world. It was an internal communication among the sisters themselves. Thus, it would be incorrect to think the sisters in any way were already trying to arrange for or looking forward to Clare's canonization with this document. This is simply a letter from the sisters who lived with Clare to other remote sisters of their order. It does not display a political purpose.

Second, the title makes clear that the document is addressed to monasteries of the Order of St. Damian. Our chapter "Who Founded the Order of St. Clare?" goes at length to distinguish between the order founded by Cardinal Ugolino (the Order of St. Damian) and the Poor Sisters living at the Monastery of San Damiano. By identifying the recipients as the "Order of St. Damian," the senders were reaching out more broadly than to just those few monasteries that shared Clare's desire for a radical and total poverty. While Clare had received papal approval of her own *Form of Life* only days before her death, her sisters at San Damiano Monastery sent this notification to all the members of the Order of St. Damian, including those who happily observed the *Rule of St. Benedict* and the *Form of Life* of either Pope Gregory IX or Pope Innocent IV.

If a curial official wrote the document as a model, then its purpose would be to provide a model and nothing more. Clare's actual details would be subservient to the goal of providing the model.

Value

The Notification of Clare's Death is perhaps the least consulted of primary sources for the life of Clare of Assisi. While it makes a few historical allusions to Clare's life, e.g., being of nobility, we attain no substantial information about Clare. Thus, it is extremely limited as a source for her life. It is more a source for the Poor Sisters' response to Clare's death and how they understood her life and death.

The fact that historians do not consider the notification an important source is evident from the dearth of studies about the document. Important medieval documents are frequently the object of literary studies of various kinds to ascertain authorship, dating, and sources. We know of no such study in English translation that could help readers assess its value. Further, we have only one manuscript containing it. Often, that causes scholars to question its reliability unless that single copy is of undoubtable reliability.

The uncertainties about the notification are of little consequence because there is little historical information to garner from it. However, it can offer students an interesting opportunity to explore the spirituality around Clare, as we will offer in a worksheet toward the end of this workbook.

The Acts of the Process of Canonization
1253
(CA:ED 141-196)

Date

The *Acts of the Process of Canonization* is indisputably dated 1253. Reasons will be explained below in the origin and purpose section.

Authorship

In an important way, the authors of the *Process* can be considered to be twenty witnesses who testified before a pontifically convoked investigation into the holiness of Clare of Assisi. The witnesses were:

Witness I — Pacifica di Guelfuccio. Clare's relative and neighbor. An intimate of Clare, who served Clare day and night upon entering San Damiano Monastery herself shortly after Clare's flight from her family home on Palm Sunday. Pacifica was the natural sister of the 17th witness, Bona di Guelfuccio.

Witness II — Benvenuta of Perugia. Sister at San Damiano Monastery. Knew Clare before she entered religious life and joined Clare at San Damiano Monastery in the first year of its establishment.

Witness III — Filippa, daughter of Lord Leonardo di Ghislerio. Knew Clare since childhood. The third to join Clare at San Damiano Monastery about 4 years after Clare moved there.

Witness IV — Amata, daughter of Sir Martino of Coccorano. Sister at San Damiano Monastery for 25 years at the time of the interview. A blood sister of Balvina de Martino, witness VII. A cousin of Clare.

Witness V — Cristiana de Sir Cristiano de Parisse. Sister at San Damiano Monastery for 7 years at the time of interview.

Witness VI   Cecilia, daughter of Sir Gualtieri Cacciaguerra of Spoleto. Entered San Damiano Monastery 3 years after Clare moved there.

Witness VII   Balvina, daughter of Sir Martino of Coccorano. Sister at San Damiano Monastery. A blood sister of Amata, witness IV. A cousin of Clare.

Witness VIII   Lucia of Rome. Sister at San Damiano Monastery.

Witness IX   Francesca, daughter of Sir Capitaneo of Col di Mezzo. Sister at San Damiano Monastery for 21 years at the time of interview.

Witness X   Agnes, daughter of Oportulo de Bernardo of Assisi. Sister at San Damiano Monastery for 33 years at the time of interview.

Witness XI   Benvenuta of Lady Diambra of Assisi. Sister at San Damiano Monastery for 29 years at the time of interview.

Witness XII   Beatrice, daughter of Sir Favarone of Assisi. Clare's youngest blood sister and sister at San Damiano Monastery for 24 years at the time of interview.

Witness XIII   Cristiana, daughter of Sir Bernardo da Suppo of Assisi. Sister at San Damiano Monastery for 34 years at the time of interview.

Witness XIV   Angeluccia, daughter of Sir Angelico of Spoleto. Entered San Damiano Monastery after Clare became sick.

Witness XV   Balvina of Porzano. Sister at San Damiano Monastery.

Witness XVI   Lord Ugolino di Pietro Girardone. Knight of Assisi who lived near San Rufino as did Clare's family.

Witness XVII Lady Bona, daughter of Guelfuccio of Assisi. Clare's distant relative and neighbor who knew Clare in her family home. Lady Bona was the natural sister of the 1st witness, Pacifica di Guelfuccio.

Witness XVIII   Lord Ranieri di Bernardo of Assisi. Husband of Clare's relative. Ranieri had unsuccessfully asked for the hand of Clare in marriage. He had several close conversations with Clare.

Witness XIX   Pietro di Damiani of Assisi. Clare's neighbor.

Witness XX   Ioanni di Ventura of Assisi. Watchman in the Favarone household who had conversations with Clare.

After the first fifteen witnesses spoke (all members of San Damiano Monastery), the entire community affirmed their report in general terms, led by Sister Benedetta di Giorgio di Ugone di Tebalduccio, who would become Clare's successor as abbess (PC XV verses 8-19). Thus, all the members of San Damiano Monastery can, in some way, also be considered contributing authors of the *Process.*

The authorship of the *Process* also needs to be considered from other perspectives. With the letter *Gloriosus Deus* (October 18, 1253), Pope Innocent IV commissioned Bishop Bartholomew Accorombani of nearby Spoleto (bishop 1236-1271) to interview the Poor Sisters at San Damiano Monastery and other citizens of Assisi regarding the holiness of Clare and her suitability for canonization. Bartholomew's team included the archdeacon Leonardo of Spoleto, the archpriest Jacobo of Trevi, two of the three famous "Three Companions" of St. Francis who were still living, i.e., Leo of Assisi and Angelo Tancredi (d. 1258), the Friar Minor Mark who was the chaplain of San Damiano Monastery, and a notary named Ser Martino.

The team started work quickly. It interviewed fifteen sisters at San Damiano Monastery on November 24 and 28, 1253, and then received a general affirmation of that testimony from Sister Benedetta and all the members of the monastery. On the 28th and 29th, the group moved to the Monastery Church of San Paolo where Bartholomew was joined by additional observers, including Sister Filippa and some other sisters, Andreolo de Bartolo, Vianello del Benvenuto Lucchese, Jacobo of Trevi, and some unnamed people. In their presence, five citizens of Assisi were interviewed.

The notary Ser Martino might be considered the "author" in the sense that he was the secretary for the Bishop. He took notes and gave form to the final document. It's important to note that he did not write down what Bishop Bartholomew said (as Francis's or Clare's secretaries did), but what the witnesses said.

However, if one examines the text of the *Process* itself, we might consider Bishop Bartholomew the author. In verses 2 and 23 of the Prologue, Bartholomew identified himself as the person commissioned by Pope Innocent IV to investigate and then recount how he accomplished the task. Even if Bartholomew did not do the recording and editing, he was the one commissioned by the pope to take the testimony. He was the one to organize the event. He must have reviewed and approved the final text. And his was the name inserted into the final document that was sent to Pope Innocent IV.

Origin and purpose

Despite the fact that Pope Innocent III had issued regulations requiring stringent investigation before canonizations at the beginning of the 13th century, Pope Innocent IV, while he was present at Clare's funeral in August 1253, intended to pray the Office of Virgins rather than the Office of the Dead. In effect, this would have immediately canonized Clare. Cardinal Rainaldo dei Conti di Segni, the cardinal-protector of the Order of St. Damian, convinced the pope to proceed at a more cautious pace, and the assembly prayed the Office of the Dead (LCl XXXVII 6-9). However, Innocent was determined to complete Clare's canonization quickly.

With the letter *Gloriosus Deus* (October 18, 1253), Innocent commissioned Bishop Bartholomew of nearby Spoleto to interview the Poor Sisters and other citizens of Assisi. This papal bull is quoted at the beginning of the *Acts of the Process of Canonization.* Bartholomew's mandate from the pope was "diligently and carefully to research her life, conversion, and manner of life, as well as the truth of all the aforesaid miracles and all their particulars according to the questions we send you included under this Bull" (PC Prologue 19).

Bartholomew wasted no time. By November 24th, he was in Assisi with his team interviewing the first thirteen witnesses who lived as nuns at the San Damiano Monastery. The text itself offers a great deal of information about the people and process. This list of notable witnesses and officials illustrates the seriousness of the process and the desire to be sure it was legally appropriate.

Value

There is little controversy about the reliability of the single manuscript we have for this important source for Clare's life. It is a 15th-century Italian translation of the original Latin. While its nature as a translation and of late origin might suggest it is not reliable, the Italian text is very consistent with the *Versified Legend* and the *Prose Legend of Saint Clare*, which used the *Process* as their primary source within two years. Thus, scholars agree about its reliability.

The fundamentals of Clare's life come from the *Acts of the Process of Canonization*. This is a different situation from the sources for Francis of Assisi's life. The *Process* from his canonization is lost. Thus, except for biographical information we can learn from his own writings and a few third-party sources, our knowledge of Francis's life begins with hagiography about him from Thomas of Celano's *The Life of St. Francis*.

The *Process* of Clare's canonization places us much closer to the primary sources for her life as they are the testimony of twenty witnesses who personally knew Clare in one way or another. While some authors believe the forces of hagiography were already at work in the memories of the witnesses (see Bynum 82-85 and Iriarte 188), the fact that we can get back to the witnesses themselves gives historians greater confidence. When you combine the testimony of all the witnesses, a rather well rounded portrait emerges.

Sources

The principle sources for the *Acts of the Process of Canonization* were the 20 witnesses whose testimony was recorded and the affirmation of Sister Benedetta and the entire community. Bishop Bartholomew of Spoleto provided some information about how the process came to be and was arranged. Innocent IV's bull *Gloriosus Deus* disclosed the guidelines given to Bartholomew by the pope.

Technical issues

When citing the various witnesses in this workbook, we use a Roman numeral to indicate the number of the witness. The first Arabic number indicates the paragraph number of that witness's testimony. Occasionally, a second Arabic number will be cited after a colon. This number refers to the verse number corresponding to the text in CA:ED. Thus, PC XII 4:9 refers to verse 9 found in the 4th paragraph of the testimony of the twelfth witness (Sister Beatrice). If the verse number is not important, the citation will appear as PC XII 4.

Cited sources and suggested reading

- Bartoli, Marco. "Historical Analysis and Psychoanalytical Interpretations of a Vision of Clare of Assisi." Trans. Madonna Balestrieri. *Greyfriars Review* 6.2 (1992) 189-209. Bartoli is one of the best sources translated into English that explains the manuscript tradition of the PC.

- Bynum, Caroline Walker. *Holy Feast and Holy Fast: The Religious Significance of Food to Medieval Women.* Berkeley and Los Angeles: University of California Press, 1987. This text describes the broader food practices of medieval religious women.

- Carney, Margaret. "Francis and Clare: A Critical Examination of the Sources." *Greyfriars Review* 3.3 (1989) 315-343. Also published in *Laurentianum* 30 (1989) 25-60. Carney's article became chapter one of her book, *The First Franciscan Woman: Clare of Assisi and Her Form of Life.* Quincy IL: Franciscan Press, 1993. Pages 21-63. Page 321 in *Greyfriars Review* contains Carney's concise summary of the witnesses' testimony about Clare's early demonstration of holiness.

- Downing, Frances Teresa. *Saint Clare of Assisi: The Context of Her Life.* Vol. 2. Phoenix AZ: Tau Publishing, 2012. Pages 239-241, 243-249 discuss Sr. Pacifica di Guelfuccio di Bernardo, the first witness. Pages 249-253 talk about Pacifica and a Sr. Balvina. However, which Balvina is confusing as there are two witnesses in the *Process* named Balvina, and an abbess at Spello was also named Balvina. Pages 254-260 talk of Sr. Filippa di Leonardo di Ghislerio di Sassorosso, the third witness. Pages 261-266 discuss Francesca, daughter of Sir Capitaneo of Col di Mezzo, the ninth witness.

- Grau, Engelbert. "Die Schriften der Heiligen Klara und die Werke ihrer biographen." In *Movimento religioso femminile e francescanesimo nel secolo XIII.* Assisi, 1980. 195-238. Grau is Carney's primary source.

- Iriarte, Lazaro. "Clare of Assisi: Her Place in Female Hagiography." Trans. Ignatius McCormick. Greyfriars *Review* 3.2 (1989) 173-206.

The Versified Legend of the Virgin Clare
1254-1255
(CA:ED 199-261)

There is a general lack of knowledge about the *Versified Legend of the Virgin Clare*. It has not attracted enough scholarly interest to provide answers to the many questions that surround it. This dearth of information is amplified for English-speakers because most of the recent research has been done in other languages. Important English summaries of the research were done by Regis Armstrong, first in a 1993 article (The Legenda Versificata) that he later summarized and updated in his 2006 introduction to the *Versified Legend* in CA:ED 197-198. However, much has happened in recent Italian (see Guida's two articles), French (see Dalarun *Claire d'Assise* for bibliography) and German (see Schneider *Klara-Quellen* 189-196 for bibliography) publications that suggest significantly different analyses.

Date

Before Armstrong's publications, most scholars believed the *Versified Legend* was written after the *Prose Legend* and that the former was dependent on the latter as a source. The most common reason for this assertion was that such was the pattern in documents about other saints. For instance, Henri d'Avranches' versified legend about Francis of Assisi was written after and dependent upon Thomas of Celano's *Life of St. Francis*, a legend in prose. The most recent collection of Italian sources about Clare still maintains this position (Boccali *Fonti Clariane* 261-262).

Armstrong appears to be among the first to date the *Versified Legend* about Clare of Assisi earlier than the *Prose Legend* and to characterize it as a source for the *Prose Legend*. He dates the *Versified Legend* no earlier than 1254 because it relies on the *Acts of the Process of Canonization* based on testimony in late 1253. Others would add that it could not be dated before December 1254 when Alexander IV was elected pope because the *Versified Legend* begins with an extensive dedication to Alexander. Armstrong believes the *Versified Legend* could not be dated later than August of 1255 because it does not mention Clare's canonization in that month. Few other scholars took the same position then, but Armstrong's analysis had tremendous impact in the English-speaking world because almost nothing else had been written about these issues in English.

In 2013, new collections of sources about Clare of Assisi appeared in both French (Dalarun *Claire d'Assise*) and German (Schneider *Klara-Quellen*). Both publications postulated that some other document predated both the *Versified Legend* and the *Prose Legend* about Clare of Assisi. In this scenario, it is probable that the preexisting document was an earlier version of Thomas of Celano's *Prose Legend of St. Clare*, which became the source for both the *Versified Legend* and Celano's own final *Prose Legend of St. Clare*. This theory sees the need for some common earlier source that imposed a thereafter consistent chronology upon the temporally disorganized information gathered in the *Acts of the Process of Canonization*. Assuming that Celano wrote that first draft based on the *Process*, these German and French-speaking scholars postulate that Celano needed to complete it (e.g., add information about the canonization) before submitting it for papal approval. We have no copy of that first draft.

The French and German collections support this scenario by noting that both the *Versified Legend* and the *Prose Legend* share much common material, but also contain information the other does not. They believe this indicates a common distinct source and then later independent development.

Other versified legends about Clare have been found that begin to appear in the 1270s. This has caused some to speculate that the *Versified Legend* we are considering could come from the same decade. However, that seems unlikely to us since the *Versified Legend* was addressed to Pope Alexander IV who died in 1261. Thus, 1261 seems the latest possible date to us. The French collection of sources dates it 1255. Marco Guida, an important scholar about sources for Clare's life and writings, gives it a possible spread of 1255-1260 (*Una Legenda*). The German collection of sources dates it between late 1254 when Alexander IV was elected pope and before August 1255 when he canonized Clare (Schneider *Klara-Quellen* 194). The German argument makes the most sense to us.

Author

Our general lack of knowledge about this versified legend is reflected in our lack of knowledge about its authorship. Armstrong believes that a curial official in Rome composed this document after the *Acts of the Process of Canonization* and a collection of miracles occurring after Clare's death arrived there. However, given the more recent uncertainty about the date and sources for the *Versified Legend,* this claim to probable authorship also is placed in question. The most prudent thing at this time is to assume nothing about a specific person as author.

Sources

There are three known sources for the *Versified Legend*, if you accept the theory that some common source predated both the *Versified Legend* and the *Prose Legend*. First is the *Acts of the Process of Canonization* which was quickly completed only months after Clare died on August 11, 1253. Second, someone, perhaps Thomas of Celano, quickly created the first draft of a legend that put the testimony of the witnesses found in the *Acts of the Process of Canonization* into chronological order. While this postulated document is lost to us, it then became a source for the *Versified Legend* and what we would come to call the *Prose Legend of St. Clare*.

At least a third source, if not more, must be accepted to account for the new information not originally found in the *Acts of the Process of Canonization* nor shared with the *Prose Legend*. At a minimum, a growing collection of miracles occurring after Clare died have to be accounted for. If the miracles were gathered into a single document, it has been lost. It is possible that the miracle stories were individual documents that have not survived. Further, both the *Versified Legend* and the *Prose Legend* have unique information which had to have come from alternate sources.

Origin

The origin of the *Versified Legend* is a curious thing to contemplate. There is no documentary evidence of it being commissioned. However, the fact that the first chapter is an incredibly idealized tribute to Pope Alexander IV, elected in 1254, suggests that the author had tremendous loyalty to the papacy. Further, we call this a *versified* legend because it is written in a poetic Latin that has meter and rhyme. It is a challenging genre to work in. Only the most accomplished authors could do it well. Even for that highly talented writer, it would be a time-consuming task. Likewise, it would mostly appeal to an educated audience, not the everyday person on the street.

Much mystery remains about the *Versified Legend*.

Value

When Regis Armstrong suggested that the *Versified Legend* predated and was thus a likely source for the *Prose Legend,* the *Versified Legend* took on enormous importance. It seemed like the first document to take the raw material of the *Acts of the Process of Canonization* and to impose on it a chronology and additional material from other unspecified sources.

However, German and French researchers have largely disproved this view. The more important document now would seem to be that preexisting first draft that was a source for both the *Versified Legend* and the *Prose Legend*. Since that draft is lost, the *Versified Legend* and the *Prose Legend* take on a more equal value. Both share the same chronology inherited from the preexisting lost draft, and each has its own unique additions gleaned from other unknown sources.

Its poetry employs biblical, theological and fanciful literary ideas and images to further interpret Clare. This includes a heavy dose of militaristic language and images that are not found in the *Prose Legend*. This versification is difficult to access in translation. The beauty of the poetry in Latin can never be replicated in another language. This is especially true of the difficult passages.

However, this heavy layer of interpretation found in the poetry should also be a warning to beginning and professional historians. Often, this interpretation is an anachronistic look back to Clare, which paints her in ways that may not be historically objective. Students doing the following worksheets will always want to ask whether the utilized images reflect the historical Clare or the idealized interpretation of her by people surviving her.

Cited sources and suggested reading

Because little recent research about the *Versified Legend* is in English, it is necessary to cite many other-language sources.

- Armstrong, Regis J. "'The Legenda Versificata': Toward an Official Biography." In *Clare of Assisi: Investigations*. Ed. Mary Francis Hone. Clare Centenary Series 7. St. Bonaventure NY: Franciscan Institute Publications, 1993. 69-93.

- Boccali, Giovanni, ed. *Fonti Clariane: Documentazione antica su santa Chiara di Assisi – Scritti, biografie, testimonianze, testi liturgici e sermoni*. Padova: Editrici Francescane, 2015. Pages 261-262 contain an introduction to the *Versified Legend*.

- Dalarun, Jacques, and Armelle Le Huërou, eds. *Claire d'Assise: Écrits, Vies, documents*. Paris: Les Éditions du CERF-Les Éditions Franciscaines, 2013. Pages 401-402 contain an introduction to the *Versified Legend*.

- Guida, Marco. *"Clara fides, clarus habitus, mores quoque clari:* la Legenda versificata di santa Chiara d'Assisi." *Frate Francesco* 80.1 (2014) 159-179 and 80.2 (2014) 461-471.

- —. *Una leggenda in cerca d'autore: la* Vita *di santa Chiara d'Assisi: Studio delle fonti e sinossi intertestuale.* Bruxelles: Société des Bollandistes, 2010.

- Schneider, Johannes and Paul Zahner, eds. *Klara-Quellen: Zeugnisse des 13. und 14. Jahrhunderts zur Franziskanischen Bewegung.* Verlag: Butzon & Bercker, 2013. Pages 189-196 contain an introduction to the *Versified Legend.*

- Uribe, Fernando. *Introduzione alle fonti agiografiche de san Francesco e santa Chiara d'Assisi (secc. XIII-XIV).* Medioevo francescano, Saggi 7. Assisi: Porziuncola, 2002.

Clara claris praeclara
The Papal Decree of Canonization
1255
(CA:ED 263-271)

Dating, authorship, origin

Pope Alexander IV canonized Clare of Assisi on August 15, 1255, just two years after her death. Alexander was the former Cardinal Rainaldo dei Conti di Segni who was the Poor Sisters' cardinal protector for many years. In that position, he was the person to accept Clare's own *Form of Life* one year before she died, before Innocent IV did so a year later.

The Papal Decree of Canonization (*Clara claris praeclara*), also called *The Bull of Canonization* (giving this work its abbreviation as BC), was issued about one or two months after the canonization ceremony for reasons we do not know. Armstrong notes that we don't know who its author was (CA:ED 262). The authorship could be of interest because of the uncommonly high poetic style of the decree. Realize that many "papal" documents were written by curial officials, but still attributed to the pope who issued them.

Sources

This decree relies on information from the *Acts of the Process of Canonization*.

Value

Clara claris praeclara offers little if any new historical information about Clare. Seldom will a decree of canonization do so. Its value is knowing that Pope Alexander IV accepted the information it contained as reliable. Thus, historians studying Clare's life are not very interested in it.

However, its poetry alone makes the document interesting for literary reasons. First among them is its intricate and prolonged musings over Clare's name, which in Latin and her native dialect of Umbrian has connotations of *clear, bright, brilliant, light, clear water, fair, clear voiced, clear image, evident, illustrious, distinguished, famous, eminent,* and *renown.*

Of particular value might be the document's portrayal of female religious leadership, admittedly from the point of view of the papacy. At many levels, this portrait is consistent with that found in Clare's own *Form of Life.*

In the end, it presents the idealized church image of a religious woman in that day, i.e., an enclosed virgin. While Clare was more concerned about poverty and a strong relationship with the Friars Minor, the papacy was more concerned about observing a strict enclosure.

The Prose Legend of Saint Clare
1255-1260
(CA:ED 277-329)

The story of the *Prose Legend* is very much tied up with the story of the *Versified Legend* related in a previous chapter. That previous chapter should be read first to better understand the questions surrounding the *Prose Legend.*

Most authors always use the word *versified* to distinguish the *Versified Legend* from the *Prose Legend.* However, many simply write the *Legend* or the *Legend of Saint Clare* without clarifying that it is the *prose* legend. Aiming to avoid as much confusion as possible, we always use the *Prose Legend* to indicate this document.

Date

There is no doubt that the *Prose Legend of Saint Clare* was not written before 1255, as it references Clare's 1255 canonization in its prologue and conclusion. It also references Clare as a saint. However, there is less certainty about the latest possible date by which it had to be written. Many authors simply list 1255 as its composition date. In Armelle Le Huërou's introduction to the *Prose Legend* in the recent French collection of sources for Clare's life and writings (Dalarun *Claire* 499-500), she dates the document between 1255-1260. The German collection of sources gives the same date spread (Schneider *Klara-Quellen* 277). There seems to be consensus that it was written shortly after Clare's canonization.

Authorship

After decades of uncertainty about the authorship of the *Prose Legend of St. Clare*, the scholarly world now shows remarkable agreement with Marco Guida (*Una leggenda*) that the author of the *Prose Legend of St. Clare* was Thomas of Celano because of both internal and external evidence. The internal evidence is the similar writing style found in the *Prose Legend of St. Clare* and Celano's known writings on Francis of Assisi. The most important external evidence is the testimony of a Poor Clare sister, Battista Alfani (d. 1523), abbess of Monteluce in Perugia. Her Italian translation of the *Acts of the Process of Canonization* and of the *Prose Legend of St. Clare* contains an *incipit* (introduction) comprised

154

of a letter Thomas of Celano wrote to Pope Alexander IV presenting to Alexander the legend he had commissioned from Celano.

Origin and Purpose

Pope Alexander IV, the former Cardinal Rainaldo dei Conti di Segni and cardinal protector of the Order of St. Damian, commissioned the *Prose Legend of Saint Clare* as part of the larger process to popularize her cult after he canonized her in August of 1255. Clearly, this indicates that the first purpose of the work was to demonstrate Clare's sanctity to the Christian public and establish the legitimacy of Alexander's decision to quickly canonize her. These facts make the legend an official document that will show the biases of the papacy and the general inclination of any document using the genre of hagiography.

Sources

As was stated in a previous chapter on the *Versified Legend,* many recent studies indicate that some lost first draft of a legend, probably written by Thomas of Celano himself, was the source for both the *Versified Legend* and what we have come to call the *Prose Legend of St. Clare.* That first draft imposed a chronology upon the temporally disorganized testimony that emerged from the *Acts of the Process of Canonization.* Thus, we can conclude that the *Prose Legend of Saint Clare* was based on the testimony from the twenty witnesses recorded in the *Acts of the Process of Canonization.* Taking the various bits of information received from each of the witnesses, the first draft wove them into a flowing narrative in more or less chronological order, which was developed by Thomas of Celano into his final *Prose Legend.*

Margaret Carney (Francis and Clare 316) claims that there are thirty-two details in the *Process* that are not repeated in the *Prose Legend of St. Clare.* On the other hand, the legend includes 20 items not originally found in the *Process.* Thus, for the most part, the *Prose Legend of St. Clare* is a massive reworking of the information already found in the *Acts of the Process of Canonization.*

However slight the number, additions not found in the *Acts of the Process of Canonization* indicate that Celano obviously had other sources as well. As one can expect from a more explicitly hagiographic work, the legend adds numerous miracles to the base of information provided in the *Acts of the Process of Canonization.* Miracles obviously have an important place in the legend as they were thought to prove the holiness of the new saint. We remain uncertain from where this new information and these miracle stories originate.

The bull of canonization, *Clara claris praeclara*, was also available to Thomas of Celano as a source, though it offers little new historical information. Finally, paragraph 11 of the preface of the legend mentions Angelo Tancredi, Leo of Assisi, and an unnamed sister at San Damiano Monastery as sources.

Thus, we can identify at least five different sources of information that contributed to the composition of the *Prose Legend of Saint Clare*:

1. *The Acts of the Process of Canonization of Clare of Assisi;*

2. A first draft legend probably written by Thomas of Celano himself;

3. The papal proclamation of Clare's canonization, *Clara claris praeclara;*

4. Angelo Tancredi and Leo of Assisi, companions of St. Francis, who are mentioned in #11 of the preface of the legend;

5. Another sister at San Damiano, also mentioned in #11 of the preface.

The first three sources are evident in the literary connections among them and the legend. The last two sources are mentioned in the preface of the legend.

Organization

The *Prose Legend of Saint Clare* is divided into two parts that are preceded by a preface. The first part relates Clare's life and concludes with her funeral. It relates many miracles reported to have occurred during her life. Many of these miracles are related in the *Acts of the Process of Canonization*, though some are new. Part two lists various miracles reported to have occurred after Clare's death and her canonization. Thus, the users of this workbook will find themselves predominantly working in the first part.

Evaluation

The *Prose Legend of Saint Clare* enjoys a positive evaluation as does most hagiography that is temporally close to the life of its subject. The legend was completed within years of Clare's death. As such, it has an importance similar to Thomas of Celano's *Life of Saint Francis* written just two or three years after Francis's death. An important difference between these two sources is that, today, we possess an important literary source for the legend about Clare, i.e., the *Acts of the Process of Canonization*. Thus, we have the *Process* about Clare, know who was in charge of collecting its data, know who else was present, importantly know who gave testimony, and know the circumstances of those giving testimony. The *Process* of Saint Francis's canonization is lost. We cannot compare Celano's first masterpiece about Francis with his *Process*. The difference between the two situations is substantial.

Since we possess the *Acts of the Process of Canonization* about Clare, we are able to compare its data to the storyline of the *Prose Legend of Saint Clare*. In so doing, we are able to see how the story was subtly and not so subtly changed. We can see what was added, subtracted, and altered. While the testimonies preserved in the *Process* include many miracles, we can see other miracles added and previously existing miracles developed. This is an amazing example of how, in only a matter of years, the pressures of hagiographic tendencies were already visibly at work.

This cautions us from assuming too easily that a source is more reliable simply because it is early and close to the historical figure who is its subject. Having said all that, we also need to admit that, in general, a source only years away from a subject's death will be more reliable than one twenty or forty years away from the death. The only source of major information that we would consider more important than this prose legend would be the *Acts of the Process of Canonization*.

Regarding notation

There is a potentially confusing situation for making references to the *Prose Legend of Saint Clare*. This work has three levels of organizational numbers: chapters indicated by Roman numerals; sections (sometimes called paragraphs) listed with large Arabic numbers at the front of a section; and verses indicated by smaller superscript Arabic numbers. Because the text uses these three numbering layers in different ways, confusion is possible unless all three numbers are used. Thus, we typically use all three numbers. So, in the example "LCl XI 16:6-7," "LCl" refers to the *Prose Legend of Saint Clare*. The Roman numeral "XI" refers to chapter eleven which talks about a miracle involving oil. The Arabic number *before* the colon, "16," refers to paragraph or section 16. The Arabic numbers *after* the colon, "6-7," refer to the verses. Occasionally, if a reference refers to the entire chapter, only the chapter Roman numeral is cited. If the section or paragraph number is sufficient, that is all that appears. So, "LCl XI" indicates all of chapter eleven. "LCl XI 16" indicates all of section 16 in chapter eleven.

Cited sources and suggested reading

- Armstrong, Regis J. "Clare of Assisi, the Poor Ladies, and their Ecclesial Mission in the *First Life* of Thomas of Celano." *Greyfriars Review* 5.3 (1991) 389-424. This article contains a lengthy discussion on whether or not Thomas of Celano was the author of the *Prose Legend of Saint Clare* (412-417). Also published in *Laurentianum* 32 (1991) 104-145. Marco Guida's arguments supersede those of Armstrong.

- Boccali, Giovanni, ed. *Fonti Clariane: Documentazione antica su santa Chiara di Assisi – Scritti, biografie, testimonianze, testi liturgici e sermoni*. Padova: Editrici Francescane, 2015. Pages 196-197 contain an introduction to the *Prose Legend of St. Clare*.

- Carney, Margaret. "Francis and Clare: A Critical Examination of the Sources." *Greyfriars Review* 3.3 (1989) 315-343.

- Dalarun, Jacques, and Armelle Le Huërou, eds. *Claire d'Assise: Écrits, Vies, documents*. Paris: Les Éditions du CERF-Les Éditions Franciscaines, 2013. Pages 499-500 contain an introduction to the *Prose Legend of St. Clare*.

- Downing, Frances Teresa. *Saint Clare of Assisi: The Context of Her Life*. Vol. 2. Phoenix AZ: Tau Publishing, 2012. Pp. 25-26.

- Guida, Marco. *Una leggenda in cerca d'autore: la* Vita *di santa Chiara d'Assisi: Studio delle fonti e sinossi intertestuale*. Bruxelles: Société des Bollandistes, 2010. Guida has established that Thomas of Celano is the author of the *Prose Legend of Saint Clare*.

- Schneider, Johannes and Paul Zahner, eds. *Klara-Quellen: Zeugnisse des 13. und 14. Jahrhunderts zur Franziskanischen Bewegung*. Verlag: Butzon & Bercker, 2013. Pages 277-292 contain an introduction to the *Prose Legend of St. Clare*.

The Doubtful *Letter to Ermentrude of Bruges* (CA:ED 420-421)

Where is the best place in this workbook to place a chapter on the *Letter to Ermentrude of Bruges*? This section on Tools focuses on writings *about* Clare that are written by other people. This letter has neither of those characteristics.

The Work section of this workbook includes works written by Clare. Not long ago, many considered the *Letter to Ermentrude of Bruges* to be a genuine letter or combination of two letters from Clare. Today, most are doubtful of Clare's authorship. So, it doesn't seem appropriate to place this chapter in the Work section. In the end, we choose to place this chapter in the Tools section simply because it has to go somewhere.

Source after source that discusses the *Letter to Ermentrude of Bruges* tells you the same story. The earliest witness to the letter is Luke Wadding's *Annales Minorum* in 1635. He claimed that Clare wrote two letters to Ermentrude, but only presented one, perhaps a summary of the two. Wadding cited no sources for this document, and no other manuscripts have been found.

Scholars find both the style and content of the letter quite different from that found in Clare's known letters to Agnes of Prague. Consequently, most scholars hold that the letter should not be included among the authentic writings of Clare. Because of this, it seems imprudent to include it in any study of Clare's spirituality. However, because you'll find many references to it on the Internet and in older books, it is necessary to briefly recount this history. If you wish to read the letter and investigate the sources concerning its authorship, see CA:ED 420-421.

Suggested reading

- Becker, Marie France., Jean-François Godet, and Thaddée Matura. *Claire d'Assise: Écrits.* Paris: Les Éditions du Cerf, 1985. 18-19.

- Grau, Engelbert and Lothar Hardick. *Leben und Schriften der hl. Klara von Assisi.* 3rd ed. Werl/Westf.: Dietrich-Coelde-Verlag, 1960. 24.

- Johnson, Timothy. "Image and Vision: Contemplation as Visual Perception in Clare of Assisi's Epistolary Writings." *Greyfriars Review* 8.2 (1994) 201-217.

- Wadding, Luke, Ed. *Annales Minorum* III. Quaracchi: Collegium S. Bonaventurae, 1635. 8-27.

WORK

About Worksheets

This section of our workbook provides you with the opportunity to study the life and writings of Clare of Assisi. We make a few introductory comments before beginning the worksheets.

First, it is our bias that people learn best by doing the work themselves. We have never found spoon-feeding to be an effective pedagogical approach. These worksheets will help you do the work by providing the primary sources for your study and a series of starter questions and/or suggestions. Read the *entire* worksheet at the beginning of your study. There may be important ideas toward the end of the worksheet to facilitate your study.

Occasionally, we provide a commentary as part of a worksheet. Generally, we do this when there is information that affects your study and comes from other scholarly works.

We also provide lists of recommended reading on numerous worksheets. Sometimes, these lists are simply for those who wish to explore a topic in greater detail. On other occasions, we strongly recommend additional readings from secondary sources because they provide essential insights into the topic.

The more work you do on these worksheets, the more you will benefit.

Second, we confess to being biased in favor of a historical approach to studying Clare. We believe a valuable spirituality can only be constructed upon good historical knowledge. Each of the worksheets provides questions and recommendations for doing historical-critical work. We enumerate here a number of common techniques that are applicable to most worksheets.

- We have previously outlined numerous characteristics of hagiography. Review them often. When you read something in the primary sources that smacks of non-historical, hagiographic influences, let your suspicions guide you. Don't blindly accept assertions or interpretations you consider historically doubtful.

- One of our favorite techniques is to compare the same story in various sources. These comparisons allow you to see what has been added, subtracted, or changed from earlier versions of the story. Always ask why these changes are occurring. Review frequently what you know about each of the various medieval sources, especially the biases that are part of each source. Consider whether a source's biases are guiding the changes in the tradition. You also will be able to see the powerful forces of hagiography adjusting stories over time. Always be suspicious of changes in a story.

- Medieval hagiography loves the miraculous. Without it, many medieval people doubted a subject's sanctity. Many world-class historians who believe in miracles acknowledge that hagiography is fraught with more miracles than are believable. Our principle is to search for the most humanly understandable rendering of a story. While that may leave us with little information about a story, it probably will leave us with a version that is reliable.

Third, we wish to emphasize that worksheets are places to begin. In our trials using this workbook, a few students made presentations in which they went through the list of questions we asked in a worksheet and provide an answer to each. This is not how we intend the worksheets to function. Our starter questions and suggestions are only intended to get you thinking and asking questions. If you are making a presentation to a group based on your study, we suggest that you organize your findings in a way that is satisfying to you and interesting to others in your group. In doing so, you may not answer a single question we list on your worksheet.

Fourth, we realize that not everyone using this book is in the same situation. If you are using it alone, do what works best for you. If you are part of a study group, we have some suggestions.

- Don't have everyone in the group do every worksheet. They take a significant amount of time, and you may not have enough time to cover most of Clare's life. We typically work with groups and generally assign the worksheets in succession to different individuals. We then ask each person to prepare a presentation to the entire group.

- Groups make for interesting and helpful dynamics in this process. After the individual's presentation, we invite other group members to respond to and evaluate the conclusions of the presenter. Often, members of the group will disagree about the conclusions and criticize each other's reasoning. We generally let this type of discussion go on for a while, especially early in the course. It teaches the participants to be critical and to think on their own. We even play the devil's advocate by asking questions of the presenter and the other participants. We use this technique to loosen up the crowd, which is often hesitant in the beginning to question another presenter. After a few presentations, we occasionally have to stop a discussion just to move on. There is only so much time for each topic.

- We find that our discussions often raise other questions about religious life, liturgy, teachings of the Church, spirituality, and values in general. We generally allow these discussions to occur when they seem manageable and we are competent to guide them. Part of the reason we study Clare's life and writings is to deepen our faith life. With that as a goal, it seems self-defeating not to allow discussion on other topics.

- Occasionally, a group leader may have an expertise that is helpful to this study process. We encourage you to share your expertise with your students. However, be careful to preserve a general atmosphere where the students feel like they are doing the majority of the work. We only present things they could not otherwise know on their own.

Fifth, each worksheet has a topic. The primary sources cited in the worksheet generally talk about many things unrelated to that topic. Occasionally, students are prone to report to their groups every bit of information provided in the worksheet's sources, even when it is unrelated to the topic. This is deadening. We encourage students to focus only on the material related to the worksheet's topic.

Related to point five is our encouragement to read "around" your worksheet's citations, i.e., before and after the cited text, if that text by itself seems out of context. Often the larger context gives the text of a citation a fuller meaning. However, in light of point five, be careful only to report on material that is directly related to the topic of your worksheet.

That's pretty much all the advice we have for you at this point. The thing to do now is to begin. If you are part of a group, divide up the first few worksheets and break up for the time being. Your next gathering promises to be an enriching learning experience.

Clare's Family

Sources

PC   I 4:10—5:16 (Pacifica)
III 28:91-92 (Filippa)
IV 16:51 (Amata di Martino)
XII 1:1-2 (Beatrice)
XVI 1:3-4; 5:16-17 (Lord Ugolino)
XVIII 4:19-20 (Ranieri)
XIX 1:1-6 (Pietro)
XX 1:1—2:5; 3:7-9 (Ioanni)

VL   V 15-16, 20-24, 31-34
BC   10:42-44, 23:99-100
LCl   I 1:1—2:11

You may also want to examine the sources in the subsequent worksheet ("The Brief Stays at San Paolo and Sant'Angelo di Panzo, Agnes Joining Clare, and Arrival at San Damiano"). For the purposes of this worksheet, only consider information about the family, especially the stories about family members trying to bring Clare and Agnes back to the family home after they entered religious life.

Starter questions and suggestions

If you are part of a small study group, you may want to assign the same person to this and the following worksheet ("Clare's Early Life"). They involve many of the same references.

Of all the people in Clare's immediate family, the primary sources give us the most information about her mother, Ortulana. However, begin by collecting as much information as possible about all her family members. Note the family's social and economic status. Determine whether we can ascertain how the family functioned.

Then focus your attention on Ortulana. List all the details you can glean about her background. The data will naturally have you focus on Ortulana's religious practices and piety. Document this thoroughly. Who might have accompanied Ortulana on her pilgrimages? Speculate about how Ortulana's religious practice might have influenced Clare. Do the medieval sources explain that influence?

Pay particular attention to the pre-birth story in which Ortulana hears a voice urging her not to fear Clare's upcoming birth. Note that childbirth was a leading cause of death for medieval women. Does this story make you think of any biblical births? In what other biblical stories does a messenger from God tell a human not to be afraid? List stories that come to your mind and explain how these similarities to biblical stories might affect a medieval reader and then a modern reader like yourself.

Note any importance given to Clare's name. This is just the beginning of many explanations of and plays on her name. Within these sources, how does her name help the reader to interpret Clare's importance?

Commentary

We know of only three girls in Clare's family. Clare was the oldest. Catherine was a little younger than Clare. Catherine joined Clare in religious life and was given the name Agnes (of Assisi) just after Clare herself fled the family home. Beatrice was quite young when Clare and Agnes left the family home. She joined Clare at San Damiano Monastery quite a bit later.

Some of the medieval sources make references to Ortulana's pilgrimage to the famous shrine of St. Michael the Archangel in Gargano, Apulia (Puglia today). It is the region that comprises the heel of geographic Italy. Michael the Archangel was among the most popular saints at the time of Francis and Clare of Assisi, and this shrine was a popular destination for pilgrims.

In his article "New Information," Arnaldo Fortini speculates that Ortulana's pilgrimage to the Holy Land most likely occurred in 1192 when peace allowed Europeans to visit Jerusalem. That would be about one year before she gave birth to Clare, her oldest child. Fortini also notes that Ortulana died before 1238 since her name is not on a list of sisters at San Damiano Monastery in that year. She had joined her daughters at San Damiano Monastery after being widowed. We cannot be more specific about when she died (Fortini, New Information 45).

Fortini's article provides a wealth of information about Clare's family, based on civil documents in Assisi. It confirms the wealth of her family (29-33) and concludes that Favarone (Clare's father) and Ortulana only had the three daughters listed in the hagiographic sources: Clare, Catherine (Agnes), and Beatrice (45). All three joined San Damiano Monastery according to the sources. Agnes later moved to the Monastery at Monticelli near Florence and probably the Monastery at Monteluce near Perugia. Increasingly, scholars believe that Agnes moved among numerous monasteries that desired the lifestyle of San Damiano Monastery in Assisi. They speculate that she might have spent around two years in each monastery and done this for about twenty years. Fortini reports that "Agnes" was the name given to Catherine by Francis when she entered religious life. She was younger than Clare and died on August 27, 1253, just weeks after Clare's death.

Using material from the *Acts of the Process of Canonization* and that found in Assisi's archives, Fortini was able to outline four generations on Clare's father's side (New Information 29). They are:

Bernardino: great grandfather

▼

Offreduccio: grandfather

▼

Favarone: father

▼

Clare of Assisi

The hagiographic and civil records leave a huge vacuum regarding Clare's father, Favarone. Arnaldo Fortini's constructed genealogy indicates that Offreduccio had five sons, including Clare's father (New Information 30). He opines that her father was seldom home, which is partially verified by how many hagiographic stories involving Clare's family do not mention him. This partially explains why Clare's uncle, Monaldo, played a much larger role in her story.

The nature of noble/knightly families at that time and place explains even more. These families were quite extended, much more akin to modern Middle Eastern Arabic families than the tight nuclear families of western countries. Medieval noble families were quite clannish, and Monaldo was clearly the leader and centerpiece of the Offreduccio family. The hagiography about Clare makes it clear that Favarone just wasn't as important as Monaldo.

Cited sources and suggested reading

- Bartoli, Marco. *Saint Clare: Beyond the Legend.* Trans. Frances Teresa Downing. Cincinnati OH: St. Anthony Messenger Press, 2010. Chapter three on "Courtesy" helps understand how Clare's family operated and situated itself in society.

- Fortini, Arnaldo. "New Information about Saint Clare of Assisi." Trans. M. Jane Frances. *Greyfriars Review* 7.1 (1993) 27-69. This is a translation of an article first published in 1953. So, "new" information is a relative term.

- Fortini, Gemma. "The Noble Family of St. Clare of Assisi." *Franciscan Studies* 42 (1982) 48-67. Gemma traces Clare's lineage back to Charlemagne and connects her family to Bona and Pacifica di Guelfuccio who were witnesses in the *Acts of the Process of Canonization.*

Clare's Early Life

Sources

PC   I 1:1—2:6 (Pacifica)
           III 2:7-10 (Filippa)
           IV 2:6 (Amata di Martino)
           XII: 1:1-3 (Beatrice)
           XIII 2:10 (Cristiana di Bernardo)
           XVI 2:5; 5:16 (Lord Ugolino)
           XVII 1:1—2:6; 4:12-15; 6:18—7:21 (Bona di Guelfuccio)
           XVIII 1:1—3:15 (Ranieri)
           XIX: 1:4; 2:7-12 (Pietro)
           XX 1:3; 2:6—5:12 (Ioanni)
VL   V 25-49
LCl   3-4

Suggestions and starter questions

If you are part of a small study group, you may want to assign the same person to this and the previous worksheet, "Clare's Family." They involve many of the same references.

The sources focus on two elements of Clare's early life that are obviously related. First, they are very intent on portraying Clare as a saintly person from the moment of her birth. Thus, her early life is portrayed as an in-home prelude to her forty-two years in the monastery. The portrayal of this holy early life also provides some information about her early family life. As students of Clare, we are interested in both. Pay particular attention to her penitential practices in her home.

Read over the various sources and give a description of Clare's natural characteristics before entering religious life. Give examples to demonstrate each characteristic.

Identify those elements in the sources that are spiritual interpretations about which the witness has no objective experience (e.g., that Clare had been sanctified in her mother's womb). How do you regard such statements?

Various sources indicate that Clare was a virgin her entire life, and Lord Ranieri tells of his own unsuccessful requests for her hand in marriage. Try to discover how virginity was perceived to be a sign of devotion to God for Clare and the witnesses who reported about her virginity. Remember how important it was to noble families to be able to grant the hands of their daughters in arranged marriages as a way to build military and economic relationships with other noble families.

Can you identify any connection between Clare's commitment to perpetual virginity, her prayer, and her ascetical practices? How do these practices relate to her idea of the passing nature of the material world? What was lasting for Clare, and how did she pursue it?

In the *Acts of the Process of Canonization* XII: 6, Beatrice, Clare's youngest sister, describes Clare's holiness by citing the following characteristics: virginity, humility, patience, kindness, necessary correction and sweet admonition of sisters, continuous prayer and contemplation, abstinence and fasting, roughness of bed and clothing, disregard of self, fervor in love of God, desire for martyrdom, and most especially love of the *Privilege of Poverty*. Other sources offer other characteristics of Clare's holiness. Some of these refer to Clare before leaving her family home and others refer to her life at San Damiano Monastery. Do you consider the same characteristics signs of holiness? Why might you and the witnesses have different opinions? Do you believe Clare was holy from an early age? Why?

The Preliminaries section of this workbook discusses the monastic, penitential, evangelical and apostolic life movements, which predated Francis and Clare, and influence them. Read that chapter and identify those signs of holiness in Clare's life that relate in some fashion to these movements. How might these movements have influenced her? Identify signs of Clare's early holiness that relate to Francis of Assisi's chosen lifestyle.

Suggested reading

- Bartoli, Marco. *Saint Clare: Beyond the Legend*. Trans. Frances Teresa Downing. Cincinnati OH: St. Anthony Messenger Press, 2010. Chapter three on "Courtesy" helps understand how the choices Clare made early in her life interfaced with social realities of her day.

- Carney, Margaret. "Francis and Clare: A Critical Examination of the Sources." *Greyfriars Review* 3.3 (1989) 315-343. Page 321 contains Carney's concise summary of the witnesses' testimony about Clare's early demonstration of holiness.

Clare's Response to Francis's Early Preaching and Their First Meetings

Sources about the Friars' Early Preaching

Test 23
1C 23, 29-30, 36-37
LJS 16, 19-20, 23
AP 15-16, 18-24, 41 b-d
L3C 33-34, 36-40, 60
LMj IV: 6
See Workbook I p. 166

Sources about Clare's First Meetings with Francis

FLCl	VI 1
TestCl	24-26
PC	I 2:5-6; 6:17 (Pacifica)
	III 1:1-3 (Filippa)
	IV 2:5-6 (Amata)
	VI 1:3 (Cecilia)
	XII 2:4-5 (Beatrice)
	XVI 3:9; 6:18 (Lord Ugolino)
	XVII 3:7-4:15 (Bona di Guelfuccio)
	XX 6:13 (Ioanni)
VL	VI
BC	6:30—7:31
LCl	5—6, 44:5
	(Compare the language of LCl 5 with that about Francis in L3C 7-8 and 2C 7.)

Starter questions and suggestions

The sources are clear that Clare embarked on an intense spiritual journey before Francis overtly influenced her. Still, the movement begun by Francis and his early companions captivated her, like others of her day. Many modern authors deduce from the primary sources that Clare and Francis began to have clandestine meetings in 1210 or 1211 when Clare was about 17 and Francis was about 29 years of age.

Describe the prominent characteristics of the friars' early example and why they captured the imagination of so many people. Into what aspirations of other people did this example tap? What did their example prompt others to do? How was Clare like and unlike others in her response to Francis and his early followers? What was the content of their discussions? Which images were used to describe Clare's choices? LCl 6 says that Clare handed herself over to the counsel of Francis after only God. Do the other sources (especially the *Acts of the Process of Canonization*) support this supposed total convergence on Francis as the originator of Clare's form of life?

Secret visits between Clare and Francis add intrigue to the more general topic of Francis's influence on others. When we first read of them, we could not help but think of Jesus and Nicodemus meeting during the night in the *Gospel of John* (3:1-21). Describe the nature of Clare and Francis's visits. Why were these meetings chaperoned? Who were the chaperones? What do the sources portray as the central themes of these visits? What was the relationship between the two people? Might these visits seem to contradict other testimony that Clare shunned contact outside her parental home? If so, what hagiographic or social reasons might authors have to portray Clare as an "invisible" person behind the walls of the family home? Who initiated these meetings? Did Clare choose her eventual lifestyle because of Francis, or would she have done so without any contact with Francis? Do the *Process* and the *Prose Legend of Saint Clare* present different perspectives about these issues?

Margaret Carney in "Francis and Clare" sees obvious differences when comparing the raw material about Clare uncovered in the *Acts of the Process of Canonization* and the re-working of that material in the *Prose Legend,* suggesting that the *Prose Legend* may have amplified what really occurred. First, Carney notes that the *Prose Legend* attributes their discernment and meetings to "the Father of spirits" (see Heb. 12:9). So, the *Prose Legend* places the impetus for the meetings *outside* of the two future saints.

She also believes the *Prose Legend* shows the two involved in very different ways. It portrays Francis as very active in these meetings, hoping to wrest Clare from the hold of the world and offering her bridal imagery to understand her vocation. This impression of Francis is amplified by the portrayal of Clare as the one responsible for the frequency of their meetings and eager to hear Francis's words that appear "to be on fire."

On the other hand, the remembrance of Bona in the *Process* simply states that Francis urged the conversion to Christ upon Clare (compare PC XVII 3-4 to LCl 5 and see Carney 323). Do you, like Carney, detect different portrayals of these secret meetings in the various sources? If so, how do you explain them? What do you consider to be the truth about these meetings?

Many witnesses in the *Process* noted Clare's perpetual virginity, and virginity as her goal in refusing proposals for marriage from prestigious suitors. How does virginity figure into the various accounts of these secret meetings? How do the subsequent actions of her flight from her familial home, struggle with family members, and eventual settlement at San Damiano express and give meaning to her virginity and vice versa?

Cited sources

- Carney, Margaret. "Francis and Clare: A Critical Examination of the Sources." *Greyfriars Review* 3.3 (1989) 315-343.

The Palm Sunday Drama and
Clare's Investiture at the Portiuncula
(probably in 1211)

Sources

PC	XII 2:5—4:7 (Beatrice)
	XIII 1:2-9 (Christiana di Bernardo)
	XVI 6:19 (Lord Ugolino)
	XVII 5:16-17 (Bona di Guelfuccio)
	XVIII 3:16 (Ranieri)
	XX 6:14 (Ioanni)
VL	VII
BC	7:31—8:33
LCl	7—8, 12:2

Sources about Bernard of Quintavalle's conversion

1C	24
2C	15
AP	10-12
L3C	27-30

Starter questions and suggestions

There has been considerable difficulty determining on which Palm Sunday Clare's departure occurred. Scholars increasingly agree it was probably 1211.

Begin by outlining the Palm Sunday drama as you believe it occurred. This story leaves many details and motivations unarticulated. Try to unpack the story as much as possible. Be clear whether your assertions are certain, probable, or possible.

Whose idea was this Palm Sunday rendezvous? Which characters were involved in this conspiracy? Why was the planning for the event so secretive? Do any of the details of the story appear to have a more symbolic meaning than a historical meaning (e.g., Clare leaving through a seldom used barred door, sometimes called the door of death)? Did Clare's entrance into religious life have any similarities to Bernard of Quintavalle's (d. c. 1242), Francis's first companion who stayed with him?

175

While five of the witnesses in the *Acts of the Process of Canonization* say Francis tonsured Clare, the *Prose Legend of Saint Clare* (8) says her hair was shorn by the hands of the brothers. Is this difference an unimportant detail? Might the difference be trying to make a symbolic point?

Commentary

Some scholars believe Clare's departure from her family home was planned by her immediate family without the knowledge of her extended family. These plans would also have included Francis of Assisi, Bishop Guido I of Assisi, Pacifica and Bona di Guelfuccio (cousins).

Padovese's article documents that the cutting of a woman's hair was often seen as a penitential act. It also could be done in repentance for a particular sin or as a symbol of entrance into religious life, which was viewed as penitential. In the case of penance for sin, it could be imposed by others or self-imposed. When attached to entering religious life, it was usually accompanied by a change of dress. Both the act of cutting a woman's hair and wearing less attractive clothing, often similar to a man's clothing, was seen as an assertion of independence from one's paternal home or husband. Thus, the act could be very provocative.

The testimony of history shows that the cutting of a woman's hair, often with attendant change of dress, was not necessarily performed by a bishop. Frequently, the person cut her own hair and changed clothes in a planned and/or solemn-religious ritual. Thus, it combined penance with initiation (see Padovese 67-74). Often, the initiation into religious life garnered the protection of church authority against those who resisted the woman's plans.

In Clare's case, remember that the earliest testimonies from the *Acts of the Process of Canonization* occurred forty-one years after the event in 1211. So, there could be some confusion as to which of the two reasons for tonsure was true for Clare. Padovese argues that Clare's hair-cutting on the evening of Palm Sunday could not have been intended as the official ritual consecration of a virgin because that could not occur during a penitential season. This contributes to Padovese's idea that sheering her hair was a penitential act (Padovese 77). He believes that Clare displaying her shorn head when her relatives came to drag her back home (see PC XVIII 3 and the Bull of Canonization 6) further verifies that she intended this as a penitential act to acquire the support of the institutional church.

Chapter two of Clare's *Form of Life* institutionalized the ritual acts of cutting the entrant's hair and setting aside secular clothing for those who entered the community. These acts should not be confused with the veiling or consecration of nuns, which required the presence of a bishop (see FLCl II 18; XI 9). These provisions in chapter two seem to apply to those entering the monastery for the first time on a probationary basis, i.e., as a novice.

Cited sources and suggested reading

- Bartoli, Marco. *Saint Clare: Beyond the Legend*. Trans. Frances Teresa Downing. Cincinnati OH: St. Anthony Messenger Press, 2010. Chapter four on "Conversion" helps understand the events surrounding Clare's departure from her parental home on Palm Sunday night. Bartoli explains how this constituted a choice of social status and identification.

- Downing, Frances Teresa. *Saint Clare of Assisi: The Context of Her Life*. Vol. 2. Phoenix AZ: Tau Publishing, 2012. Pages 54-59 discuss tonsure as an act of penance.

- Fortini, Arnaldo. "New Information about Saint Clare of Assisi." Trans. M. Jane Frances. *Greyfriars Review* 7.1 (1993) 27-69. This is a translation of an article first published in 1953. So, "new" information is a relative term.

- Padovese, Luigi. "Clare's Tonsure: Act of Consecration or Sign of Penance?" Trans. Madonna Balestrieri. *Greyfriars Review* 6.1 (1992) 67-80.

The Brief Stays at San Paolo and Sant'Angelo di Panzo, Agnes Joining Clare, and Arrival at San Damiano

Sources

TestCl	6-17, 24-32
PC	XII 4:8—5:14 (Beatrice)
	XVI 6:20 (Lord Ugolino)
	XVIII 3:17-18 (Ranieri)
	XX 6:14—7:17 (Ioanni)
VL	VII:35—IX
BC	8:33—9:36
LCl	IV 8:12–VI 10:12 (Clare's journey)
	(Note that chapter 10 is erroneously listed on page 287 of CA:ED while it should be listed as starting at the top of page 289.)
	XVI 24:1—26:31 (Agnes's flight some days later)
Fortini	(*Francis of Assisi*) 341-349

Starter questions, suggestions and commentary

After her tonsure and investiture at the Portiuncula, Clare needed a place to live. Surely, living with the friars was not acceptable as this would be a scandalous arrangement. Thus, it seemed that either Francis or Bishop Guido arranged for Clare to first stay at San Paolo delle Abbadesse in Bastia. Marco Bartoli's *Clare of Assisi* (49) gives a great deal of information about San Paolo. It was a monastery with vast lands that were sources of income. Its members were noble women dedicated to prayer. They had male and female servants who wore a different habit, did different work, and were considered at a different social level.

If Clare had intended to stay at San Paolo, it would have been as a servant since she had already given away her dowry that was required to enter as a nun. Fortini adds that the monastery enjoyed a privilege of excommunication of anyone interfering with or maltreating its inhabitants (*Francis of Assisi* 341-345). Many believe that Clare left San Paolo because the monastic lifestyle did not suit her. This is a reasonable speculation given her later insistence on total and radical personal and corporate poverty.

After a short time, Clare moved to Sant'Angelo di Panzo on Mount Subasio. While the exact nature of life there cannot be ascertained, some authors believe the women lived a type of Beguine observance, i.e., lay penitents living together, but more active than nuns in a monastery. Francesco Santucci believes Sant' Angelo was smaller, simpler and closer to San Damiano. There is even more uncertainty about why Clare eventually left Sant'Angelo. As a foundation of penitents, it seemed much closer to Clare's intentions. Could she have wanted a foundation much more explicitly connected to the Friars Minor? Much later, Sant'Angelo would join the new Order of St. Damian founded by Cardinal Ugolino. (See Bartoli 57-58 for more information about Sant'Angelo and our Chapter "Who Founded the Order of St. Clare?" for information about the Order of St. Damian.)

After her blood sister Agnes joined her, Clare finally moved to San Damiano, just below and outside the walls of Assisi, which Francis had previously restored during his conversion. Realize that at that time, San Damiano looked nothing like the complex today. Then, it was essentially a chapel with a small attached residence for a priest.

Outline the events of Clare quickly moving from one place of refuge to another. Why did Clare never seem to intend either San Paolo or Sant'Angelo as a permanent dwelling place? With the Palm Sunday drama apparently so well planned, why was there such tentativeness about a subsequent dwelling place for Clare? What was Francis's role in these events? Why was Clare's soul "not at rest" (LC1 10) until she arrived at San Damiano?

Agnes's escape is only found in the *Prose Legend of Saint Clare*. Was her movement into religious life as well planned as Clare's? What do you think was the nature of Clare and Agnes's conversations before Clare fled on Palm Sunday? Had Clare and Agnes conspired about Agnes's decision? The *Prose Legend* portrays Clare and Agnes's encounters with their family at each of these places as a test that demonstrated their determination. Note that the story of Agnes's entrance already portrayed Clare with super human powers.

What might have been Francis's role in Agnes's decision? Why is no mention of Francis made in the story of Agnes's escape? Why was Francis, who was involved in Clare's escape, so absent from their confrontations with their family? While Francis gave Clare counsel, it seems Clare was making the decisions about her own destiny. In this regard, how might Clare's relationship with Francis be like Francis's relationship with Bishop Guido I of Assisi, Cardinal Ugolino, or Cardinal John of St. Paul? Do these stories portray Clare as "founding" anything?

What about Clare attracted both women and men to the Franciscan movement? Since Clare is portrayed as inspiring men as well as women (PC XX 7; LC1 10), could she be considered a founder of the First Order?

While Francis and Clare undoubtedly contributed to the institutional development of their own and each other's foundations, we prefer to think of them as founders of a movement rather than institutions. What might be the differences between these two ways of understanding Francis and Clare as founders? (Consult the chapter "Who Founded the Order of St. Clare?")

Cited sources and suggested reading

- Bartoli, Marco. *Clare of Assisi.* Trans. Frances Teresa Downing. Quincy IL: Franciscan Press, 1993.

- Downing, Frances Teresa. *Saint Clare of Assisi: The Context of Her Life.* Vol. 2. Phoenix AZ: Tau Publishing, 2012. Pages 60-71 are about San Paulo; pages 72-76 are about Sant'Angelo di Panzo; pages 117-120 are about Clare's relationship with Bishop Guido I (c. 1195-1212) and Bishop Guido II of Assisi (1212 – c. 1228).

- Fortini, Arnaldo. "New Information about Saint Clare of Assisi." Trans. M. Jane Frances. *Greyfriars Review* 7.1 (1993) 27-69. This is a translation of an article first published in 1953. So, "new" information is a relative term. This article contains much information from the archives of Assisi about Clare's extended family, San Paolo and Sant'Angelo. A genealogical chart is provided on page 30. Do *not* confuse this article with Fortini's book, *Francis of Assisi*, which is the work cited at the beginning of this worksheet.

- —. *Francis of Assisi.* Trans. Helen Moak. NY: Crossroad, 1992. 341-345.

- Santucci, Francesco. "Sant'Angelo di Panzo Near Assisi." Trans. Lori Pieper. *Greyfriars Review* 8 (1994) 219-238.

Francis's Prediction that the Poor Sisters Would Live at San Damiano

Sources

L3C   24
2C   13, 204
TestCl 6-17

Starter questions and suggestions

While some hagiography about Francis rebuilding the Church of San Damiano also notes that the Poor Sisters would someday live there (1C 18-20; 1.5C 8; LJS 13), only L3C, 2C, and Clare's *Testament* include a prediction by Francis that this would happen.

Scholars see a variety of hands in the composition of Clare's *Testament* (see our chapter on Clare's *Testament*). Many consider it to be a collection of sayings from throughout her life. Obviously, they would have required editing. Could the comment about this prediction be attributed to an editor who was filling in the blanks? Given the controversy over how Clare's *Testament* may have been composed, is it significant that no other writing of Clare references this prediction by Francis about San Damiano? Note that Clare's *Testament* acknowledges the prophecy as showing God's mercy and love.

Consider that Clare was not present when this prediction was made. Hagiography loves predictions that are read back into a text from the perspective of a later time. It is a common technique used to achieve the hagiographic goal of proving someone's holiness through the ability to see into the future.

Could Clare in her *Testament* simply be accepting what was written about herself and the other Poor Sisters in the hagiography about Francis? Could she have heard of this prediction earlier from Francis himself or others? Some scholars believe Clare is the source of this memory about Francis's prediction and specifically for its insertion into the *Legend of the Three Companions*. If Clare wasn't the source, who else could be the source? Why does no hagiography before L3C include the prediction?

Clarify what you believe to be true in this story. From a hagiographic point of view, what is the purpose of including this story in the legend?

Suggested reading

• Dalarun, Jacques. *The Misadventure of Francis of Assisi*. Trans. Edward Hagman. St. Bonaventure NY: Franciscan Institute Publications, 2002. Pages 75-88 discusses memories about San Damiano.

Clare's Divestiture

Sources about Clare's divestiture

PC   II 22:74-77 (Benvenuta of Perugia)
           III 31:104 (Filippa)
           XII 3:6 (Beatrice)
           XIII 11:31-34 (Cristiana di Bernardo)

Sources about Francis's response to the Gospel

1C	22
LJS	15
L3C	25
LMj	III 1
Matt	10:7-14 (Parallels found in Mark 6:8-11 and Luke 9:1-5; missionary discourse to the twelve)
Luke	10:1-6 (Missionary discourse to seventy-two disciples)

Workbook I 164-165, 205-206

Sources about Bernard of Quintavalle's response to the Gospel

1C	24
AP	10-12
L3C	27-29
2C	15, 109
LMj	III 3
Mark	10:17-22 (Parallels found in Matt 19:16-22 and Luke 18:18-23)
Luke	9:1-6
Matt	16:24-28 (Parallels found in Mark 8:34-38 and Luke 9:23-27)

Workbook I 164-165, 206-207

Starter questions and suggestions

The four sources about Clare's divestiture indicate that she gave up everything including her dowry and part of her sister Beatrice's dowry before entering religious life. While the first three witnesses simply state the fact of Clare's total divestiture, the thirteenth witness (Cristiana di Bernardo) gives interesting information about her family wanting to buy

Clare's inheritance from her. How does Clare's response to their desires reflect her understanding of poverty for the sake of the Gospel? How does it connect the vow of poverty to a relationship with poor people?

Armstrong writes in note "a" on CA:ED 47 that Francis used the word *paupertas* (poverty) only 16 times in all of his writings while Clare does so 41 times in hers and frequently with adjectives: *sancta* or *sanctissima (16x), summa* or *altissima (5), beata (3), pia (1),* and *stupenda (1).* That's an incredible statistic given that we have many more writings by Francis than we have by Clare. How might the topic of Clare's divestiture reflect her underlying value of poverty?

We find no literary connections between the stories about Clare's divestiture and those about the manner in which Francis and his early followers chose to "leave the world" and enter a form of religious life. However, we do see similar motivations in Clare, Francis and Bernard of Quintavalle (the first follower of Francis who permanently joined him) as they discerned their vocations and decisively took steps to realize them. Take note of the similarities you find in the vocational journey of these three early Franciscans.

Finally, consider the relationship between Clare's divestiture of her dowry and her investiture at the Portiuncula during the Palm Sunday Drama (see previous worksheet). By sheering her hair and entering religious life, Clare's political and economic value as a marriageable woman was lost to her family.

The Virtues that Characterized Clare's Life

Sources

LR   IV—VI

1-4LAg While the letters of Clare to Agnes of Prague will be studied
        in a subsequent worksheet, we recommend that you read them
        now simply to examine references to the five premier virtues of
        Clare: virginity, humility, obedience, service, and poverty (listed
        in LCl 10-14).

FLCl   VI—VIII

PC   I 3:7; 10:30; 12:35—13:39 (Pacifica)
        II 1: 2-3; 3:11-14; 22:74-77 (Benvenuta of Perugia)
        III 9:23-27; 13:35—14:38; 31:103-105 (Filippa)
        VI 2:7-9; 7:23-25 (Cecilia)
        X 6:16—7:25; 11:47-49 (Agnes)
        XII 2:5—3:6; 6:17-20 (Beatrice)
        XIII 10:29—11:34 (Cristiana di Bernardo)
        XVI 2:7-8 (Lord Ugolino)

VL   X—XII

BC   1:3-4, 9
        2:12
        6:27-30
        7:31-32
        9:37-38
        10:42
        12:52-53
        13:54-59
        14:63
        15:65-67
        17:74-77
        24:101

LCl   VI 10:1—IX 14:18
        (note that CA:ED erroneously lists paragraph 10 as starting on
        page 287 when it should start on the top of page 289)

Starter questions and suggestions

The *Prose Legend of Saint Clare* picks out five of Clare's virtues from
the documents before it and portrays them as inseparable in characterizing

185

Clare's religious life. They are virginity, humility, obedience, service, and poverty. Nearly every line of every page of Clare's writings or the hagiography about her discusses her virtue in some way. So, it is a challenge to select a small manageable group of sources that can adequately lead to an appreciation of these virtues and their interaction.

To avoid being overwhelmed by the sheer number of sources for this worksheet, we suggest that you begin by writing down several questions or points about each of these five virtues *before* reading the sources listed above. You already have had sufficient exposure to Clare's writings and hagiography to have formed some opinions and impressions about her. In order to highlight the difference between Clare's moment in history and our current experience, answer each of your questions or describe each of your points from your modern understanding. Then record under each question/point the answers that you find about Clare as you read the listed sources. At the end of your reading, examine what you have collected and compose a statement that answers each of your questions from Clare's or her hagiographers' point of view. Finally, list any new questions or points that surfaced for you as you read the sources about Clare.

If you are presenting your results to a group, ask the members to answer your questions for themselves *first*. Then, go on to describe what you learned was true about Clare. Finally, with your group, compare and contrast the two groups of answers, one medieval and the other modern.

These are possible questions or points that might help you execute this worksheet. We suggest that you write down each question or point you select at the top of a separate piece of paper so that you have enough room to complete the project.

1. These are example questions you could ask about celibacy or virginity. Consider similar specific questions about each of the five essential virtues. Was Clare celibate her entire life? In what way is virginity or celibacy virtuous? How is virginity *essential* to Clare's way of life? How is virginity associated with following Christ? How are virginity and marriage to Christ related? While some sources about Clare's life use images of marriage, virginity and being a bride of Christ, it's curious that Clare's own *Form of Life* does not. Why might that be? A clue may be in how Clare's *Form of Life* came into being. See our section on Clare's *Form of Life* to better understand this.

2. Note how many witnesses say that Clare's virtue was renowned in Assisi before and after her entrance into religious life. How do the sources characterize the impressions of people around her? How do others respond to Clare's example?

3. Note statements in the sources that link two or more virtues. How do they fit together or interact? Discern how the various virtues might help to define or describe the other virtues.

4. Note statements in the sources that explain why these five are so important for Clare and the Poor Sisters. Why aren't other virtues as prominent in the sources? Note that LCl 12 calls humility the foundation of Clare's entire way of life. Explain this.

5. Compare the legislation about poverty found in chapters 4, 5 and 6 of the *Later Rule* of Saint Francis with that found in chapters 6, 7 and 8 of Clare's *Form of Life*. How are they alike and dissimilar? Does Clare's text show any literary dependence on Francis's text? On page 47 of CA:ED in note "a," Armstrong observes that Francis used the word *paupertas* (poverty) only 16 times in all of his writings while Clare does so 41 times in hers and frequently with adjectives: *sancta* (holy) or *sanctissima* (most holy) (16x), *summa* or *altissima* (highest) (5), *beata* (happy or blessed) (3), *pia* (honest, pius or devout) (1), and *stupenda* (beautiful or amazing) (1). What might this indicate to you?

6. Finally, compare chapters 6, 7 and 8 of Clare's *Form of Life* with the material found in the hagiographic material cited above. How are they alike and dissimilar? Does the hagiography show an awareness of Clare's *Form of Life* which achieved papal approval only days before she died?

We recommend that you consult the chapter entitled "Medieval Religious Women" to assist you in shaping and answering your questions.

Clare's Dream of Drinking at Francis's Breast

Sources

FLFr
LR   VI: 7-8
PC   III: 29 (Philippa) relates the dream
       IV: 16 (Amata) confirms the dream
       VI: 13 (Cecilia) confirms the dream
       VII: 10 (Balvina de Martino) confirms the dream

Commentary

Caroline Walker Bynum's book *Holy Feast and Holy Fast* is invaluable for completing this worksheet. References in this commentary refer to that work, which is an excellent source for any reader desiring to better understand the late medieval context for this dream.

Just before and during Clare's life, spiritual writing increasingly became more graphically concerned with physicality. This concern regarded both the physicality of believers and Jesus. Consequently, theological reflection on Jesus began to shift from a focus on the Resurrection and the Incarnation in a more abstract form to a focus on the historical particularities of the Incarnation, Jesus's birth, and his crucifixion. This shift reflected late medieval concern with the poverty of Christ, expressed in the Word of God forsaking its divine privilege to join itself to a broken humanity and, thus, to save that humanity. Consequently, Eucharistic theology also shifted emphasis from receiving in the communion experience to seeing at the consecration (53-54).

Food became an important spiritual image during this historical period, especially for women mystics. The nurturing dimension of food is equally evident to people of the 21st century as to those of the 13th. However, it is important for us to also appreciate the late medieval growing association of the Eucharist as a food that was increasingly the physical crucified flesh of Jesus. The ancient notion of Eucharist as a meal in which all the participants corporately became the Body of Christ gave way to a medieval idea of sharing in the physical sufferings of the crucified Christ through seeing or consuming the consecrated host. Thus, the notion of sharing in the sufferings and poverty of Christ was linked with the nourishing qualities of receiving communion and *ocular communion*, i.e., seeing the host (53-55).

In a time when reception of communion by the laity (that included all female religious) was becoming less frequent and even suspect in some quarters, the feminine spiritual aspiration to be united with Jesus expressed itself in alternate ways, including visions of and meditations on the physical Christ, often associated with Eucharistic elements like consecrated hosts (139). A significant number of these recorded visions and meditations included individuals nursing at the breast of Jesus (150).

When consideration is given to the late medieval belief that a woman's breast milk was associated with her own blood, this image of nursing at Jesus's breast overflowed with meaning. Jesus was nurturing and life giving. Further, this act of nurturing (associated with Jesus's blood as food) associated the recipient with his suffering and crucifixion. Thus, many of the beliefs and aspirations associated with the penitential, evangelical, and apostolic life movements were fulfilled through this image (see the earlier chapter in this book on those movements).

For Clare to nurse at the breast of Francis would simply seem to be an extension of this late medieval image of Jesus. This is hardly surprising since Francis himself had been physically united in hagiography with the suffering and crucified Jesus through the stigmata. Thus, the image of Clare suckling at the breast of Francis was akin to Clare at the breast of Jesus. It focused on Francis as a valid intermediary in that experience. It also demonstrated that Clare, in her enclosed way of life, was also connected to the poor and humble crucified Christ, and thus within the penitential, evangelical, and apostolic life movements of her day which influenced the formation of her lifestyle, especially her radical expression of poverty. (Bynum, in *Holy Feast*, summarizes these points in her introduction (1-9) and then elaborates each of the points in subsequent chapters. Consult her table of contents to learn about specific aspects mentioned in this chapter.)

Note that Bynum holds that Francis of Assisi in the 13th century, and Richard Rolle and Henry Suso in the 14th were the most extreme male examples of this type of affective spirituality most characteristic of women at that time (94-112).

Starter questions and suggestions

This dream of Clare presents many emotional challenges to modern readers. The idea of a woman suckling at the breast of a man is fraught with gender confusion. Despite this, Clare makes an important point about her spiritual life by relating the dream. Beginning students need to move beyond the uncomfortableness of the images in the dream to understand its meaning and importance.

While the dream is not explicitly mentioned in Francis's *Form of Life Given to Clare*, that document presents a basis for the dream. In his *Form of Life*, Francis promises loving care and solicitude for Clare and her followers, and LR VI: 8 extends that promise by saying that future brothers will do the same. It is this promised care that is expressed by the suckling nourishment of the dream.

Considering the background offered above, write a positive explanation of the dream as Clare and those of her time would have understood it. List succinctly the spiritual claims that this dream makes about who Francis of Assisi was for Clare, what their relationship was, and how those realities fit into Clare's *Form of Life* at San Damiano Monastery.

Reread the accounts of Clare's dream and explore what it can mean for people living in the 21st century. Are there other images you might use to express a similar spiritual assertion today? Compose your own made-up dream that would express the same feelings and spiritual imaginations of Clare, but in a modern way more accessible to people today. Compare and contrast your dream with that of Clare. Relate these matters to your study group and facilitate a considerable conversation to get the many aspects of this dream out on the table.

Note that this story does not occur in the *Prose Legend* or the *Versified Legend*. What could be the reason? Might its gender confusing images have bothered an official hagiographer writing for a pope?

Cited sources and suggested reading

- Bartoli, Marco. "Historical Analysis and Psychoanalytical Interpretations of a Vision of Clare of Assisi." Trans. Madonna Balestrieri. *Greyfriars Review* 6.2 (1992) 189-209. A similar analysis is found in Bartoli's *Clare of Assisi*. Trans. Frances Teresa Downing. Quincy IL: Franciscan Press, 1993. Pages 141-157.

- Bynum, Caroline Walker. *Holy Feast and Holy Fast: The Religious Significance of Food to Medieval Women.* Berkeley and Los Angeles: University of California Press, 1987. Both of Bynum's books listed here are groundbreaking works on the understanding of late medieval women's spirituality. Many of our comments reflect entire chapters in this book. Chapter one, "Religious Women in the Later Middle Ages," describes the social and religious situation of medieval women vis-à-vis spirituality. Chapter two, "Fast and Feast: The Historical Background," describes the changes in fasting, and Eucharistic practice and meaning at the time. Chapter six, "Food as Control of Self," disputes that dualistic thinking was the primary motivation for late medieval ascetical practices of women and asserts that the desire to unite oneself to the suffering Christ was the primary motivator. Chapter eight, "The Meaning of Food: Food as Physicality," and chapter nine, "Woman as Body and as Food," examine the connections between the human physicality of Christ, especially in his birth and crucifixion, the growing physical understanding of Eucharist, and the late medieval notion of female physicality. Bynum has written many helpful works on medieval women's spirituality, more of which are found in the bibliography for the chapter section "Medieval Religious Women: Modern Food Practices."

- —. *Jesus as Mother: Studies in the Spirituality of the High Middle Ages.* Berkeley and Los Angeles: University of California Press, 1982. Clare's image of a nursing Francis relates to chapter four "Jesus as Mother, Abbot as Mother: Some Themes in Twelfth-Century Cistercian Writing."

- Carney, Margaret. "Francis and Clare: A Critical Examination of the Sources." *Greyfriars Review* 3.3 (1989) 315-343.

- —. *The First Franciscan Woman: Clare of Assisi and Her Form of Life.* Quincy IL: Franciscan Press, 1993.

- Petroff, Elizabeth. *Medieval Women's Visionary Literature.* New York: Oxford University Press, 1986.

Clare and Francis's Relationship
After Moving to San Damiano

Sources

Other worksheets on:
>   Clare's Dream of Drinking at Francis's Breast
>   Francis's *The Canticle of Exhortation to Saint Clare
>   and Her Sisters*
>   Francis's *Last Will Written for the Poor Ladies*
>   Clare's *Testament*

FLFr	
ER	XII 1—XIII 2
LR	XI
CtExh	
Last Will	
1C	18-20, 37, 116-117
1.5C	8, 18, 89 (do not confuse with the section on miracles)
LJS	13-14, 23, 72
AP	7, 41
AC	13
	83-85 (tells about the composition of the CtExh and CtC)
L3C	24, 60
2C	13, 90, 108, 112-114, 204-207
2MP	86, 90, 95
FLCl	I 1-5
	VI 1-15
BlCl	6
TestCl	Entire document
PC	I 2:5-6; 6:17-18; 8:22-25 (Pacifica)
	II 8:26-29; 15:47-52 (Benvenuta of Perugia)
	III 1:1-2; 29:93-98 (Filippa)
	IV 2:5-6; 5:12-15; 16:51 (Amata)
	VI 1:1-6; 13:37-38; 15:45-50 (Cecilia)
	VII 10:21 (Balvina de Martino)
	X 7:22-25 (Agnes)
	XII 2:1—5:14 (Beatrice)
	XVI 3:9; 6:18-20 (Lord Ugolino)
	XVII 3:7-11 (Bona di Guelfuccio)
	XVIII 3:14-18 (Ranieri)

	XX 6:13-16 (Ioanni)
VL	VI 1—VII 35
	IX 1-2
BC	6:27—9:41
LCl	III 5:1—V 9:17
	(paragraph 10 is misplaced in CA:ED; paragraph 9
	comprises all of chapter V)
	VIII 12:1-4
	XII 17:1-12
	XVI 26:30
	XX 30:8
	XXI 31:1-7
	XXII 32:4-7
LMj	V 5
	XII 2 (The only source for this story)
	XIII 8 (about Clare seeing Francis's stigmata)

Starter questions and suggestions

This is an enormous worksheet. If you are working in a group, you might want to assign two participants to it. Many stories are related in these sources. Stay focused on the relationship between Francis and Clare. It is easy to wander into many unrelated aspects of the stories. Further, no other worksheet contains so many questions and suggestions from us. Some paragraphs simply list question after question. We purposefully do this to expand your consideration of the topic. Remember that our questions are places to begin your study. We do not expect you to answer each of them, especially during a study group presentation.

This worksheet refers you to four other worksheets. They provide valuable information that is not repeated here. It is especially important to understand the questions surrounding the authorship of Clare's *Testament* that are explored in that worksheet. We recommend reviewing those worksheets before reading the other listed sources.

This worksheet covers a wide range of stories involving Clare and Francis. They include the early years of their conversions, the middle years when the sources portray Francis as more distant from Clare, and Francis's final years including his death when the warmth of their relationship seemed to return. Placing stories into one of these timeframes can help understand them better.

Here is a list of particular stories we suggest you consider exploring in those sources:

- Using the San Damiano Chapel as a metaphor for Clare
- Francis's early thoughts on the spiritual abilities of the early Poor Sisters
- Francis's role in Clare's escape from her parental home
- Francis's consultation with Sylvester, Clare and her sisters about his future life
- Clare becoming an abbess between 1215 and 1216
- Francis sending Brother Stephen to be cured by Clare
- Clare's frequent use of Francis's *Office of the Passion*
- Francis's concern about the severity of Clare's penances
- Francis sending five candidates to Clare
- The sermon in ashes
- Francis allegedly founding three orders and providing plans of life for each

Examine as many of these stories as you have time for. Date the stories. Attempt to establish what is historical about each story. Create a narrative for each of the stories based on the information provided in the various sources. Later, review all the stories and attempt to summarize the nature of the relationship between Clare and Francis. Consider whether Francis primarily influenced Clare, Clare primarily influenced Francis, or they mutually influenced each other. These questions are often raised in modern writings about Clare and Francis.

Marco Bartoli counts thirty-two references to Francis by Clare in her writings. There are none about Clare in the writings of Francis (*Beyond the Legend* 97). Jacques Dalarun in *Francis of Assisi and the Feminine* agrees that Francis never mentioned Clare's name in his writings, while Clare specifically mentioned Francis at least 13 times in her writings (29). He uses this as a partial basis for concluding that the relationship between the two saints from Assisi was asymmetrical. Describe how it might be asymmetrical.

Clare clearly saw Francis as an important inspiration in her vocational decision making. Did Francis see his role in the same way? Obviously, Clare did not exercise an equivalent role in Francis's conversion, which occurred some years earlier. How would you describe Clare's later influence on Francis's vocation?

Note that the *Prose Legend of St. Clare* relates only a little about Francis, and most of that at the beginning, i.e., during Clare's conversion. However, the *Acts of the Process of Canonization* displays a greater role for Francis. What could this mean? How might the politics of female religious life at the time have influenced this? Consult our previous chapter entitled, "Who Founded the Order of St. Clare?"

While the ER prohibited friars from receiving the obedience of any woman and discouraged even other kinds of interaction, Clare twice reported in her *Form of Life* that she promised obedience to Francis. How can this apparent discrepancy be explained?

Despite Francis's infrequent later interaction with Clare, she continued to invoke the memory of Francis after his death. In some ways, it seems she was one of the most important agents preserving his memory. How might that be true? Consider this especially in regard to the nature of Franciscan poverty.

On what was Clare and Francis's friendship based? What was the nature of trust and confidence between them? Was one of them dominant (e.g., the teacher) over the other? Do Francis and Clare show emotional attachment to one another? What about Clare does Francis admire? What about Francis does Clare admire? What writings did Francis send to Clare and the Poor Sisters? Were any writings sent to Clare alone, not including the other sisters? What was the nature of their physical presence to each other? Who inspired whom? Who showed whom concrete ways of living their charism? What names, descriptions and titles does each one use for the other? Which of these names, descriptions and titles predominate? How did they influence each other's vocation?

Do the different legends about Francis and Clare present a different tone to their relationship? Do the various legends show Clare and Francis more involved with each other before or after Clare settled at San Damiano?

Note that *The Canticle of the Creatures* and *The Canticle of Exhortation to Saint Clare and Her Sisters* were written while Francis was staying at San Damiano in the final years of his life. Tell the story of their composition and how they are related to his time near San Damiano Monastery.

Cited sources and suggested reading

- Bartoli, Marco. *Clare: Beyond the Legend.* Trans. Frances Teresa Downing. Cincinnati OH: St. Anthony Messenger Press, 2010. Chapter seven on "Asymmetrical symmetry: Clare and Francis" presents a critical and straightforward analysis of how the two saints from Assisi influenced each other.

- Brunette, Pierre. "Clare and Francis: A Saintly Friendship." Trans. Edward Hagman. *Greyfriars Review* 11.2 (1997) 185-227.

- Bynum, Caroline Walker. *Holy Feast and Holy Fast: The Religious Significance of Food to Medieval Women.* Berkeley and Los Angeles: University of California Press, 1987.

- Carney, Margaret. "Francis and Clare: A Critical Examination of the Sources." *Greyfriars Review* 3.3 (1989) 315-343. This article attempts to answer questions about the relationship between Francis and Clare. Having less to do with their affective "friendship," the article focuses on whether or not Clare had a determinative role on the development of not only the Poor Sisters, but the entire Franciscan movement, including the Friars Minor.

- Dalarun, Jacques. "Francis and Clare of Assisi: Differing Perspectives on Gender and Power." *Franciscan Studies* 63 (2005) 11-25.

- —. *Francis of Assisi and the Feminine.* Saint Bonaventure NY: Franciscan Institute Publications, 2006.

- Guida, Marco. "La pericope clariano-damianita de *Vita beati Francisci* VIII, 18-20: un'aggiunta all'opera di Tommaso da Celano?" *Collectanea Franciscana* 77 (2007) 5-26.

- Peterson, Ingrid. "Clare of Assisi: Hidden Behind Which Image of Francis?" in *Francis of Assisi: History, Hagiography and Hermeneutics in the Early Documents.* Ed. Jay Hammond. New York: New City Press, 2004. 39-63.

Francis's *Canticle of Exhortation to Saint Clare and Her Sisters*

Sources

CtExh
AC   83-85
2MP   90

Commentary

This canticle is also called the *Audite* because of the first Italian word of the text which means "listen." Its existence was first known in 1922 when Ferdinand Delorme published a newly discovered florilegium about Francis of Assisi, *The Assisi Compilation*. It discussed the text without reproducing it (AC 85). The text itself was first published in a 1977 Italian collection of early Franciscan documents. That same year, Giovanni Boccali published a critical edition of the *Audite*.

There is general agreement that Francis of Assisi wrote this canticle in 1225 when he also wrote the first of three parts of his *Canticle of the Creatures*. Already quite sick, Francis was staying in a hut near San Damiano Monastery for recuperation when he wrote both canticles.

The text of this canticle is an example of emerging rhythm and rhyme in early Italian dialects, in this case Umbrian. It is very difficult if not impossible to communicate this effect in translations. These characteristics also lead one to wonder whether music was ever attached to the canticle, though no musical notation survives.

Starter questions and suggestions

Read the sources about the composition of the canticle and understand the story around it. If you're presenting to a study group, prepare introductory comments about that situation.

How does Francis address the Poor Sisters? How does that name relate to his image of Jesus? What are the main themes addressed in the canticle? Can you generalize from these themes Francis's central concerns? Explore the paradoxes presented in the canticle. How do they express Francis's message?

If you are presenting to a study group, be sure to have two different people in the group slowly read the canticle. Different readers often present different interpretations or emphases.

Cited sources and suggested reading

- Boccali, Giovanni. "Parole di esortazione alle 'poverelle' di San Damiano." *Forma sororum* 14 (1977) 54-70. Republished as "Canto di esortazione all 'poverelle' di San Damiano." *Collectanea Franciscana* 48 (1978) 5-29.

- Delorme, Ferdinand. "La 'Legenda Antiqua S. Francisci' du ms. 1046 de la bibliothèque communale de Pérouse." *Archivum Franciscanum Historicum* 15 (1922) 23-70, 278-332. Republished as *La "Legenda antiqua S. Francisci": Texte du ms. 1046 (M. 69) de Pérouse.* Paris: La France Franciscaine, 1926.

- Godet-Calogeras, Jean-François. "From Brother Francis to the Poor Sisters of San Damiano: What Is Left of Their Correspondence?" In *Her Bright Merits: Essays Honoring Ingrid J. Peterson, OSF."* Eds. Mary Walsh Meany and Felicity Dorsett. Spirit and Life 17. St. Bonaventure NY: Franciscan Institute Publications, 2012. 61-81. Godet-Calogeras writes about the *Audite* on pages 71-77.

- Schmucki, Octavian. "The Rediscovery of the Canticle of Exhortation *Audite* of St. Francis for the Poor Ladies of San Damiano." Trans. Ignatius McCormick. *Greyfriars Review* 3.2 (1989) 115-126.

Francis's *Last Will Written for the Poor Ladies*

Sources

ER   VII, VIII, IX and XII 4
LR   IV, V and VI
Last Will
2LAg
FLCl   I 4, VI, VII, VIII
            (Consult all of FLCl VI, VII and VIII for the bigger picture
            of the Poor Sisters' poverty.)

Commentary

Francis's so-called *Last Will Written for the Poor Ladies* is only found embedded within Clare's own *Form of Life* (FLCl VI 7-9). Clare reported that Francis wrote this to her just days before he died in 1226.

Starter questions and suggestions

In the previous worksheet on the *Canticle of Exhortation to Saint Clare and Her Sisters*, we encouraged you to pay attention to how Francis addressed the Poor Sisters. Note how, in his *Last Will* for the Poor Sisters, he describes himself. Is the description like or unlike that given to the sisters in the *Exhortation*? What is the relationship between Francis's self-identity and qualities of Jesus? How does this fit in with the message of the penitential, evangelical, and apostolic life movements?

Try to find references to "perseverance" in Clare's second letter to Agnes of Prague. Did Francis offer to Clare and the Poor Sisters advice similar to what Clare gave Agnes? Did Clare and Francis use similar scriptural allusions? What's different? What's similar?

In the verses of Clare's *Form of Life* that follow Francis's imbedded *Last Will Written for the Poor Sisters* (i.e., FLCl VI 10-15), note how Clare responded to the admonition of Francis. She provided more direction about poverty in chapters VII and VIII. Compare Clare's prescriptions with those in Francis's *Earlier Rule* (VII, VIII and IX) and *Later Rule* (IV, V and VI). How are the prescriptions of Clare similar and dissimilar to Francis's prescriptions?

Francis admonished his brothers to never accept the obedience of a woman (ER XII 4). So, what should we make of Clare's assertion that she promised obedience to Francis's command about poverty? How does Clare understand that she and the Poor Sisters are fulfilling Francis's directions? Note that Clare reports a more general and decisive promise of obedience to Francis and his successors in FLCl I 4.

Suggested reading

- Godet-Calogeras, Jean-François. "From Brother Francis to the Poor Sisters of San Damiano: What Is Left of Their Correspondence?" In *Her Bright Merits: Essays Honoring Ingrid J. Peterson, OSF."* Eds. Mary Walsh Meany and Felicity Dorsett. Spirit and Life 17. St. Bonaventure NY: Franciscan Institute Publications, 2012. 61-81. Godet-Calogeras writes about Francis's *Last Will Written for the Poor Ladies* on pages 77-80.

The Poor Sisters View Francis's Corpse

Sources

1C	116-117
1.5C	89
AC	13
LMj	XIII: 8

Starter questions and suggestions

First, note that this story only occurs in the hagiography about Francis of Assisi. No source associated primarily with Clare contains any story about Francis's death or his body being brought to San Damiano for viewing by the Poor Sisters and Clare. What might this mean?

The Assisi Compilation alerts us that Clare was already in poor health by the time of Francis's death, though she would live for another 27 years. Her health was so bad at this time that the author believed Clare herself was at the point of death.

If working with a group, relate the events of this last visit between Francis and Clare. What images are used to describe each of them? What side comments are made in this story that disclose the nature of the relationship between Clare and Francis? After Francis seemed to avoid visiting Clare so often during his life, why would such an effort be made to bring his body to San Damiano before burial? Note that the strictness of the enclosure was relaxed so that the Poor Sisters could have a more proximate experience with Francis's body. What might this further indicate about Clare's observance of the enclosure?

Note that LMj XIII:8 claims that Clare was one of those to see Francis's stigmata. It is the only early source to make that claim. How do you evaluate this claim in light of its late inclusion (1262) into the hagiography about Francis of Assisi?

Suggested reading

- Godet-Calogeras, Jean-François. "Thomas of Celano 1.5: Where have Clare and the Sisters gone?" *Franciscan Connections: The Cord – A Spiritual Review* 67.4 (2017) 6-10.

Clare's Physical Penances

Sources

3LAg   29-41
PC   I 7:19—8:25 (Pacifica)
        II 4:15—8:29 (Benvenuta of Perugia)
        III 3:13—6:17 (Filippa)
        IV 5:12—6:16 (Amata di Martino)
        X 1:1-3; 7:22-25; 11:47-49 (Agnes)
        XI 5:38-39 (Benvenuta of Assisi)
VL   XV (entire chapter)
BC   65-70
LCl   XII 17:1— XIII 19:2

Commentary

We believe this is one of the most difficult worksheets in our workbook. This is because the hagiography about Clare is full of stories about her physical penances that appall many modern readers. The beginning student is left with a strong impression that Clare was an extreme ascetic. This impression needs to be balanced with an understanding of medieval expectations for its female saints. Thus, we recommend that you review our earlier chapter "Medieval Women: Medieval Food Practices" before completing this worksheet.

Starter questions and suggestions

There is little doubt that Clare practiced physical mortification to a high degree, perhaps more so than Francis. This is often hard for modern people to understand but is a fact that cannot be denied. List the various mortifications that Clare practiced. Equally important, find motivations for these practices within the texts.

Two are quite evident. One is the desire to imitate the poor and humble Christ who suffered so much. Analyze that motivation. Consider how a person might understand the value of sharing in another's suffering. Compare Clare's practices to modern people who fast in solidarity with hungry people in another part of the world. Rice Bowl is a common example. How are these practices of benefit? Is such a practice for the benefit of the person practicing them, the benefit of Christ or the benefit of the one with whom we are in solidarity? Is it a physical, economic, social or religious value? Why might Clare seek to so literally imitate Christ? Write a positive explanation of Clare's motivation in performing these ascetical practices.

A second possible motivation is less often recorded in the sources. The *Prose Legend of Saint Clare* notes that Clare's mortifications left her flesh so dead that she was able to be occupied with prayer and praise. Note that this motivation is primarily found in hagiography about Clare and not in her own writings. This dynamic reminds us of the Capuchins' Seventh Plenary Council on the theme of minority held in Assisi in 2004 (www. ofmcap.org). Its fourth proposition declared that Franciscan poverty and minority constitute Franciscan freedom. How might this be true today or in the time of Clare? Explain how mortification might make someone free to do something else. Compare these ideas to St. Paul of Tarsus's idea that true freedom is not the ability to do whatever we want, but the ability to become who we want to be in light of our baptism into Christ.

Hagiography often uses models of holiness to prove to the reader that its subject is holy. These patterns are found in numerous already venerated saints who follow a common pattern. For instance, there is a martyr model, a missionary bishop model, a monastic founder model, and many more. Some believe that around the time of Francis and Clare an angelic model was beginning to emerge. This model was based on the belief that good angels were holy because they were constantly in the presence and service of God. So, the angelic model of holiness strove to show how the subjects of hagiography were like the angels and, thus, worthy of saintly veneration.

A key to doing this was the consideration that angels are bodiless beings. Thus, they were not tied down to the requirements of a human body. So, if a hagiographic subject could be portrayed as not needing food, sleep, sex or other bodily needs and comforts, he or she began to appear "angelic." There were also positive angelic characteristics that might be applied in the use of this model. Subjects of hagiography might levitate like flying angels, bilocate because their bodies did not limit them, know the hearts and thoughts of mere mortals, etc. The third witness in the *Acts of the Process of Canonization*, Sister Filippa, actually says in 6:17 "Her life was totally angelic." Is it possible that Clare's mortifications were exaggerated to make her appear more angelic?

Several sources note that both Francis and the bishop of Assisi instructed Clare to take some food each day, thus moderating her fasting pattern. Some of the sisters who testified in the *Acts of the Process of Canonization* also noted that they feared for Clare's health because of her fasting, not understanding how she could live on so little food. These passages suggest an inappropriateness to Clare's fasting practice that was cited in these sources to illustrate her sanctity. However, it sets up values in opposition: fasting vs. obedience. Could this be a double standard by the sources? How do you reconcile these seemingly opposing interests of the sources? It's also interesting that Francis himself needed to be admonished about excessive fasting. Is Francis duplicitous in admonishing Clare while he himself hardly observed the warning himself? Finally, do you think the fasts and admonitions were exaggerated for hagiographic purposes? If so, explain.

A totally different explanation is provided in the *Prose Legend of Saint Clare* 18:15. There, Thomas of Celano says that Clare fasted so we the readers could marvel at what we cannot do. This suggests that Clare had superhuman assistance in performing her fasts and invites us to view Clare more as someone chosen by God for special things than as a person whose human power and constitution allowed her to fast so severely. If this perspective is true, how might it change answers to other questions listed above in this worksheet?

Finally, list your conclusions about Clare's mortifications and how they might or might not inspire you.

Suggested reading

See the suggested reading list in our chapter entitled "Medieval Women: Medieval Food Practices."

Mercenaries Invade San Damiano

Sources

PC	II 20:69-72 (Benvenuta of Perugia)
	III 18:59-65 (Filippa)
	IV 14:46-49 (Amata, daughter of Sir Martino of Coccorano)
	IX 2:4-22 (Francesca)
	X 9:41-42 (Agnes)
	XII 8:26-28 (Beatrice)
	XIII 9:26 (Cristiana di Bernardo)
	XIV 3:7 (Angeluccia)
	XVIII 6:22 (Ranieri)
VL	XX the entire chapter
LCl	21:1—22:16

Commentary

During the ancient Roman Empire, "Saracens" referred to nomadic people living in the deserts of the Middle East. People in the Middles Ages generally adopted it to refer to Muslims, and that is how it is used in these stories about Clare.

It often surprises readers to learn that Muslim warriors were present in Italy in the 13th century. It does need some explanation. These were not Muslim armies seeking to conquer Italy for some Muslim power. Instead, they were bands of mercenaries who happened to be Muslims and worked for Frederick II, the Holy Roman Emperor who was often at odds with the popes of his day. In this story, Frederick used the Muslims to disrupt things for the increasingly independent Commune of Assisi. We prefer to call these bands of marauders "mercenaries" to avoid any hint of interreligious conflict.

It is amazing that so many witnesses in the *Acts of the Process of Canonization* relate this story. It is among the best-known stories about Clare today, from which comes a feature of her iconography, a pyx or more commonly a monstrance.

Begin by noting the variations in the story related by various witnesses in the *Process*, the *Versified Legend* and the *Prose Legend*. Determine whether the variations make any difference. Why might the differences have occurred? Pay special attention to changes that occur *after* the witnesses in the *Process*.

Next, note that this story is being related in the *Process* as a proof of the power of Clare's prayer. Could this be a feature that fits into the angelic model of holiness discussed in the chapter on Clare's mortifications? Regardless, what does this story suggest about Clare's relationship with God? Does the reassuring voice that Clare hears in some of the versions deliver a message as important to the reader as to Clare and her other sisters? Why would Clare ask that the reassuring voice not be revealed to others until after she died? Does this cause you to question the objectivity of the voice? What are the religious values at stake in the story? What do you see as a modern lesson from the story?

Clare's Letters to Agnes of Prague

Introduction

We know of four letters written by Clare of Assisi to Agnes of Prague. There could be more, but we don't have them and don't know for sure that they ever existed. We do know for sure that Agnes of Prague also wrote to Clare. However, none of those letters survive. We can only guess what they might have said by how Clare responded in the letters we have. We also have some letters Agnes wrote to other people besides Clare. They help to understand the general concerns of Agnes but are of limited value in this study for beginners.

Many authors are quick to point out that Clare's letters to Agnes are "occasional writing" by which they mean written in response to specific events or requests. They are not literary treatises in letterform. Thus, they are not that different from the letters of St. Paul of Tarsus to various early Christian communities. We cannot expect Clare's letters to provide a comprehensive treatment of issues involving early female Franciscan spirituality and practice. Clare only writes what helps to answer one or another of Agnes's questions. On some occasions, Clare expresses some of her own thoughts before answering Agnes's questions (Van den Goorbergh and Zweerman 7).

To fully appreciate Clare's letters to Agnes, it is helpful to have a broad awareness of several topics that fill in the blanks within the letters. An important development was the Church's drive to normalize female religious life into a more manageable institution that had a firm financial basis. This form of female religious life enforced a strict enclosure and practiced strict fasting regulations, things that were not at the heart of Clare's concerns. The uniqueness of each monastery was allowed in the form of papal exemptions, a legal procedure Clare would use to achieve her *Privilege of Poverty* but which never left her feeling secure in her position about absolute poverty. Papal policy sought to establish a secure financial foundation for each monastery through endowments. Clare's desire for a total and radical personal and corporate poverty was the antithesis of that goal.

Clare's identity was tied to a close relationship with the Friars Minor. This was a mixed bag for Roman officials who sometimes hoped the Friars Minor would assume spiritual responsibility for the Order of St. Damian but at different times appointed others in the Church to provide that care. While some friars desired such a relationship with the Poor Sisters, the leadership of the Friars Minor generally resisted such responsibility. Agnes of Prague bought into Clare's vision. Their correspondence is largely around these issues in relationship to the Church.

There also are particular developments in this struggle that need to be understood. First is the foundation of the Order of the Poor Ladies of the Valley of Spoleto or of Tuscany, the first order founded specifically for women in the Church by Cardinal Ugolino dei Conti di Segni. Later, Clare and the Poor Sisters at San Damiano Monastery joined it or were forced to join it. At that point, Cardinal Rainaldo dei Conti di Segni announced its new name: the Order of St. Damian. This took advantage of the PR and branding possibility offered by the growing respect and fame of Clare of Assisi and her San Damiano Monastery in Assisi.

Clare's reception of the *Privilege of Poverty* in 1228 from Pope Gregory IX was another important development. It was later extended to St. Francis Monastery in Prague at Agnes's request. This privilege was really an exemption from provisions in Cardinal Ugolino's *Form of Life* that allowed corporate ownership and endowments. Pope Innocent IV attempted to solve many ongoing problems by his own *Form of Life* which largely failed. Finally, Clare received approval of her own *Form of Life*, though only a handful of monasteries received permission to follow it.

These were the issues, struggles and events that gave shape to Clare's letters to Agnes of Prague. We strongly advise readers to review our earlier chapter entitled "Who Founded the Order of St. Clare?" for a fuller treatment. Doing so allows you to better understand these letters. A helpful bibliography is also provided there. Here, we provide additional information before providing worksheets designed to help you study the letters on your own.

Cited sources and suggested reading

- Downing, Frances Teresa. *Saint Clare of Assisi: The Context of Her Life*. Vol. 2. Phoenix AZ: Tau Publishing, 2012. Pp. 15-16.

- Van den Goorbergh, Edith A. and Theodore H Zweerman. *Light Shining Through a Veil: On Saint Clare's Letters to Saint Agnes of Prague*. The Netherlands: Peeters, 2000.

Agnes's Life

Scholars believe Agnes of Prague was born in 1211 to King Premysl Otto-kar I of Bohemia and Queen Constance (c. 1180 – 1240), and died in 1282. Prague was the capital of Bohemia, which encompassed the western por-tion of the modern Czech Republic.

In accord with the custom of her day, Agnes was betrothed at an ear-ly age in political arrangements by her father. She was first betrothed to Boleslaus of Silesia when she was three years old. Agnes moved to Silesia in the southwestern part of modern Poland and the northern part of the modern Czech Republic, as also was customary. However, Boleslaus died a few years later, before they were old enough to marry, and Agnes re-turned to Prague. There, she continued her education in a Premonstraten-sian monastery.

Later, Agnes was engaged to Henry (1211 – 1242), the then ten-year-old son of the Holy Roman Emperor, Frederick II. Again, in order to be raised near her betrothed, she moved to Austria where Henry was schooling. In a surprising development, Henry married the daughter of Duke Leopold of Austria, their host. The appearance of a conspiracy to address new po-litical goals by Frederick and Leopold infuriated Ottokar who threatened war over the scuttled marriage. Agnes is believed to have participated in dissuading her father from such violent retribution.

Agnes's life was typical of many women from powerful families in regard to betrothal. Arranged marriages had primarily political goals. Our modern notions of romantic love being part of marriage were hard-ly a prerequisite. In many situations, women were abused—physically, sexually, and emotionally. Childbearing and birthing were dangerous ex-periences for women. Noble women's situations precluded the possibility for them to easily be involved in ventures other than childbearing, child raising, housekeeping, and providing entertainment for husbands and their friends or acquaintances. These realities provided motives for many women to avoid marriage.

However, the single life was suspect for women in most cases. One of the few honorable ways to avoid marriage was to enter religious life. Pow-erful and wealthy families often resisted this, as the marriage of a daughter helped to achieve important political, economic, and military goals. Still, religious life emerged as Agnes's goal during the next few years of her life, and her father acquiesced over the years. After returning from Austria,

Agnes received two more proposals: one from the royal family of England (Henry III); the other from Frederick II himself after becoming widowed. All requests were denied, apparently with the support of her father, and Agnes spent the rest of her life in Prague. Agnes's rejection of proposed marriage to Frederick II became a subject of Clare's letters to her.

We know of several events that most probably influenced Agnes's direction toward Franciscan religious life. In 1225 the Friars Minor arrived in Prague and related stories about Francis and Clare of Assisi. Around the same time, Agnes learned about the activities of her cousin, Elizabeth of Hungary (1207-1231), who married into the ruling family of Thuringia (located in the central part of modern Germany). After her husband died, Elizabeth became a lay penitent associated with the Franciscans and dedicated herself to helping poor people. She became one of the most popular saints of the day.

In 1232, Agnes received land from her brother Vaclav (Wenceslaus in English), then ruler of Bohemia, for a hospice benefiting the poor, a friary for the Friars Minor, and a monastery for the future Franciscan Poor Sisters in Prague. When the monastery building was nearing completion, Agnes successfully petitioned Pope Gregory IX that she be allowed to establish a monastery of the Order of St. Damian in Prague. Together with seven women from the wealthiest Prague families and five sisters from a St. Damian monastery in Trent, Agnes entered that Monastery of St. Francis in 1234.

The entrance day is typically identified as June 11, 1234. Clare's first letter to Agnes appears to have been written slightly before or on the occasion of the opening of St. Francis Monastery. It congratulates Agnes and celebrates her new project. Gregory IX approved the establishment of this monastery in his missive *Sincerum animi*, dated August 31, 1234. A few days later, he issued a second bull under the same name that was a message to John, the Franciscan minister of Saxony. *Sincerum animi* named Agnes abbess of the foundation.

As time progressed, it appeared that Agnes and her community encountered the same obstacles to living a radical personal and corporate poverty as their sisters in Assisi. On May 18, 1235, Gregory IX wrote to Agnes in *Cum relicta saeculi* that St. Francis Hospice in Prague was to remain tied to St. Francis Monastery. He no doubt believed that he was placing St. Francis Monastery on a sound financial footing by establishing this endowment. In so doing, he was simply following the same policy that he previously implemented in central and northern Italy to economically stabilize female monasteries there.

Agnes had to be horrified at the affront to her core charism of total individual and corporate poverty, shared with Clare and San Damiano Monastery in Assisi. This issue became the impetus for Clare to write her second letter to Agnes of Prague between 1235-1238.

The issue of the sisters' poverty and ownership of the hospice must have been a touchy matter. Regis Armstrong lists sixteen letters of Gregory IX about the matter dated from 1234 through 1238 (Starting Points 27, n 32). Eventually, Agnes would prevail, and on April 15, 1238 Pope Gregory IX issued *Pia credulitate tenentes* accepting her renunciation of the hospice, its rights, and its revenues. The letter also affirmed that the Poor Sisters in Prague could not unwillingly be forced to accept possessions in the future. This was the same *Privilege of Poverty* that Clare received for San Damiano Monastery in 1228. In both cases, the privilege was granted only to the one monastery.

Care for St. Francis Hospice was turned over to the Knights of the Cross with the Red Star. On May 5, 1238, Pope Gregory also made concessions about fasting because of the harsh climate in Prague (*Pia meditatione pensantes*). A third papal bull essentially encouraged Agnes in her chosen way of life (*De conditoris omnium*). It almost appears as if the pope had learned of her discouragement and need to be uplifted.

However, Pope Gregory's tone changed on May 11, 1238 when he denied Agnes's request for her own form of life and reasserted that St. Francis Monastery in Prague, like all in the Order of St. Damian, follow the *Rule of St. Benedict* and his own *Form of Life* (*Angelis gaudium*). So, like Clare, Agnes was forced to live with a rule and form of life that envisioned corporate ownership through an endowment, while having a papal exemption or privilege that disallowed anyone from forcing ownership on her.

Later, Innocent IV issued various papal bulls that continued to exempt Agnes's monastery from various parts of the *Benedictine Rule* and the *Form of Life* given by Ugolino. These typically moderated fasting regulations because of the harsh Bohemian winters. However, on August 6, 1245, Innocent IV issued his own *Form of Life*, which removed reference to the *Benedictine Rule* and placed The Order of St. Damian under Francis of Assisi's *Later Rule*.

Innocent IV's *Form of Life* remained unacceptable to those desiring radical and absolute poverty because it once again assumed ownership of property and endowment. Two days before Clare of Assisi died, Innocent approved her own *Form of Life* for San Damiano Monastery, and it is commonly believed, though not documented, that Innocent allowed St. Francis Monastery in Prague to observe the same in 1254 (see Downing page 218).

The remainder of Agnes life had little bearing on the writings or hagiography of Clare of Assisi.

An excellent summary of Agnes's life is found on pages 184-214 of Frances Teresa Downing's *Saint Clare of Assisi: The Spirituality of Her Letters: Letter Four.* Vol. 4. Pages 215-220 provide a short chronology of Agnes's life and events leading up to her canonization.

Agnes of Prague died in 1282 and was canonized on November 12, 1989 by Pope John Paul II.

Cited sources and suggested reading

Unfortunately, the primary sources for the life of Agnes of Prague have not been translated into English. Perhaps the two best modern sources are Jaroslav Nemec's *Agnese di Pragua* and J. Polc's *Agnes von Böhmen 1211-1282.* Nemec provides an Italian translation of the *Legenda B. Agnesae Bohemiae.* The following additional sources provide information in English.

- Armstrong, Regis J., ed. and trans. *Clare of Assisi: Early Documents (The Lady).* Second Revised Edition. New York: New City Press, 2006. Armstrong's introduction to *The First Letter to Agnes of Prague* includes the basics of Agnes's life (39-42). Notes and introductions for all four letters contain additional details (43-58). Various papal bulls from Gregory IX to the Poor Clares in Prague provide clues about Agnes's life at St. Francis Monastery (351-364).

- —. "Starting Points: Images of Women in the Letters of Clare of Assisi to Agnes of Prague." In *Clare of Assisi: Model for Franciscan Women.* Ed. Ann Carville. Spirit and Life 1. St. Bonaventure NY: The Franciscan Institute, 1991. 17-54. Subsequently published in a revised version in *Greyfriars Review* 7.3 (1993) 347-380 and in *Collectanea Franciscana* 62 (1992) 63-100. Citations in this book come from the edition of Ann Carville.

- Downing, Frances Teresa. *Saint Clare of Assisi: The Spirituality of Her Letters: Letter Four.* Vol. 4. Phoenix AZ: Tau Publishing, 2017. Pages 185-214 provide a narrative of the life of Agnes of Prague, while pages 215-220 provide a simple chronology of events leading to her canonization on November 12, 1989.

- Klaniczay, Gábor. *Holy Rulers and Blessed Princesses: Dynastic Cults in Medieval Central Europe.* Trans. Eva Palmai. Cambridge: Cambridge University Press, 2002.

- Marini, Alfonso. *Agnese di Boemia*, Rome: Istituto Storico dei Cappuccini, 1991.

- Mueller, Joan. "Clare of Assisi and the Agnes Legend. A Franciscan Citing of St. Agnes of Rome as *Mulier Sancta*." *Studies in Spirituality* 8 (1998) 141-161.

- Nemec, Jaroslav. *Agnese di Pragua*. Assisi: Edizioni Porziuncula, 1982.

- Pitha, Petr. "Agnes of Prague—A New Bohemian Saint." *Franziskanische Studien* 72 (1990) 325-340.

- Polc, J. *Agnes von Böhmen 1211-1282: Königstochter, Äbtissin, Heilige.* München: R. Oldenbourg, 1989.

The Example of Agnes of Rome, Martyr

Agnes of Rome and a handful of other early Roman virgin-martyrs were popular saints during the medieval period. In part, this is evidenced by the fact that when Pope Innocent III shortened the texts of the Liturgy of Hours so that it could be prayed quicker and contained in a portable breviary, the Office for St. Agnes of Rome was largely untouched (Mueller, *Clare's Letters* 107). Her importance at the time was so great that the Liturgy for the Consecration of Virgins actually focused more on Agnes than Mary, the Mother of Jesus.

Agnes of Rome was a young woman who vowed celibacy or virginity as a way to express her intense devotion to Christ, which she described as being the bride of Christ. When the son of an unbelieving Roman official took a fancy to Agnes, he attempted to win her hand in a variety of ways without success. Forlorn, he returned home, but his father threatened to accuse Agnes of blasphemy for refusing to sacrifice to the Roman goddess Vesta or to deliver her to a brothel in order to socially discredit her.

In the end, God protected her, and when the son of the official appeared at the brothel, he miraculously died. Later, through Agnes's prayers, the son revived and became a believer. Nonetheless, because pagan temple priests considered Agnes a sorceress, they pressured officials to execute her by burning. When the fires turned on the spectators but left Agnes alive, a sword was driven into her throat, killing her.

Agnes's legend, office, and popular devotion remained strong from ancient through medieval times. Her bride-of-Christ spirituality that was the basis for her committed virginity became the prevailing motivation for other committed virgins to follow. Artwork throughout the Christian West and especially in monasteries of women frequently depicted her, her martyrdom, and her spiritual marriage to Christ. Through her legend, committed virgins in the West would easily and instinctively link martyrdom with their virginity.

Joan Mueller twice wrote extensively on Clare's sources about the Agnes of Rome *Legend*. One is *Clare's Letters to Agnes: Texts and Sources* (107-148; published in 2001) and the other *A Companion to Clare of Assisi: Life, Writings, and Spirituality* (169-208; published in 2010). Mueller convincingly shows how the four letters are replete with quotations, paraphrases and allusions to the *Legend of Saint Agnes of Rome* (cf. Mueller's chart in *Clare's Letters* on 142). Mueller's earlier work favors Clare's more direct access to the Agnes of Rome *Legend*, while Mueller's later work argues with certainty that Clare knew of Agnes's *Legend* through popular culture and the lessons of the Office of Matins for the Feast of Saint Agnes of Rome, Martyr (196).

Regardless of the precise means through which Clare of Assisi became familiar with the Agnes of Rome *Legend*, it remains obvious that praying the office and being exposed to popular devotion to Agnes of Rome reinforced those images for Clare. Finally, Clare's explicit reference to St. Agnes of Rome in her fourth letter to Agnes of Prague makes it clear that Clare considered Agnes of Rome a model for the Poor Sisters' life, whether in Assisi or in Prague (4LAg 8).

Despite the debate among scholars about the exact sources for Clare's language, it is clear that the four letters from Clare cannot be accurately understood unless her allusions to Agnes of Rome are understood. The translation and extremely ample footnotes in Mueller's works on the letters are the best tools leading to that understanding. Mueller's books also include an English translation of *The Legend of Saint Agnes of Rome* by Julie Fleming (253-265 in *Clare's Letters*, and 199-208 in *A Companion*).

It is easy to imagine two reasons for which Clare would have wanted to invoke Agnes of Rome in her letters. First, Agnes of Rome was *the* model of consecrated virginal life in the Church at the time. Secondly, the fact that the Roman Agnes was the patron saint of Agnes of Prague makes these references a requirement.

Cited sources and suggested reading

- Mueller, Joan. *Clare's Letters to Agnes: Texts and Sources.* St. Bonaventure NY: Franciscan Institute Publications, 2001. Mueller provides (1) an original translation of the four letters of Clare of Assisi to Agnes of Prague, (2) introductions to the letters in general and each individual letter, (3) copious notes on the texts, (4) the original Latin texts facing the translation, (5) a list of sources for Clare's texts, (6) cross-references, (7) analyses of the sources for Clare's letters including those about Agnes of Rome, and (8) an English translation of *The Legend of Saint Agnes of Rome*. Highly recommended.

- —. *A Companion to Clare of Assisi: Life, Writings, and Spirituality.* Leiden: Brill, 2010.

Papal Bulls Affecting Clare of Assisi, Agnes of Prague and Other Monasteries of the Order of St. Damian

Papal bulls or letters from the time of Clare of Assisi and Agnes of Prague give us great insight into the correspondence between the two women. While we have no letters from Agnes to Clare and possibly not all the letters from Clare to Agnes, writings by Clare and various popes and cardinals give us insight into the issues among the two women and the Church. A partial list and brief description of relevant papal bulls and documents follow for easy reference. When the title of a document is cited within this workbook, the reader can come to this collection to learn more about it. The list is also helpful for understanding Clare's *Form of Life*.

The names of the bulls come from the first few words of the document. It should be noted that the papal curia used many stock letters to respond to the enormous number of requests it received. Thus, many documents have the same name and must be distinguished by the dates of issuance. While there are other papal bulls affecting San Damiano Monastery in Assisi and St. Francis Monastery in Prague, we list here those that help us better understand the writings of Clare.

Here, we provide summaries of the bulls, but CA:ED 333-387 contains many entire papal bulls from Popes Honorius III, Gregory IX, and Innocent IV. It can be helpful to read the entire bulls or our summaries dated just before any of the four letters of Clare to Agnes of Prague to learn whether Clare was addressing some theme already addressed by one of the popes and/or a concern of Agnes. It also can be profitable to do this reading in as few sittings as possible. This approach helps the reader discern the major concerns that are repeated, thus becoming themes.

Important themes include these. First, it's obvious that papal policy settled into a position that all female monasteries founded at this time would observe the *Rule of St. Benedict* and the *Form of Life* given by Cardinal Ugolino (later Pope Gregory IX). This arrangement allowed monasteries to own property or other forms of endowment as a means to support themselves. Later, Pope Innocent IV issued his own *Form of Life* that eliminated reference to the *Rule of St. Benedict* and designated the *Later Rule* of St. Francis as the foundational document for these monasteries, including the interpretation of their vows. However, it will be obvious when you study Clare's letters to Agnes of Prague and summaries of the papal bulls below that not even this satisfied women who desired a total and more radical poverty. Clare and Agnes are the two most obvious examples.

216

Second, the other half of this legal framework was that the local customs and preferences of monasteries would be treated through papal exemptions. The papal bulls summarized below are a testimony that the papal curia was very busy churning out bulls granting such exemptions. Rome preferred this model to approving unique and particular rules or forms of life that would just confuse the governance of religious women. Rome wanted as few rules as possible, which made supervision from the center easier.

Other important themes to emerge from the papacy were the primacy of the enclosure and strict observance of fasting as ideals of female religious life. Pope Gregory IX appeared to be exceptionally strong about these points. The popes also were quick to remove these female monasteries from the oversight of local bishops. Papal bull after papal bull moved responsibility for female monasteries to the papacy, leaving mostly sacramental responsibilities and other spiritual care to the local bishop.

A final struggle was the relationship between the Friars Minor and the myriad groups of enclosed women. The women often lamented the ebbing relationship that they believed was promised by Francis of Assisi. The friars increasingly resisted the responsibility of pastoral care as burdensome and limiting other ministries. The papacy would have liked the friars to assume more pastoral care of female religious, but also wanted the friars free to do other ministry that it considered important. The papal bulls disclose a back and forth process on this issue, never resolved to anyone's satisfaction.

Relevant bulls and documents are listed below.

Aug. 27, 1218   *Litterae tuae nobis* by Pope Honorius III
(CA:ED 71-72)
to Cardinal Ugolino dei Conti di Segni.

Pope Honorius gave Cardinal Ugolino authority to establish female monasteries subject to the Bishop of Rome. This was a game changer. Before this, female religious houses were more independent in their charism and under the supervision of the local bishop. This papal bull marked the beginning of a new papal policy to exempt female monasteries from the control of local bishops and clergy, and to form them into a single religious order specifically for women under the control of the papacy. Cardinal Ugolino had already acquired land and established monasteries at

Monticelli near Florence and Monteluce near Perugia under this arrangement. These would later choose to follow a form of life similar to that of San Damiano Monastery in Assisi, always a frustration for Ugolino.

Dec. 9, 1219   *Sacrosancta Romana Ecclesia* by Pope Honorius III (CA:ED 336-339)
to the abbess and nuns of the Monastery of St. Mary of the Holy Sepulcher of Monticelli near Florence.

Pope Honorius accepted ownership of the land of this monastery, appeasing the nuns' request not to own property. However, he insisted that the *Rule of St. Benedict* and Ugolino's *Form of Life* be the official governing documents of the monastery. Nevertheless, in the style of San Damiano Monastery in Assisi, Monticelli didn't exercise the option to own property as these two documents allowed. This became the repeated pattern of several subsequent papal bulls.

A symbolic annual payment of one pound of wax was to be made to the Diocese of Florence, which in effect meant the monastery was freed from any significant payment to the diocese. While the pope reserved to himself oversight of the monastery, the local bishop of Florence was to exercise pastoral care for the monastery. This was another pattern that followed in many subsequent bulls to female monasteries.

The content of this bull was very typical for female monasteries that were under the direct protection of the papacy. What made this bull unique was allowing the regular observance associated with San Damiano Monastery in Assisi, i.e., not exercising the right to hold property.

This bull was originally issued July 27, 1219, but found with a postscript dated December 9, 1219. Similar documents were issued to the sisters at Gattaiola and Siena on September 19, 1222. That raised to at least four the number of female monasteries observing a radical poverty through exemption.

1220, after Holy Week: Letter from Cardinal Ugolino dei Conti di Segni to Clare of Assisi
(CA:ED 129-130)

This cannot be called a "bull" because Ugolino was not yet pope. In it he emotionally expressed his desolation at having to depart from Clare and San Damiano Monastery after having spent Holy Week there, and return to his ministry,. He related how his encounter with Clare heightened his sense of personal sinfulness and begged for Clare's prayers that he be forgiven.

Sept. 24, 1222   *Sacrosancta Romana Ecclesia* by Pope Honorius III
(CA:ED 340-343)
to the abbess and nuns of the Monastery of Saint Mary at Monteluce near Perugia.

This bull essentially granted the same things as the bull by the same name sent to the monastery at Monticelli in 1219. However, its allowance of the regular observance of San Damiano Monastery was not explicit though clear from later documents.

Dec. 14, 1227   *Quoties cordis* by Pope Gregory IX
to the general minister of the Friars Minor.

This bull charged the general minister of the Friars Minor with the care of the *pauperes moniales reclusae* (poor enclosed nuns), which included monasteries belonging to what would be called the Order of St. Damian.

1228 (Jan.-July)   *Deus Pater* by Pope Gregory IX
(CA:ED 131-132)
to Clare of Assisi and the enclosed nuns of San Damiano in Assisi.

Like his 1220 letter to Clare after spending Holy Week at San Damiano, this letter from the now-pope was unusual because of its intimacy, personal approach, and lack of typical pontifical formality. It is difficult to completely understand all the assumptions underneath the text of the letter. At some levels, it appears to be a letter simply asking for Clare and the sisters' prayers after he had been elected pope.

At another level, historians wonder whether some of the allusions in the letter reflected the personal history between Clare and Gregory. After describing the sisters as daughters and spouses of Christ, he encouraged them to change from something that had been bitter for them to something sweet. He tied this to the sufferings of Christ, which had great appeal to almost any enclosed woman at the time. He then encouraged the sisters to forget past negative experiences as he himself had done. Was he asking Clare and her Poor Sisters to go along with the papal plan for endowment of female monasteries?

Aug. 18, 1228

Matribus sororibus by Cardinal Rainaldo dei Conti di Segni
(CA:ED 133-134)
to the abbesses and communities of the Order of St. Damian

Rainaldo announced that he had been appointed the new cardinal protector of 24 female monasteries in central and northern Italy. For the first time, we see the new order of Ugolino called the Order of St. Damian instead of the Order of the Poor Ladies of the Valley of Spoleto or of Tuscany, and San Damiano Monastery in Assisi at the top of the list. This is the first documentary evidence that the papacy assumed San Damiano Monastery into Ugolino's new order. Rainaldo further noted that a Friar Minor named Filippo had been appointed visitator to the monasteries in the place of Brother Pacifico.

Sept. 17, 1228

Sicut manifestum est by Pope Gregory IX
(CA:ED 87-88)
to Clare and the other sisters living at San Damiano Monastery in Assisi

Clare's request is summarized in the first part of the letter, i.e., to be dedicated to God alone; to give up any temporal concern; to sell everything and give it to the poor; to have no possession of any kind; and to cling to the footsteps of Jesus who became poor for our sake. Gregory didn't declare the Poor Sisters of San Damiano to be absolutely poor but to be free from coercion to accept property. It seems Gregory always hoped the sisters would outgrow this exemption and eventually accept a form of endowment as he planned for all female monasteries in his new order. This bull became known as the *Privilege of Poverty.*

Sept. 28, 1230   ***Quo elongati*** by Pope Gregory IX
(FA:ED I 570-575)
to the Friars Minor

This bull responded to various questions that the friars in chapter had surrounding their rule and Francis's Testament. Among the clarifications, Gregory ruled that Friars Minor needed papal permission to visit even monasteries associated with Clare of Assisi, and not only those of the new Order of St. Damian that did not have a connection to the Friars Minor. This crushed Clare who considered regular contact with Friars Minor essential to her Franciscan identity.

In protest, she dismissed not only Friars Minor who offered pastoral care (as *Quo elongati* prescribed), but also the friars who begged for the benefit of the Poor Sisters in San Damiano Monastery, a decision that amounted to a hunger strike involving all the sisters. Though we cannot locate a papal document abrogating this decision, the *Versified Legend* (XXIX 63-72) and the *Prose Legend of St. Clare* (XXIV 37:7-10) testify that Gregory, upon hearing of Clare's hunger strike, abrogated this provision, placing the care of the Poor Sisters at San Damiano Monastery in the hands of the general minister of the Friars Minor. This witness cannot be traced back to any of the twenty witnesses in the *Acts of the Process of Canonization.* However, the witness of the legends is credible since some resolution must account for the return to previous practice.

Aug. 30, 1234   ***Sincerum animi*** by Pope Gregory IX
(CA:ED 351-352)
to Agnes of Prague.

Gregory IX began this letter by extolling Agnes of Prague and her brother-king, Vaclav, for their devotion. He then described Agnes's entrance into a contemplative lifestyle by using images of Agnes the Martyr, which permeated the ritual of the day for the dedication of virgins and upheld the current theology of celibacy for cloistered women.

The letter affirmed that Vaclav donated to the Church the land on which was built the hospice and monastery of St. Francis in Prague. The main point of the letter, however, was to appoint Agnes the abbess of the new monastery and to authorize her to dispense the community from the rule's directives about fasting and the wearing of shoes and mantles.

A day later (31 August 1234) a second text with virtually the same message was addressed to John who was minister of Saxony and to Thomas who was custos in Bohemia (found only in the Franciscan Institute edition of CA:ED at 360-361).

May 18, 1235   *Cum relicta saeculi* by Pope Gregory IX
(CA:ED 353-354)
to Agnes and the nuns at St. Francis Monastery in Prague.

This bull ensured that the monastery had a regular income derived from the Hospice of St. Francis. The bull even gave permission to increase those assets. This message certainly alarmed Agnes who sought to live the radical poverty she believed Francis and Clare of Assisi espoused. It likely convinced Agnes to be freed of the *Rule of St. Benedict* and the *Form of Life* given by Ugolino in favor of her own rule or form of life. This conflict would be an issue in Clare's remaining letters to Agnes of Prague, as both women sought resolution of the same issue.

July 25, 1235   *Prudentibus virginibus religiosam* by Pope Gregory IX
(https://epistolae.ccnmtl.columbia.edu/letter/833.html)
to St. Francis Monastery in Prague.

The bull again gave official recognition to the foundation of St. Francis Monastery in Prague. Though this bull talks about the poverty of the sisters, it gave them an allocated income from St. Francis Hospice for their sustenance. The hospice's huge endowed properties were listed. This arrangement very much reflected Gregory IX's plan to financially support all female monasteries at the time. This was exactly what Agnes of Prague did not desire, as she wanted to live after the style of Clare of Assisi at San Damiano Monastery.

Feb. 9, 1237   ***Licet velut ignis*** by Pope Gregory IX
(CA:ED 354-355)
to monasteries of the Order of St. Damian.

Ugolino's *Form of Life* (1219) already took a strict approach to fasting. This bull further mandated that nuns of the Order of St. Damian no longer eat meat, according to the *Rule of St. Benedict* and in imitation of Cistercian nuns. This was hard on monasteries that embraced a stricter poverty like San Damiano Monastery in Assisi. Because of their desired poverty, they didn't have the land to grow the vegetarian food they needed. Many scholars believe Pope Gregory viewed severe fasting as the highest form of perfection. That attitude can be seen in many of his papal bulls about fasting in female monasteries.

However, this requirement to abstain from meat was especially hard in northern climates like that of Prague. While Italy could grow vegetables almost all year long, Prague could not. In northern climates, the consumption of meat helped to bridge the lack of winter produce. Also, Mediterranean climates had non-meat-based oils, like olive oil. Northern climates typically relied on animal fat for oil. This difficult papal requirement for northern climates resulted in many requests for exemptions.

April 9, 1237   ***Cum sicut propositum*** by Pope Gregory IX
to St. Francis Monastery in Prague.

It allowed the abbess to give dispensations about fasting, clothing, and shoes, after consulting with the visitor.

April 14, 1237   ***Omnipotens Deus*** by Pope Gregory IX
to the Knights of the Cross with the Red Star

This bull established the independence of the sisters in Prague from St. Francis Hospice. Control of the hospice was given to the Knights of the Cross with the Red Star who following the *Augustinian Rule*. Agnes would have rejoiced at this news, wanting to separate the monastery from the endowed income of the hospice, though she still had to live with the *Benedictine Rule* and Ugolino's *Form of Life*.

This bull acknowledged that Agnes helped found two groups: The Knights who cared for the poor at the Hospice and were not considered poor themselves; and the Monastery of St. Francis that was absolutely poor and Franciscan. This indicated that Agnes did not think everyone needed to be Franciscan, but if you were, you should be poor. Despite his decision in this bull, Gregory disliked the separation of the hospice and monastery as unsustainable in the long run.

April 15 1238   ***Pia credulitate tenentes*** by Pope Gregory IX
(CA:ED 356-357)
to Agnes and the nuns of St. Francis Monastery in Prague.

Reaffirmed the separation of St. Francis Hospice (with its vast endowment) from St. Francis Monastery, and granted the Privilege of Poverty to the Monastery of St. Francis, as already enjoyed by San Damiano Monastery in Assisi. This meant that the monastery could not be forced to accept possessions. It did not require St. Francis Monastery to reject possessions. Surely, Gregory hoped that someday St. Francis Monastery would grow tired of this exemption and accept property. Short of having her own rule, this was the most desired situation for Agnes. However, she continued to resist being assigned the *Rule of St. Benedict* and Ugolino's *Form of Life*, which allowed ownership.

May 5, 1238   ***Pia meditatione pensantes*** by Pope Gregory IX
(CA:ED 357-358)
to Agnes and the nuns at St. Francis Monastery in Prague.

This was another letter imposing rules for fasting, clothing and shoes. It reaffirms that the abbess at St. Francis Monastery in Prague could grant dispensations from fasting and moderate the clothing of the nuns, presumably because of the climate. The rules for fasting are nearly identical to those given by Clare in 3LAg (29-37). How this connection occurred is uncertain, but it could not be coincidental. These rules showed the prudent approach of Clare to fasting.

May 9, 1238

De conditoris omnium by Pope Gregory IX
(CA: 358-360)
to Agnes and the nuns at St. Francis Monastery in Prague.

This papal letter seems intended to encourage Agnes, just as Clare's third letter to Agnes was. We wonder whether Agnes was suffering from doubts and anxieties. The pope introduced the image of the mirror in relationship to Agnes's life, just as Clare would in her 3LAg (12-13).

This is the first papal mention of Francis of Assisi as the founder of the three Franciscan orders called "Fratrum Ordo Minorum, Sororum inclusarum et poenitentium collegia." Previously, *The Life of St. Francis* by Julian of Speyer (LJS 13), written between 1234-1235, identified Francis as the founder of the Poor Ladies at San Damiano Monastery without discussing a third order. Clare also identified Francis as founder in her *Form of Life* (I:1-5; VI:1-10).

May 11, 1238

Angelis gaudium by Pope Gregory IX
(CA:ED 360-362)
to Agnes of Prague.

After receiving so much encouragement just two days earlier, Agnes learned from the pope that her request for her own Franciscan *Form of Life* was denied. The pope cited the confusion caused by so many rules in use at the time. Gregory directed Agnes of Prague to use his own *Form of Life* with the *Benedictine Rule* as was done at San Damiano Monastery in Assisi. Gregory noted that the *Privilege of Poverty* should be enough to satisfy Agnes, as it does Clare. Clare likely would have disagreed with Gregory on this point as she continued to petition for her own form of life until just days before her death. Obviously, this entire arrangement satisfied neither Clare nor Agnes.

Gregory emphasized the value of obedience over poverty. He opined that Francis had given them just "milk" (i.e., Francis's original and simple *Form of Life*) while Gregory's *Form of Life* was for those more advanced in the spiritual life.

While Clare in Assisi sustained a more moderate fasting regime, Agnes seemed to have begun to observe the strict fasting rules of Ugolino's *Form of Life* and the *Rule of St. Benedict*, which were very difficult in the climate of Prague. Hearing this, Clare seemed motivated to write 3LAg to Agnes in which she urged Agnes to greater prudence.

Dec. 18, 1238   ***Ex parte carissima*** by Pope Gregory IX
(CA:ED 362-363)
to Agnes and the nuns of St. Francis Monastery in Prague.

This bull reflected the more moderate fasting rules that Clare included in her third letter to Agnes. The pope gave Agnes discretion in deciding which fasting rules to observe, including fasting on feasts falling on Fridays, striving to be in communion with the Crucified One.

May 31, 1241   ***Vestris piis supplicationibus*** by Pope Gregory IX
(CA:ED 363-364)
to all abbesses and monasteries of the Order of St. Damian.

Gregory assured all monasteries of the Order of St. Damian that Friars Minor could enter their monasteries and listed specific instances: for maintenance, to save them from fire, to protect them from thieves and to celebrate sacraments. This was an important victory for Clare of Assisi and Agnes of Prague who wanted a close relationship with the Friars Minor, while the friars often sought to minimize their growing responsibilities to the sisters.

This is an example of Gregory, in his sunset years, relaxing restrictions on the enclosure after a career of strictly enforcing them. It was a time when Gregory was in fierce conflict with the Holy Roman Emperor, Frederick II, and sought the help of Agnes in convincing her king-brother Vaclav to come to the side of the papacy.

Dec. 21, 1241   *Ad audientiam nostrum* by Pope Gregory IX to the bishops of the whole world

Gregory attacked women not observing the enclosure and calling themselves "Sisters Minor." He assured the reader that these were not the same as the women at San Damiano Monastery in Assisi who surely were enclosed. This denunciation helps to explain why enclosed women in Italy who desired a Franciscan identity stayed clear of calling themselves "sisters minor," a title that otherwise would closely connect them to the "Friars Minor."

Pope Innocent IV followed-up with similar complaints about unenclosed women in 1246 (2x), 1250, 1251, and 1257. Clearly, Rome saw this movement as a serious threat to its program to regularize female religious life under the title Order of St. Damian and within an enclosure.

This made it all the more spectacular when Isabelle of France was allowed to call her enclosed Franciscan women at Longchamps (outside Paris) "Sisters Minor" in the 1263 version of her *Form of Life*, after failing to receive permission to do so in the 1259 version. This way of associating with the Friars Minor and her emphasis on minority rather than poverty distinguished Isabelle from Clare and Agnes of Prague, and alerts students that there was more than one female approach to a Franciscan identity.

NB: When Gregory IX died in 1241, Clare and Agnes had accomplished three impressive things: (1) the Privilege of Poverty; (2) permission to follow moderate fasting rules; and (3) permission for Friars Minor to enter the enclosure for various reasons, including confession, preaching and other sacraments. These were amazing feats considering the papal policy of Gregory IX.

Nov. 13, 1243   *Piis votis omnium* by Pope Innocent IV to Agnes and the nuns of St. Francis Monastery in Prague.

It confirmed previously granted exemptions from Ugolino's *Form of Life* to St. Francis Monastery because of harsh weather in Prague. However, it reaffirmed the Ugolinian solution of imposing the *Rule of St. Benedict* and Ugolino's *Form of Life*.

Nov. 13, 1243   *In divini timore nominis* by Pope Innocent IV
                       (CA:ED 371-373)
                       to Agnes of Prague.

It granted various exemptions from the *Rule of St. Benedict*, but denied Agnes's repeated request to annul obedience to that rule. Innocent called the *Rule of St. Benedict* the greatest approved rule for religious. He then told the sisters to quit requesting their own form of life.

Aug. 21, 1244   *Cum universitate vestrae* by Pope Innocent IV
                       (CA:ED 373-374)
                       to Agnes and the nuns at St. Francis Monastery in Prague.

In divini timore nominis was not successful in calming the anxiety of Agnes and her sisters about observing the *Rule of St. Benedict*. Innocent attempted to put Agnes of Prague at greater ease by declaring that the *Rule of St. Benedict* only applied to Agnes and her sisters in their observance of obedience, the renunciation of personal property and perpetual chastity, i.e., the three personal vows that every approved rule required. Of course, this did not address the question of corporate property and endowments that Innocent hoped would support the monastery.

Oct. 21, 1245   *Vestris piis supplicationibus* by Pope Innocent IV
                       (CA:ED 374-375)
                       to the abbesses and nuns of the Order of St. Damian.

Repeats what was granted to all monasteries of the Order of St. Damian in the May 31, 1241 papal bull of Gregory IX by the same name, but extended the reasons for Friars Minor to visit the sisters, including for visitation and preaching. It gave a more general approval for the Friars Minor to visit and enter the enclosure.

Nov. 13, 1245

Solet annuere by Pope Innocent IV
to the abbesses and nuns of the Order of St. Damian.

This bull reaffirmed that all monasteries of the Order of St. Damian were to follow the *Form of Life* given by Cardinal Ugolino in 1219 in conjunction with the *Rule of St. Benedict*. Innocent issued several bulls with the same name and message until he issued his own *Form of Life* for the Order of St. Damian.

1246 -1251

Cum harum rector by Innocent IV
to various church officials

Innocent IV issued various papal bulls by this name over many years condemning the Sorores Minores (Sisters Minor), an unenclosed group of women who were inspired by the example of Francis of Assisi and the Friars Minor. They were often confused with the Poor Sisters at San Damiano Monastery in Assisi. Innocent and Gregory IX before him considered strict enclosure essential to female religious life and sought to eradicate these unobservant groups. Pope Alexander IV also issued similar bulls with the same name later.

July 12, 1246

Licet olim quibusdam by Pope Innocent IV
to the general and provincial ministers of the Friars Minor

It acknowledged the request of the Friars Minor to lessen their commitment to the care of the nuns of the Order of St. Damian.

Aug. 6, 1247

Cum omnis vera religio by Innocent IV
(CA:ED 89-105)
to the abbesses and nuns of the Order of St. Damian.

With this papal bull, Innocent IV issued his own revised *Form of Life*. Importantly, he eliminated reference to the *Rule of St. Benedict*. Instead, Francis of Assisi's *Later Rule* (1223) became the fundamental legislation for the Order of St. Damian.

Comparing this form of life to that of Ugolino, one can see many additions that illustrate the many requests for exemptions and the dissatisfaction of many nuns with Ugolino's *Form of Life*. It may also illustrate Innocent's frustration with so many requests for exemption. However, in the end, Innocent's new *Form of Life* was not received well either, indicating how hard it was to centralize the diverse female monasteries at the time. It also demonstrated that those devoted to a radical and total corporate and personal poverty would not be satisfied by anything less than their own form of life enshrining those values explicitly. Clare of Assisi and Agnes of Prague were the most visible examples.

Innocent's *Form of Life* also considerably relaxed fasting regulations. It permitted the sisters to eat much more food than the *Privilege of Poverty* made possible. Each monastery was to have a procurator. While this document seemed to establish closer ties between the Friars Minor and the Poor Ladies, in fact it only required the Friars Minor to care for the spiritual needs of the sisters and not any physical needs. This meant they no longer had to provide brothers to beg for the sisters. Again, this made the *Privilege of Poverty* difficult if not impossible to observe.

In the end, Innocent IV's *Form of Life* was largely ignored by the sisters. The friars refused to accept responsibility for the women, as Innocent envisioned. On June 6, 1250, in *Inter personas*, Innocent told sisters in the Order of St. Damian that they didn't have to observe his *Form of Life* and could return to the care of Cardinal Rainaldo as cardinal protector.

Aug. 23, 1247   *Quoties a nobis* by Pope Innocent IV
to the abbesses and nuns of the Order of St. Damian.

This bull repeated that of Aug. 6, 1247, in which Innocent issued his own *Form of Life,* abrogating earlier rules.

June 6, 1250   **Inter personas** by Pope Innocent IV
to Cardinal Rainaldo, protector of the Order of St. Damian.

This bull declared that monasteries in the Order of St. Damian were no longer required to follow Innocent

IV's *Form of Life*. Monasteries were free to return to observance of Ugolino's *Form of Life* if they desired.

Sept 16, 1252   ***Quia vos*** by Cardinal Rainaldo dei Conti di Segni
(CA:ED 108-126)
to Clare and the nuns at San Damiano.

Quia vos is embedded in Pope Innocent IV's approval of Clare's *Form of Life* (*Solet annuere*), beginning with #2 of the Prologue through the first sentence of the conclusion after chapter 12.

Through this document, Cardinal Rainaldo approved Clare's own *Form of Life* for San Damiano Monastery in Assisi alone. It removed San Damiano Monastery from the Order of St. Damian and called the sisters "the Order of Poor Sisters that Blessed Francis founded." Francis of Assisi was designated their founder. Members were no longer called "Poor Ladies" or "nuns," but "Poor Sisters." However, the Holy See continued to treat San Damiano Monastery as if it were part of the Order of St. Damian.

Aug. 9, 1253   ***Solet annuere*** by Pope Innocent IV (CA:ED 108-126)
to Clare and the Poor Sisters at San Damiano.

This papal bull mostly contains Cardinal Rainaldo's *Quia vos*. Thus, it gave papal approval to Clare's *Form of Life* just days before she died. However, even though San Damiano Monastery had its unique form of life, Rome continued to deal with it as if it were part of the Oder of St. Damian.

Oct. 18, 1253   ***Gloriosus Deus*** by Pope Innocent IV
(CA:ED 141-143)
to Bishop Bartholomew of nearby Spoleto.

Innocent commissioned Bishop Bartholomew to interview the Poor Sisters at San Damiano Monastery and other citizens of Assisi as part of the process of canonization of Clare of Assisi. *Gloriosus Deus* is found within the prologue of the *Acts of the Process of Canonization* (prologue: 3-22).

1255	***Clara claris praeclara*** by Pope Alexander IV (CA:ED 263-271) to all bishops

This is the bull of canonization of Clare. One or two months after Clare's canonization on August 15, 1255, the text was released. Why it was delayed is unknown. See our chapter on *Clara claris praeclara* in the Tools section of this Workbook.

July 27, 1263	***Beata Clara virtute clarens nomine*** by Pope Urban IV (Can be found in many pre-Vatican Council II editions of constitutions for the various Poor Clare groups.) to the Order of St. Clare.

This bull contained Urban's own *Rule* for what he began to call the Order of St. Clare.

Dec. 31, 1266	***Solet annuere*** by Pope Clement IV to the sisters living at the Proto-Monastery in Assisi.

A reaffirmation of Clare's *Form of Life* for them. From a strictly legal point of view, this continued to place the sisters at the Proto-Monastery outside of the Order of St. Damian that Urban IV first called the Order of St. Clare in 1263. However, in reality, observance of Clare's *Form of Life* was considered more of an exemption, and, within years, even the Proto-Monastery took on Urban's *Rule*.

Suggested reading

- CA:ED 333-387 contains complete translations of many papal bulls from Honorius III, Gregory IX, and Innocent IV.

- Hone, Mary Francis. *St. Clare of Assisi and Her Order: A Bibliographic Guide*. Clare Centenary Series 5. St. Bonaventure NY: The Franciscan Institute, 1995. Includes a partial list of papal and other documents sent to the Order of St. Damian and its individual monasteries. Some important papal bulls are missing. Many of its dates vary from those provided in other sources. This list verifies the enormous number of exemptions granted to sisters observing Ugolino's *Form of Life*, which might help us understand why Innocent IV issued his own form of life in frustration.

- Knox, Lezlie. "Audacious Nuns: Conflict Between the Franciscan Friars and the Order of Saint Clare." *Church History* 41 (2000) 41-62.

- Pásztor, Edith. "The Popes of the Thirteenth Century and Women Religious." Trans. Ignatius McCormick. *Greyfriars Review* 7.3 (1993) 381-405.

Clare's *First Letter to Agnes of Prague* 1234

Sources

1LAg

Commentary

Most scholars accept 1234 as the date of this first known letter from Clare to Agnes of Prague. At that time, Clare was in her early 40s and had lived at San Damiano Monastery for about 22 years. Agnes was about 23.

Though Agnes's brother, King Vaclav, gave her land for a religious foundation in 1232, Agnes first entered St. Francis Monastery in Prague on June 11, 1234 with seven wealthy Praguer women and five women from a monastery in Trent. This first letter appears to have been written on the occasion of their entrance into religious life for several reasons. It uses many texts from the rite for consecration of a virgin. That would include many images surrounding Agnes the Martyr of Rome. The references to Agnes of Rome chosen by Clare focus on the fidelity of Agnes of Rome to her bridegroom, i.e., Christ, rather than on the bravery of her martyrdom, as is appropriate to the situation of Agnes of Prague.

Note that, in this first letter, Clare addresses Agnes with the formal version of *you*, i.e., *vos*, instead of the familiar *tu*. In medieval times, the formal pronoun was used with nobility and the familiar pronoun with those on an equal, lower, or more familiar basis. Though Clare was from a noble family in Assisi, she was nowhere near the rank of the daughter and sister of Kings from Bohemia. In the last three letters, Clare will switch to using *tu*, indicating her greater familiarity with Agnes at those times.

Starter questions and suggestions

Read through this letter in a single sitting to familiarize yourself with its general content and style.

Read the letter a second time, listing the dichotomies offered in its images, scriptural passages, and allusions, e.g., the things of time vs. the things of eternity; the things of heaven vs. the goods of earth; living in the glory of earth vs. ruling with Christ in heaven; etc. Clare apparently lived within the worldview of these dichotomies. Write a page-long essay explaining Clare's perspective as revealed in this list of dichotomies. Present this summary in positive language, being as persuasive as Clare was in her letter.

Next, turn your attention to appropriating this medieval text for use today. Reflect on how people today visualize our world in different ways. Clare's dichotomous language seemed to present only two options, i.e., either being totally for or against something. Modern people tend to be more pluralistic, i.e., they see more options and nuances. Within Clare's letter, identify ideas which you think have meaning for people today. Explain those ideas in modern language in another page-long composition.

Remember that the first letter to Agnes was likely written as Agnes and her sisters were entering their new monastery in a moment of intense anticipation. Explore how Clare's language would appeal to the women in Prague at that moment. In your second written reflection, try to apply the enthusiasm Clare expressed for her sisters in Prague to those joining Franciscan religious life today.

Personally, we have a bias about dichotomous language, which you need not share. We find it too often limits our imaginations by reducing possibilities to only two choices. It often neglects the complexity of reality. Too often it forces readers or listeners to choose when no choice is necessary. Having said that, we also appreciate how the starkness of dichotomous language can shock us in a positive way to take stock of what's going on in our world and lives. It can keep us from becoming complacent or lukewarm.

In light of this positive understanding, we too want to offer some dichotomies in the form of questions about Clare, her spirituality, and her approach to life. We don't expect answers to these either-or questions. Rather, we hope framing the questions in this way will help you to clarify your own reception of Clare's message. After considering this list of questions, you may want to review or even rewrite the short papers we suggest above: In persevering toward total poverty, was Clare virtuous or stubborn? Was she enlightened or obsessed? Did she simply reflect her era or was her understanding objectively true? Was Clare a fundamentalist or a prophet? You may have other similar questions to consider.

This letter references a "sacred exchange" as was common at the time. This reference was to a business agreement or contract, i.e., this for that. Through this analogy, the person entering religious life gave all to the poor in exchange for a greater return here and in heaven. Explore how Clare expressed Agnes's exchange in this first letter. Imagine how you would use exchange language when talking to a person today. In light of this, consider making changes to your two essays.

Finally, this first letter introduces the metaphor of the Poor Sisters as brides of Christ. Van den Goorbergh and Zweerman (55-67) note that this image is not primarily about abstinence from earthly marriage, but growing in an undivided (i.e., pure) service to Christ. Recall that in medieval times, wives were often and ideally viewed as committed to the projects of their husbands. By being brides of Christ, Agnes of Prague and Clare of Assisi were expressing their total service to Christ (i.e., their purity). Modern people think of marriage as a union of equals. How can Clare's medieval idea be translated into suitable modern language?

Cited sources and suggested reading

- Cited sources and suggested reading for all four letters are listed at the end of this chapter.

Clare's *Second Letter to Agnes of Prague* 1235-1238

Sources

2LAg

Starter questions, suggestions, and commentary

Many of our starter questions and suggestions for this letter first require some commentary. Thus, we combine those two sections in this worksheet.

Dating:

Scholars give widely varying assessments about the date of this letter. Most judgments fall between 1234-1239 and frequently include a dating range. 1235-1238 is the most favored range. Clare's second letter was obviously written after what we believe was her first letter to Agnes. It clearly is a response to questions raised by the developing community in Prague.

Papal documents:

Numerous papal bulls were issued around the time Clare wrote this second letter. Thus, we recommend that you familiarize yourself with those documents. You can do that in two ways. First, you could review the description of those documents that we provide earlier in this chapter. A second approach could be to read the complete documents in CA:ED 351-363. Focus on papal bulls from 1234 through 1238.

While all the papal bulls within the date-range are interesting, we recommend you pay special attention to:

- *Sincerum animi* (30 August 1234);
- *Cum relicta saeculi* (18 May 1235);
- *Pia credulitate tenentes* (15 April 1238);
- *Angelis gaudium* (11 May 1238).

Next, read Clare's second letter to Agnes of Prague in a single sitting. Do not stop to take notes or to check references. Simply receive the overall message of the letter as it strikes you, keeping in mind the sisters' struggle with the papacy over property and corporate poverty. Recall that Agnes likely had previously sent Clare a letter asking for advice about how to organize her life of poverty in Prague in light of opposing papal desires.

Write a short essay describing the state of this struggle at the time this second letter was written.

The poor and humble Christ:

Spirituality at the time of Francis and Clare was increasingly focused on the humble human situation of Jesus, particularly his birth and death. Many concluded that to be like Christ meant to imitate his poverty, humility, and physical suffering in increasingly radical and economic ways. Francis and Clare were among the most radical interpreters in this approach.

In a second reading of this letter, pay attention to the image of the poor and humble crucified Christ used throughout the letter. The image begins on the theological level. As the Word of God made flesh in the Incarnation, Christ gave up the privileges of divinity to become human and to save humanity by bringing it back to God. This self-emptying is the theological expression of Christ's humility and poverty. Many in the day of Clare and Agnes believed this poverty also was expressed in the physical way Jesus and his mother lived on earth.

Write a brief summary exploring Clare's use of the image of the poor and humble Christ. Then consider how helpful her understanding is today. Prepare a page-long reflection on how you would appropriate this image today. As an alternate exercise, identify and write about the image of Christ that speaks to you. Note how your appropriation is different from Clare's and attempt to explain why there are differences.

The bride of Christ:

First, review our chapter section "Medieval Religious Women: Nuptial Spirituality" for a general introduction to this theme.

Clare imaged Agnes as a bride of Christ in her first letter. This second letter continues to use it as the central image interpreting Agnes's way of life. Perhaps a difficulty in appreciating this metaphor as Clare did is our different attitudes toward marriage. We suspect that most people today would first think of the romantic and sexual components of modern marriage. In medieval times, marriages of noble and wealthy people were more likely to be arranged than chosen by two consenting adults madly in love. The case of Agnes of Prague, the recipient of Clare's letters, makes the point well.

Agnes's multiple engagements (see our earlier section on "Agnes's Life) highlight numerous practices and attitudes toward marriage in her time and place that bear repetition. First, women were often viewed as property: owned by fathers who could trade their hand for political, social, military, or economic advantage. The women had no rights and little choice in the matter. Thus, wives were bound to *serve* their husbands. This service included sexual relations, childbearing, child rearing, care for the house, entertainment of her husband's guests, and the general advancement of the husband's well-being and goals. Love had little value in itself, and, if it existed in marriage, might be considered incidental. While the bride took on the rank of her husband, she was often dependent on his generosity to enjoy the fruits of that rank.

Given this framework, the metaphor of the Poor Sisters being brides of Christ is not primarily about expressing a love with God through sexual imagery. Rather, the metaphor primarily expresses the total dedication of oneself to the service of the beloved (Christ) and working for his goals. Within this understanding, the metaphor still encompasses an exclusiveness or faithfulness sexually envisioned in modern attitudes toward marriage. The difference is that the medieval person would typically see these characteristics present in the exclusive and faithful *service* of the bride to her husband.

Given the literal ways people within the penitential, evangelical and apostolic life movements were interpreting Jesus's poverty, it is not surprising that Clare and her followers would talk of themselves as poor and humble servants and handmaids of Christ. However, despite their humility and poverty, the brides of Christ were to be considered noble ladies taking on the rank of their spouse, i.e., Christ who was King (cf. UltVol 2; 1LAg 2, 4, 7, 12; 2LAg 1; 3LAg 1-2; TestCl 79; BlCl 6). Clare was clear in asserting that those who shared in the poverty and humility of Christ will share in his glory (2LAg 18-21).

A variety of exercises can help to enter into the image of the Poor Sisters as brides of Christ. Review the first two letters again and list all the paradoxical statements that you encounter about being Christ's spouse. For instance, Christ's love makes Agnes chaste; his touch leaves her pure; and his union with her preserves her virginity (see 1LAg 8). After writing down these paradoxical statements, notice the different meanings of the various terms. List the fundamental insights of these paradoxes. Also notice what about these passages makes it difficult for modern people to assimilate them.

Remember your beginning:

This second letter uses another image that requires some explanation for modern readers: the biblical Rachel. In 2LAg 11, Clare admonished Agnes to be "mindful of your resolution like another Rachel always seeing your beginning" (cf. Gen 29:16). Clare was referencing early fathers of the church and medieval writers who interpreted Rachel allegorically as a symbol of contemplation.

Recall the story of Jacob working for his uncle Laban to win the hand of his second daughter, Rachel. In a trick, Laban gave Jacob the hand of his oldest daughter, the half-blind Leah. So, Jacob continued to work for Laban so that he might become husband to both sisters, including the one he loved from the beginning, Rachel. Barren for a long time, Rachel was portrayed as one who steadfastly "saw the beginning," as her name indicates (ra'ah, "to see"; halel, "to begin"). Thus, Rachel was a figure who tied together contemplative insight with reaffirmation of earlier commitments.

On the other hand, Leah's name was understood to mean "laborious." Thus, early Christian theologians allegorically understood Leah as the active dimension of Christian life and Rachel as the contemplative dimension, much like Martha and Mary in Christian tradition (Luke 10:38-42). Thus, Clare's reference to Rachel encouraged Agnes to be a contemplative who was faithful to her original vision for St. Francis Monastery in Prague. This was a poignant reference since it appeared that those who sought to "help" Agnes by providing endowments actually threatened Agnes's original goal of imitating the poor and humble Christ. A more detailed analysis can be found in Regis Armstrong's informative article "Starting Points," from which much of this information is gleaned (26-36).

Read Clare's second letter once again and note how the images of Rachel and Leah help Clare to make her points.

Clare's plan for prayer:

The Rachel image also identified Agnes as a contemplative. Interestingly, this second letter offers what might be the most reliable description of Clare's approach to prayer. She admonishes Agnes and her sisters: "O most noble Queen, gaze upon [Him] (Christ), consider [Him], contemplate [Him], as you desire to imitate [Him]" (2LAg 20). The same pattern was treated eighteen years later in 4LAg 15-23, suggesting that it was a steadfast framework for Clare.

An important link in this process was between prayer and imitation of Christ. For Clare, the first three stages of prayer made imitation possible. Clearly, the poor and humble Christ was the figure being gazed at, considered, contemplated and imitated. So, Rachel illustrated how Agnes could be fixed on her original goal of imitating the poor and humble Christ by making him the object of her prayer. Understanding the structure of Clare's prayer helps to appreciate this connection.

The practice of lectio divina grew in popularity through the monastic tradition and reached an important high point during the High Middle Ages. While many variations in this style of prayer are found, it was and is primarily characterized by three main steps: to read, to meditate, and to contemplate. Typically, the first stage involved reading a biblical text. The second step of meditation involved the use of one's imagination to insert oneself into the text. The practitioner might use the five senses to investigate the scene of the reading or take on the roles of characters in the reading, discovering their feelings and experiences. The third step was a quiet contemplation, in which the practitioner silenced her or his imagination while sitting in a quiet presence to the text and any action of God flowing out of the experience. While many monastic authors talked about how lectio divina would change a practitioner's life, most considered that action as a *consequence* of the prayer; only a few describe it as *part* of the prayer.

Clare's four-step description of prayer began with the typical monastic understanding. However, she changed some of the steps' names. *Reading* became *gazing*, a change that made sense if you recall that few medieval people could read. Thus, gazing at a physical or mental image might have been applicable to more practitioners in Clare's day than reading the text itself. *To consider* was Clare's term for *meditation*. Her name for the third stage, contemplation, was the same as in most medieval descriptions of lectio divina. Thus, though she changed some terms, her first three stages were quite typical.

What makes Clare stand out is the unequivocal addition of *imitation* as a fourth and final step of prayer. Even a casual reader of Clare's letters can see that Clare's purpose for gazing at the poor and humble Christ was to learn how to take on his divine life and manner of being. Clare prayed over Christ so that she could become like him. That transformation, imitation or action was *part of the prayer* not a consequence of the prayer.

Reflect on what each of the four verbs from 2LAg 20 might mean: gaze, consider, contemplate, and imitate. How would you explain the process in modern language? Is there any logic to the order of the verbs? Attempt to use this method in your own prayer. After the experience, journal about how you experienced it. Report on your experience to your study group. Lead the group in a discussion of how Clare's pattern is or might be helpful to them.

Clare's *Third Letter to Agnes of Prague*
1238

Sources

3LAg

Commentary

Clare's third known letter to Agnes has two major parts. The second part addressed previous questions from Agnes about fasting at San Damiano Monastery in Assisi. It would seem that Agnes was confused by pontifical fasting guidelines received either through the *Rule of St. Benedict*, Ugolino's *Form of Life*, or papal bulls on fasting. You can review papal bulls written between 1237 and 1238 in an earlier section of this chapter. You could also read the complete bulls in translation in CA:ED 354-363.

However, when reading this third letter from Clare, one receives the impression that fasting practices were not the foremost thing on Clare's mind. Her answers on fasting are at the end of the letter and constitute less than half the letter. Even the introductory phrase, "Now concerning those matters that you have asked me to clarify..." (29), leaves the impression that, while this may have been the reason for writing, it was not the topic Clare most wanted to discuss.

Instead, it seems that two linked papal bulls touched the spiritual aspirations of Agnes that Clare wanted to address. One papal bull represented a victory; the other, a setback. The papal bull *Pia credulitate tenentes* (15 April 1238) was electrifying. It was the thrilling papal bull that allowed Agnes and her sisters in Prague to fully implement absolute corporate poverty in imitation of the poor and humble Christ by not receiving any endowment from the St. Francis Hospice. This decision came after several years of correspondence between Agnes and the Apostolic See, and placed St. Francis Monastery in Prague on the short list, with San Damiano Monastery in Assisi, of monasteries granted this "privilege" by the papacy.

It would seem from Pope Gregory's response that Agnes's brother, King Vaclav, wrote to the pope in 1237 supporting his sister's request for divestiture. There is little doubt that Gregory's troubles with Holy Roman

Emperor Frederick II pressured him to accede to Vaclav's requests for his sister, since Gregory sought Vaclav's support against Frederick.

However, Gregory's subsequent bull, *Angelis gaudium*, denied Agnes's request for her own form of life. Approval of her own form of life or rule would have satisfied Agnes much more than the exemption granted earlier in *Pia credulitate tenentes*. In some ways, *Angelis gaudium* seemed to take away with one hand what *Pia credulitate tenentes* had given with the other hand. Clare's third letter to Agnes began by addressing an Agnes who might have needed encouragement.

That accomplished, Clare still needed to respond to Agnes's specific questions about fasting at San Damiano Monastery. Understanding the fasting regulations of the day can be a very confusing task for moderns. Rather than detailing them all, generalizations serve the needs of a beginning student today. First, the *Rule of St. Benedict* as supplemented for women by Ugolino's *Form of Life* laid down rather strict fasting and abstinence rules. Gregory's bull *Licet velut ignis* (February 9, 1237) reinforced the toughness of the rules in the tradition of the Cistercians.

These stricter rules were very burdensome for the sisters in Prague, as the climate did not include many conditions that made stricter fasting possible in the Mediterranean Basin. Clare's third letter clearly recommended moderation to Agnes, suggesting that Agnes may have been a bit obsessive about following rules to the letter. In *Pia meditationes pensantes* (May 5, 1238) Gregory allowed Agnes as abbess to make prudent judgments about fasting and other ascetical practices. Eventually, he also wrote a letter of encouragement to Agnes (*De conditoris omnium* of May 9, 1238).

It is important to appreciate the predominant medieval view of fasting. Less a discipline to achieve spiritual growth, it was increasingly viewed as a way of participating in the sufferings of Christ whom the sisters served as spouses (see Van den Goorbergh & Zweerman 206). This also explains why fasting exceptions were frequently recommended for the sick or aged. They already were participating in the sufferings of Christ.

Given the interplay among these various letters from a pope, a king, and Clare, we feel confident assigning 1238 as the date of this third known letter from Clare to Agnes of Prague, probably after *Angelis gaudium* of May 11, 1238.

Starter questions and suggestions

Read this third letter and observe how it develops many of the themes already introduced in the first two. In particular, we point out that 3LAg 13 states, "Place your heart in the icon of the divine substance and transform your whole self through contemplation into an image of his Godhead." Note that while 2LAg and 4LAg are typically cited to observe Clare's style of prayer (gazing, considering, contemplating, and imitating), this citation from 3LAg provides a quite concrete expression of the dynamic of that process. Why contemplate? Because it changes you. This text asserts that it changes you into what you contemplate.

We will suggest several exercises in the next section which involve both 3LAg and 4LAg.

Clare's Letters to Agnes of Prague

Clare's *Fourth Letter to Agnes of Prague*

Sources

4LAg
TestCl 19-23

Commentary

Clare's fourth and final known letter to Agnes of Prague was written in 1253, fourteen years after the previous one and just months before Clare died. The text itself gives little explicit evidence about what occasioned the letter. However, the heightened eschatological expression of the letter suggests that Clare's pending death was most likely the reason. It has the feel of a last will and testament.

Clare already introduced the metaphor of a mirror in her third letter to Agnes. That image became the central image in this fourth letter. Cited sources explaining its use in this letter include Armstrong (Mirror Mystic), Johnson, and Van den Goorbergh & Zweerman (218-219).

Medieval mirrors did not reflect the sharp, well-defined images that our modern mirrors do. In fact, by modern standards, we might consider the dull and fuzzy reflections of medieval mirrors to be more of a good shine than a reflection. Consequently, medieval people would naturally pay more attention to the mirror itself, typically a twisted and polished piece of metal placed within a frame. It became the subject of hundreds of medieval documents on the spiritual life, and Clare obviously found it useful to convey her message to Agnes.

The mirror itself is as important as the image reflected by the mirror. It is important to clarify that Christ is not the reflected image, but the mirror itself, i.e., the reflector. By gazing at Christ (the mirror) we see an image of ourselves as we are meant to be. Once we have gazed upon Christ and have seen the image of what we ourselves can be when "reflected" by Christ, we can then imitate him. This is the connection Clare makes in 2LAg 20: prayer leads to and ends with the imitation of Christ.

The mirror metaphor is akin to the notion of seeing yourself in the eyes of your lover. The lover reflects you back to yourself, but in an image transformed by the love of the beloved. In the process, one receives a new and different image of oneself.

Once this initial image is understood, Clare goes further by exchanging the terms. After our own contemplation and imitation of Christ have transformed us, we ourselves become mirrors for others. Others can gaze on us, as they can on Christ, and see a reflection of whom they can be. This is made possible by our own imitation of Christ, made possible by our contemplation of Christ. The process is endless. Clare returned one last time to the theme of becoming a mirror to others in her *Testament* (19-23).

Clare's mirror mysticism observes three dimensions to a medieval mirror: (1) in the border we see the poverty of the Incarnation; (2) at the "surface" or intermediate section we view the humility of his ministry; and (3) at the center or depth of the mirror we contemplate the unspeakable charity of the passion (4LCl 18-23).

Starter questions and suggestions

Read the fourth letter in a single sitting without taking notes, getting a sense of the flow of the letter. Then reread the third and fourth letters, taking notes about how the mirror image helps Clare to explain contemplation and imitation of Christ to Agnes. As in some of the earlier exercises, note the nature of Christ's image that Clare is contemplating and attempting to imitate (i.e., the poor, humble and charitable Christ). Write a short explanation of how the mirror image helped Clare to appropriate this image of Christ. Then, identify your own favorite portraits of Christ. How are they different from Clare's? How would you plug your images of Christ into the metaphor of the mirror? What would you concretely do to imitate the Christ in your image?

Medieval mirror spirituality may be difficult for moderns to understand because we use mirrors to see and study ourselves, not another. Is there a different modern way of understanding the same thing? Explain.

Clare's Letters to Agnes of Prague

Bringing the Letters Together

After looking at the four letters individually, it's helpful to look at them together. We propose four different ways of approaching this task.

Metaphors, images and values

The letters touch upon a great number of metaphors, images, and values. List the important ones you recall from the letters. Reread the letters if that's necessary to capture a larger list. Do not include elements that seem tangential or unimportant to the letters' intent. For instance, do not include most of the prescriptions about fasting found in the final portion of the third letter. Our simple list includes:

Mirror

Poverty

Humility

Contemplation

Bride of Christ

Perfection

Imitation of Christ

Celibacy

Enclosure

Next, write half a page about each item, explaining it within the medieval context in which Clare lived. Use a different piece of paper to describe each item.

After composing and explaining your list, look for connections among the items in your list. If writing helps you to be clear about your ideas, write a short paragraph about each of the connections you perceive.

Return to the pages on which you described each element. In the lower half of each page, explain its metaphor, image or value in modern language. Explore why a modern appropriation of each item might be different from a medieval one.

If you are working with a study group, present your work orally or by distributing copies of your various pages. Because your work was intentionally sparse, you should expect your study group to have many questions. This situation is an opportunity to engage the entire study group in a larger discussion that expands the understanding of each item and its relationship to the others. You should also expect study group members to want to include items that you did not. That's fine, but make them do similar work on their items. Let this discussion go on for as long as possible, since it will help everyone better understand what was at stake in Clare's letters to Agnes.

Dichotomies

Clare often viewed her life in strikingly dichotomous terms: one thing in opposition to another. Her first letter includes these dichotomies:

> the things of time vs. the things of eternity;
> the things of heaven vs. the goods of earth;
> living in the glory of the earth vs. ruling with Christ in heaven.

We already suggested exploring these and other dichotomies in our sections on the first two letters. Do it again now for all four letters, adding new ones especially from the third and fourth letters. Begin by write down each dichotomy on a separate paper. Explain how the terms might be used in different ways to draw out the contrast. Again, limit yourself to half of the page so you are forced to be concise.

Then, as you did for the metaphors, images, and values, attempt to write a modern appropriation of each dichotomy in the lower part of each page. Again, use your own work as a stimulus to a study group discussion.

Unexpected opposites

Another project is to collect the various unexpected or paradoxical opposites in the letters. For instance,

> Christ's love makes Agnes chaste;
> his touch leaves her pure; and
> his union with her preserves her virginity (cf. 1LAg 8).

However, love should lead to broken chastity (celibacy), touch to broken purity, and unity to broken virginity. So, in Clare's view, Agnes is both loved and chaste at the same time. It's worth another reading of the letters to list as many opposites as possible.

Explore the different meanings of the words at play in each paradox. Think of scriptures that use the same kind of paradoxical language. What is the fundamental insight of these texts in Clare's letters and in the Gospels? Become aware of how Clare's use of these paradoxical opposites is difficult for you to appreciate. Would you change the way Clare expressed these ideas? How?

New metaphors

A final project for this chapter could be to list metaphors of your own invention that express for you Clare's relationship with Christ. Invite your study group to do the same. Explain them.

Cited sources and suggested reading for worksheets on all four letters

- Armstrong, Regis J. "Clare of Assisi: The Mirror Mystic." *The Cord* 35.7 (1985) 195-202.

- —. "Starting Points: Images of Women in the Letters of Clare of Assisi to Agnes of Prague." In *Clare of Assisi: Model for Franciscan Women.* Ed. Ann Carville. Spirit and Life 1. St. Bonaventure NY: The Franciscan Institute, 1991. 17-54.

- —. "Women in the Letters of Clare." *Greyfriars Review* 7.3 (1993) 347-380. Previously published in *Collectanea Francescana* 62.1-2 (1992) 63-100.

- Bell, Rudolph. *Holy Anorexia.* Chicago: University of Chicago Press, 1985. This text describes the broader food practices of medieval religious women.

- Blastic, Michael W., Jay M. Hammond, and J. A. Wayne Hellmann, eds. *The Writings of Clare of Assisi: Letters, Form of Life, Testament and Blessing.* Studies in Early Franciscan Sources 3. St. Bonaventure NY: Franciscan Institute Publications, 2011.

- Bradley, Ritamary. "Backgrounds of the Title *Speculum* in Medieval Literature." *Speculum* 29 (1954) 100-115.

- Brunelli, Delir. "Contemplation in the Following of Jesus Christ: The Experience of Clare of Assisi." *The Cord* (2002) 154-170.

- Burfield, Brian. "Reflections in the Mirror: The Images of Christ in the Spiritual Life of Saint Clare of Assisi." Master's thesis. St. Bonaventure NY: Franciscan Institute, 1990.

- Bynum, Caroline Walker. *Holy Feast and Holy Fast: The Religious Significance of Food to Medieval Women.* Berkeley and Los Angeles: University of California Press, 1987. This text describes the broader food practices of medieval religious women. See other sources by Bynum on the topic in our earlier chapter, "Medieval Religious Women: Medieval Food Practices."

- —. "Women Mystics and Eucharistic Devotion in the Thirteenth Century." *Women Studies* 11 (1984) 179-214. On pages 201-203, Bynum relates how *imitatio* became more literal and physical, and was the basis of a new religiosity that included "a sense of imitation as becoming or being."

- Cherewatuk, Karen and Ulrike Wiethaus, eds. *Dear Sister: Medieval Women and the Epistolary Genre.* Philadelphia: University of Pennsylvania Press, 1993.

- Chinnici, Joseph. "Francis and Clare: The Vocation of Exchange." In *Proceedings of the Annual Federation Council Conference,* August 20-22, 1987.

- Constable, Giles. *Letters and Letter Collections.* Typologie des sources du moyen âge 17. Turnhout: Éditions Brepols, 1976.

- Cusato, Michael. "Elias and Clare: An Enigmatic Relationship." In *Clare of Assisi: Investigations.* Ed. Mary Francis Hone. Clare Centenary Series 7. St. Bonaventure NY: The Franciscan Institute, 1993. 95-115. Pages 97-101 include background on 2LAg.

- Delio, Ilia. "Identity and Contemplation in Clare of Assisi's Writings." *Journal of Studies in Spirituality* 14 (2001) 139-152.

- —. "Mirrors and Footprints: Metaphors of Relationships in Clare of Assisi's Writings." *Studies in Spirituality* 10 (2000) 167-181. Reprinted in *Laurentianum* 41 (2000) 455-471.

- Downing, Frances Teresa. *Saint Clare of Assisi: The Context of Her Life.* Vol. 2. Phoenix AZ: Tau Publishing, 2012.

- —. *Saint Clare of Assisi: The Spirituality of Her Letters: Letter Four.* Vol. 4. Phoenix AZ: Tau Publishing, 2017.

- Doyle, Eric. "Discipleship of Christ in St. Clare's Letters to Blessed Agnes of Prague." *Franciscan Christology: Selected Texts.* Trans. and Ed. Damian McElrath. St. Bonaventure NY: The Franciscan Institute, 1980. 14-39.

- Evans, Ruth Agnes. "Relationship with Christ in Clare's Letters to Agnes." *The Cord* 59.2 (2009) 165-195. A profound reflection on all four letters.

- Flanagan, Eileen. "Medieval Epistolary Genre and the Letters to Agnes of Prague." In *An Unencumbered Heart: A Tribute to Clare of Assisi 1253-2003.* Eds. Jean-François Godet-Calogeras and Roberta McKelvie. Spirit and Life 11 (2004) 51-53.

- Hellmann, J. A. Wayne. "Genres of Spiritual Writing." In *The New Dictionary of Catholic Spirituality.* Ed. Michael Downey. Collegeville: The Liturgical Press, 1993. 922-930.

- Johnson, Timothy. "Clare, Leo, and the Authorship of the Fourth Letter to Agnes of Prague." *Franciscan Studies* 62 (2004) 91-100.

- —. "'To Her Who Is Half of Her Soul': Clare of Assisi and the Medieval Epistolary Tradition." *Greyfriars Review* 11.1 (1997) 23-40. Also published in *Magistra* 2.1 (1996) 24-50.

- —. "Visual Imagery and Contemplation in Clare of Assisi's 'Letters to Agnes of Prague.'" *Mystics Quarterly* 19.4 (1993) 161-172.

- Karper, Karen. "The Mirror Image in Clare of Assisi." *Review for Religious* 51 (1992) 424-431.

- Leclercq, Jean. "St. Clare and Nuptial Spirituality." Trans. Edward Hagman. *Greyfriars Review* 10.2 (1996) 171-178.

- Ledoux, Claire Marie. *Clare of Assisi: Her Spirituality Revealed in Her Letters.* Trans. Colette Joly Dees. Cincinnati OH: St. Anthony Messenger Press, 2003.

- Lynn, Beth. "Early Friars and the Poor Ladies in Conversation: *Scripta Leonis* and the Writings of Clare: A Common Matrix of Evangelical Contemplative Life for both Men and Women." *The Cord* 45.1 (1995) 21-30.

- McFague, Sallie. *Metaphorical Theology: Models of God in Religious Language*. Philadelphia: Fortress Press, 1982. This text deals with metaphor in general and then applies it to religious and theological language.

- Mueller, Joan. "Agnes of Prague and the Juridical Implications of the Privilege of Poverty." *Franciscan Studies* 58 (2000) 261-287.

- —. *Clare of Assisi: The Letters to Agnes*. Collegeville MN: Glazier, 2003. An exceptional popular treatment of the letters without the scholarly aspects of the Franciscan Institute text.

- —. *Clare's Letters to Agnes: Texts and Sources*. St. Bonaventure NY: Franciscan Institute Publications, 2001. Mueller provides (1) an original translation of the text, (2) introductions to all the letters and each individual letter, (3) copious notes on the text, (4) the original Latin text facing the translation, (5) a list of sources for Clare's texts, and (6) cross-references. Highly recommended.

- Peterson, Ingrid. "Clare of Assisi: Espoused to the Crucified." In *A Leaf from the Great Tree of God: Essays in Honour of Ritamary Bradley*. Toronto: Peregrina Publishing, 1994. 156-172.

- —. "Clare of Assisi's Mysticism of the Poor Crucified." *Greyfriars Review* 9.2 (1995) 163-192. Also published in *Studies in Spirituality* 4 (1994) 51-78.

- Schlosser, Marianne. "Mother, Sister, Bride: The Spirituality of St. Clare." *Greyfriars Review* 5 (1991) 233-249.

- Tavormina, M. Teresa. "Of Maidenhood and Maternity: Liturgical Hagiography and the Medieval Ideal of Virginity." *American Benedictine Review* 31.December (1980) 384-399. Besides providing general information about the cited topic, Tavormina provides specific information about the cult of the Roman virgin martyr Agnes of the third or fourth century. She quotes from Agnes's legend and the rite for the consecration of virgins. Clare uses both of these sources in her letters to Agnes. This is an accessible resource for people who only read English.

- Van den Goorbergh, Edith. "Clare's Prayer as a Spiritual Journey." *Greyfriars Review* 10.3 (1996) 283-292. Also published in *The Way Supplement* 80 (1994) 51-60.

- Van Den Goorbergh, Edith A. and Theodore H Zweerman. *Light Shining Through a Veil: On Saint Clare's Letters to Saint Agnes of Prague*. The Netherlands: Peeters, 2000.

The Forms of Life Given to Clare

Introduction

Naming the documents that governed the Poor Sisters at San Damiano Monastery in Assisi can confuse readers. Many older authors used the terms "form of life" and "rule" interchangeably. However, some scholars today think "form of life" was a term used for the guiding documents of new religious groups like the Beguines heavily located in the Lowlands and the Humiliati of Milan. These documents were less formal and comprehensive than the "rules" of the traditional orders like the Benedictines.

Further complicating things, Ugolino gave his *Form of Life* as a supplement to the *Rule of St. Benedict* (FLHug 3). In our modern understanding, that arrangement would make his document more like constitutions than a rule. However, it's also important to realize that use of the *Rule of St. Benedict* for female religious during Clare's time was often more symbolic than practical. The papacy was granting so many exemptions that the integrity of that rule as a guiding document can be seriously questioned. For instance, we have a papal document that claimed the only thing in the *Rule of St. Benedict* that was binding was observance of the three vows (*Cum universitate vestrae* of August 21, 1244 by Pope Innocent IV). Yet Clare, who wanted a radical personal and corporate poverty, even questioned observance of the vow of poverty according to the *Rule of St. Benedict*. In our analysis, Ugolino's *Form of Life* seems more important for new female religious at the time than the *Rule of St. Benedict*.

Regardless, CA:ED consistently uses the term *form of life* for the various documents guiding the Poor Sisters at San Damiano Monastery over Clare's lifetime. We do the same in this workbook, though revert to the term *rule* for any fundamental document written after Clare's own *Form of Life* was approved in 1252 by Cardinal Rainaldo.

It is impossible to study Clare's *Form of Life* in exactly the same manner William proposed for Francis's rule in his previous workbook (Workbook I, 175-192). The reason is that Francis's rule was a single document that developed extensively between 1208 and 1223, i.e., from Francis and Bernard of Quintavalle's reception of gospel directives to his *Later Rule*. In the first workbook, William talked about "glimpses" of Francis's rule, which are like snapshots at various stages of its integral development. The glimpses have textual connections—one form emerging from the previous form.

The history of Clare's *Form of Life* is quite different. Rather than a single developing text, Clare's group lived with a succession of distinct forms of life. While there is some continuity of content among these forms of life, they cannot be considered an organic literary development of a single document. Furthermore, in some areas, the various forms of life under which she lived contained ideas totally opposed to her vision for herself and her sisters.

In studying the history of the forms of life Clare lived with, it is necessary to consider the following documents written in the indicated years:

- *The Form of Life* given by Francis of Assisi (1212-1213)
- *The Form of Life* given by Cardinal Ugolino (1219)
- *The Privilege of Poverty* by Pope Gregory IX (1228)
- *The Form of Life* given by Pope Innocent IV (1247)
- *Clare's Form of Life* (1252)

The historical circumstances of Clare's *Form of Life* were also different from that of Francis. Francis received oral approval of his rule from Innocent III before the Fourth Lateran Council (1215), which forbade new rules within the Church. Thus, Francis was able to continue the development of his rule, a glimpse of which we have in 1221 (*The Earlier Rule*), and the final papally approved glimpse in 1223 (*The Later Rule*).

Clare did not receive oral or written approval for a rule or form of life before the Fourth Lateran Council. Thus, she was expected to accept one of the rules for women circulating at the time. There were four, two of which were not well suited to contemporary use in Italy (Pachomius's and Basil's). The remaining two were those largely chosen by western groups, i.e., Augustine of Hippo's or Benedict's (see Godet 22-23). Cardinal Ugolino essentially forced San Damiano Monastery in Assisi to live with the *Benedictine Rule* and his own *Form of Life*. However, those documents allowed corporate ownership of properties with their revenues. Clare's vision of absolute poverty, in imitation of Jesus, precluded that. So, Clare embarked on an incredible journey that eventually led to the approval of her own *Form of Life* in 1252. The remainder of this chapter charts that long and involved process.

The Form of Life Given by Francis of Assisi
1212-1213
(CA:ED 118)

Sources

FLCl 6:3-4
TestCl 33

Starter questions, suggestions, and commentary

Both Clare's *Form of Life* and *Testament* testify that, early on, Francis provided a *Form of Life* to the Poor Sisters of San Damiano Monastery in Assisi. It has not survived independently and is only found embedded within Clare's own *Form of Life* (VI: 3-4). This passage from Clare's *Form of Life* certainly does not preserve Francis's entire text (Godet 73). Clare's *Testament* affirms that it sought to preserve poverty for the Poor Sisters (33-35). Most likely, Clare and the Poor Sisters considered the *Form of Life* given by Francis and their own lived experience as sufficient to guide their life. No more comprehensive rule was part of their early reality.

While the Augustinian and Benedictine rules allowed other religious women to share their common goods and develop a means of supporting themselves, Clare's way was radically different. Seeking to unite themselves with Christ by sharing in his poverty and humility, the Poor Sisters renounced all individual and common ownership, and the means to secure an income as, for example, through endowment or land.

Although Francis's *Form of Life* was symbolically important, we wonder about its practicality. It attests that Francis was impressed with Clare and her companions' ability to live the penitential and poor life-style that he espoused. It also confirms that Francis promised a perpetual relationship between the two Franciscan Orders. However, it really says nothing of that life, except through its admiration of Clare's ability to live poorly and penitentially.

As a reader and student, your tasks around this document are quite simple. First, note that it exists. Second, realize that it is found only in FLCl VI 3-4, and then only as a fragment. Read the text and imagine what else might have been included and how it could guide the early Poor Sisters at San Damiano Monastery. Note how this situation was different from other monasteries of enclosed women who accepted one of the commonly available rules. If you are working with a study group, invite the group to discuss the text and its situation.

Suggested reading

- Godet-Calogeras, Jean-François. "From Brother Francis to the Poor Sisters of San Damiano: What Is Left of Their Correspondence?" In *Her Bright Merits: Essays Honoring Ingrid J. Peterson, OSF."* Eds. Mary Walsh Meany and Felicity Dorsett. Spirit and Life 17. St. Bonaventure NY: Franciscan Institute Publications, 2012. 61-81. Godet-Calogeras writes about the *Form of Life* given by Francis of Assisi on pages 65-70.

The (Doubtful) *Privilege of Poverty*
Ascribed to Innocent III

Sources

PC	III 14:37-38; 32:106 (Filippa)
	VII 8:18 (Balvina of Martino)
	XII 6:17-20 (Beatrice)
VL	XII 20-25
BC	1:4 (Note that paragraph 1 is accidentally not noted in CA:ED)
LCl	IX 14:9-11

Commentary

Before the 1990s, most historians believed that Pope Innocent III issued a *Privilege of Poverty* to Clare of Assisi before he died in 1216. Significant research since then has disproved such a document ever existed. New students are likely to be confused about this because of their access to older articles and books. Because this issue is so complicated, we do not expect readers of this workbook to approach this section as a worksheet. Instead we hope to explain the controversy and list the primary sources above that are involved. Let's try to unravel the mystery.

The first witness to a document entitled the *Privilege of Poverty* written by Pope Innocent III is the *Prose Legend of Saint Clare*, which was composed between 1255-1260. Earlier documents do not mention Innocent. Within months of Clare's death (1253), the *Acts of the Process of Canonization* was recorded in which three of the twenty witnesses referred to the *Privilege of Poverty* but neglected to mention its author. The subsequent *Versified Legend* and the bull of canonization (*Clara claris praeclara*) also mention the privilege without naming its author. Before the 1990s, most historians assumed that these earlier sources referred to Innocent III, first mentioned between 1255-1260 in LCl. Later, when a copy of the *Privilege* was found, it too was assumed to be the text written by Innocent III in 1216.

During and after the 1990s, historians began to wonder from where the *Prose Legend* learned that the author was Innocent III. All these documents freely mention sources in other places, especially that of Pope Gregory IX. Why would they neglect to mention Innocent III in this case? Soon, historians had other doubts about his authorship.

Early belief that Innocent III wrote a *Privilege of Poverty* in 1216 was further based on the Messina Manuscript, which included a copy of the bull issuing the privilege. It identifies the author as "Innocent." Since the *Prose Legend* mentions Innocent III as the author, most believed that the bull preserved in the Messina Manuscript was written by Innocent III in 1216. Like Gregory IX's *Privilege of Poverty* (1228), this bull also was called *Sicut manifestum est*.

Later in the 1990s, Werner Maleczek discredited the authenticity of the Messina Manuscript in a lengthy article. Subsequent research rees-tablished the authenticity of the manuscript, dating it no later than 1270 when Leo of Assisi likely died (see our subsequent chapters "Clare's *Testament*" and "*The Blessing of Clare* "). However, the doubt that Innocent III authored *the Privilege of Poverty* persisted. The strongest objection was the simple observation that there was no apparent reason for a *Privilege of Poverty* in 1216.

In the early years at San Damiano Monastery, Clare considered herself to be living under a *Form of Life* given by Francis of Assisi, which praised the Poor Sisters for their radical poverty. They had no reason to ask the papacy for an exemption from corporate ownership. A reason didn't exist until 1219 when Ugolino began his new order of female religious that would live under the *Rule of St. Benedict* and his own *Form of Life*. Those doc-uments allowed and encouraged female monasteries to establish endow-ments and own property as a way to financially secure themselves. This was the first time Clare and the Poor Sisters at San Damiano Monastery had a reason to fear for their way of life including radical poverty.

Still, we have no firm evidence that Clare and the Poor Sisters of San Damiano Monastery were part of that order or lived under its arrangement until 1228 when Cardinal Rainaldo listed San Damiano Monastery in this new order, for the first time called "The Order of St. Damian" (*Matribus sororibus* on August 18). Clearly in 1228, Clare had reason to ask for an exemption from the undesirable elements of the *Rule of St. Benedict* and Ugolino's *Form of Life*. Pope Gregory IX granted this in the same year, something that then made historical sense (*Sicut manifestum est* on Sep-tember 17, 1228). It became known as the *Privilege of Poverty*.

Catherine Mooney's *Clare of Assisi and the Thirteenth-Century Church* presents an appealing analysis that early witnesses like the Messi-na Manuscript actually refer to a reaffirmation by Innocent IV of the *Privilege of Poverty* first issued by Gregory IX (1228). She reasons that Innocent IV's document was granted just before Clare's death when she feared losing her cherished privilege of radical poverty. Thus, Mooney argues that early witnesses misidentify the "Innocent" in the papal bull as Innocent III. In fact, it was Innocent IV (161-169). An English translation of an edition simply naming Innocent is in CA:ED 86, note b.

The final puzzle is why Thomas of Celano's *Prose Legend* states that Innocent III granted the privilege. Perhaps the best hypothesis is that the oral tradition leading up to the *Prose Legend* was already getting confused about which Innocent was involved. No other evidence explains it. As the only source stating Innocent III issued the privilege, the *Prose Legend* simply appears to be in error.

Today, few scholars accept the existence of a *Privilege of Poverty* written by Innocent III, as Thomas of Celano's *Prose Legend* first reported.

Cited sources and suggested reading

- Alberzoni, Maria Pia. *Clare of Assisi and the Poor Sisters in the Thirteenth Century.* St. Bonaventure NY: Franciscan Institute Publications, 2004.

- —. "'Nequaquam a Christi sequela in perpetuum absolve desiderio' [I will Never Desire in Any Way to be Absolved from the Following of Christ]: Clare between Charism and Institution." *Greyfriars Review* 12.Supplement (1998) 81-121.

- Andenna, Cristina. "Chiara d'Assisi: Alcune Riflessioni su un problema ancora aperto." *Rivista di Storia e Letteratura Religiosa* 34 (1998) 547-579.

- —. "Chiara d'Assisi. La Questione dell'Autenticitá del <<Privilegium Paupertatis>> e del Testamento." *Tavola Rotonda. Rivista di Storia della Chiesa in Italia* 51 (1997) 595-597.

- Cusato, Michael. "Elias and Clare: An Enigmatic Relationship." In *Clare of Assisi: Investigations.* Ed. Mary Francis Hone. Clare Centenary Series 7. St. Bonaventure NY: The Franciscan Institute, 1993. 95-115. The part about Clare and *the Privilege of Poverty* is from 101-115.

- —. "From the *Perfectio Sancti Evangelii* to the *Sanctissima Vita et Paupertas:* An Hypothesis on the Origin of the *Privilegium Paupertatis* to Clare and Her Sisters at San Damiano." *Franciscan Studies* 64 (2006) 123-144.

- Gennaro, Clara. "Clare, Agnes and the First Sisters: from the "Pauperes Dominae" of San Damiano to the Poor Clares." Trans. Lori Pieper. *Greyfriars Review* 9.3 (1995) 259-276.

- Godet, Jean-François. "A New Look at Clare's Gospel Plan of Life." Trans. Edward Hagman. *Greyfriars Review* 5.Supplement (1991) 1-84.

- Knox, Leslie. *Creating Clare of Assisi: Female Franciscan Identities in later Medieval Italy.* The Medieval Franciscans 5. Leiden: Brill, 2008. 10-12.

- Kuster, Niklaus. "Clare's Testament and Innocent III's Privilege of Poverty: Genuine or Clever Forgeries." Trans. Nancy Celaschi. *Greyfriars Review* 15 (2001) 171-252.

- Maleczek, Werner, "Questions about the Authenticity of the Privilege of Poverty of Innocent III and of the Testament of Clare of Assisi." *Greyfriars Review* 12.Supplement (1998) 1-80.

- Mooney, Catherine. *Clare of Assisi and the Thirteenth-Century Church: Religious Women, Rules, and Resistance.* Philadelphia: University of Pennsylvania Press, 2016. An excellent summary of current research on the history of the "Order of St. Clare" through the 1260s. Mooney breaks new ground in suggesting that the commonly discounted *Privilege of Poverty* once thought to be issued by Innocent III may actually have been issued by Innocent IV (161-167); that Cardinal Rainaldo (later Alexander IV) was the main force behind the failure of Innocent IV's *Form of Life* (1247) and not Clare of Assisi's resistance (135-160); and that Cardinal Rainaldo may have had a more substantial and definitive role in the final redaction of Clare's *Form of Life* than previously thought (161-196).

- Rusconi, Roberto. "The Spread of Women's Franciscanism in the Thirteenth Century." Trans. Edward Hagman. *Greyfriars Review* 12.1 (1998) 35-75.

The Form of Life Given by Cardinal Ugolino
1219
(CA:ED 75-85)

Dating and Authorship

There is no doubt that Cardinal Ugolino dei Conti di Segni is the author of this *Form of Life* which he intended as a supplement to the *Rule of St. Benedict.* For a long time, many scholars believed this document was dated 1219 even though the oldest known manuscript containing it was dated 1228. In 2008, Giovanni Boccali (*Cum omnis vera religio* 435-477) published an edition that he convincingly dated 1219, allowing us to certainly use the same date here.

Commentary

We know that the original version of this *Form of Life* was written shortly after a letter from Pope Honorius III in August 1219, *Litterae tuae nobis,* exempting nuns in central and northern Italy from local episcopal and civil control, and placing them directly under the jurisdiction of the papacy. Some editions of this *Form of Life* use Ugolino's papal name, Gregory, in the opening line because for a long time the oldest manuscript was from 1228, one year after Ugolino became pope.

Cardinal Ugolino was the nephew of Pope Innocent III (1198-1216) who verbally approved Francis of Assisi's *Primitive Rule* in 1209 or 1210 and was Bishop of Rome when Clare entered San Damiano Monastery in Assisi. Ugolino served Innocent's successor, Honorius III (1216-1227), as a papal legate in central and northern Italy during which he also was the cardinal protector of the Friars Minor. He became Pope Gregory IX (1227-1241) after Honorius and remained very involved with Franciscan men and women.

Both Honorius and Ugolino were concerned for the physical wellbeing of religious women. As papal legate and later as pope, Ugolino worked to free nuns from the interfering control of local ecclesiastical and civil authorities. He worked to provide them with a plan of life that contemporaries would consider both religious and reasonable. For this reason, Ugolino generally judged Clare and Agnes's ideal of absolute poverty as unrealistic. Since many female monasteries were closing because of insufficient financial support, Ugolino and Honorius sought to establish an endowment (usually of land) for each monastery's support.

With his *Form of Life,* Ugolino hoped to stabilize female religious life in central and northern Italy. However, it hardly satisfied Clare of Assisi or Agnes of Prague. Instead, it was a huge disappointment to them. Their agitation caused the two to exchange letters. As much as their correspondence was borne out of consternation, we can be grateful for it today as, otherwise, we would have very little actually written by Clare herself.

Clare obediently accepted documents given to her by the papacy. Still, she shrewdly noted that her Poor Sisters only had to observe their required norms. She correctly observed that Ugolino's *Form of Life* neither required nor prohibited absolute poverty. She simply decided with her Poor Sisters not to exercise the option of corporate ownership. However, there is no doubt that Clare and her Poor Sisters felt threatened by the intentions of the papacy in this regard. So, it should not be surprising that in 1228, the year in which we first find San Damiano Monastery listed among the members of Ugolino's Order of St. Damian (*Matribus sororibus*), Clare also obtained the *Privilege of Poverty* from Gregory IX (*Sicut manifestum est*).

It is important to realize that Ugolino's *Form of Life* was not written specifically for Clare at San Damiano Monastery in Assisi. Instead, it was written for a group of female monasteries in central and northern Italy under the jurisdiction of Cardinal Ugolino. They constituted the first order totally composed of women, called the "Order of the Poor Ladies of the Valley of Spoleto or of Tuscany." Later, in 1228, Cardinal Rainaldo called them the "Order of St. Damian" in his letter *Matribus sororibus.*

Ugolino's *Form of Life* was intended to guide their lives in tandem with the *Rule of St. Benedict* and reflected a great deal of influence from the Cistercian reform of Benedictinism. As such, it gave importance to the enclosure, fasting, physical penances, and traditional monastic prayer forms. However, more importantly to Clare and Agnes, it assumed that monasteries would own property as a source of income. This was one of the reasons Honorius III and Cardinal Ugolino, concerned about the financial instability of many monasteries, chose the *Rule of St. Benedict* for these women.

It is important to realize that while poverty was the primary concern of Clare, Ugolino was most concerned about strict observance of the cloister and fasting. Number 4 of his *Form of Life* (CA:ED 76) states that this enclosure was lifelong and only to be broken for a sister to help start or build up a different monastery. Ugolino strongly linked enclosure, virginity, fasting and the spiritual marriage to Christ. In medieval society, the seclusion of noble women was very important to preserve their virginity and thus their "value" in arranged marriages. In female religious life, the metaphor of marriage to Christ was also very important. Thus, so too was enclosure which preserved and demonstrated the nun's total dedication to Christ as spouse.

Starter suggestions

We must always keep in mind that Clare did not write this *Form of Life*. Still, it is important to study because Clare lived with it for many years, and eventually clashed with Ugolino after he became Pope Gregory IX over the issue of her absolute poverty in imitation of Christ. To better understand how and why this *Form of Life* so disappointed Clare, read it carefully and list aspects that don't strike you as Franciscan in inspiration or practice. Note elements discussed in this commentary. You may want to hold onto your notes from this exercise to compare them later with Clare's own *Form of Life* first approved by Cardinal Rainaldo in 1252 and later by Pope Innocent IV just days before she died.

Cited sources and suggested reading

- Boccali, Giovanni. "La 'Cum omnis vera religio' del Cardinale Ugolino: *Forma vite* primitiva per San Damiano ed altri monasteri." *Frate Francesco* 74 (2008) 435-477.

The Forms of Life Given to Clare

The Privilege of Poverty of Pope Gregory IX
1228
(CA:ED 87-88)

Sources

Many of the sources cited above for the doubtful *Privilege of Poverty* by Innocent III talk about a privilege without naming Innocent. They more likely refer to the certain *Privilege of Poverty* authored by Gregory IX in 1228. Those sources are also included here. It would be valuable to read our commentary about the doubtful document for this section as well.

1-4LAg	See commentary below
PrPov	
PC	I 13:38-39 (Pacifica)
	II 22:74-77 (Benvenuta of Perugia)
	III 14:37-38; 32:106 (Filippa)
	VII 8:18 (Balvina of Martino)
	XII 6:17-20 (Beatrice)
VL	XII 1-50
BC	1:4 (Note that paragraph 1 is accidentally not noted in CA:ED)
	17:74-77
LCl	IX 13:1—14:18

Dating and Authorship

There is no doubt that Pope Gregory IX, the former Cardinal Ugolino, issued this privilege or exemption to San Damiano Monastery in his papal bull *Sicut manifestum est* on September 17, 1228. Note that the privilege was *only* extended to San Damiano Monastery. The bull is preserved at the Protomonastery in Assisi.

Commentary

Though we include Gregory IX's *Privilege of Poverty* in this chapter on the forms of life given to Clare, we need to be clear that the privilege is *not* a form of life. It is an exemption from elements in Ugolino's *Form of Life* that allowed the ownership of land and other forms of endowment. To be clear, let us state that Clare already shrewdly realized that Ugolino's *Form of Life* neither required nor prohibited ownership. However, Clare obviously sensed conflict in the future over this issue and likely requested the privilege before agreeing to become part of the Order of St. Damian that lived under the *Rule of St. Benedict* and Ugolino's *Form of Life*. Because the *Privilege of Poverty* clarified the nature of life at San Damiano Monastery, we include it in this chapter.

We have already explained that, in the beginning, Clare and her Poor Sisters were satisfied to follow the simple *Form of Life* given by Francis and their own lived experience. When San Damiano Monastery became part of the Order of St. Damian (certainly by 1228), its Poor Sisters began to live with Cardinal Ugolino's more substantial *Form of Life* that he wrote in 1219. It encouraged endowments that often included rent paying lands. Ugolino believed this contributed to the stability and sustainability of female religious life.

This Roman policy also sought to make women's religious life in the region more homogenous, minimizing differences. It is easy to see how upsetting the approach was to Clare, who was famous for her desire to own absolutely nothing in imitation of the radical poverty of Christ visible in the Incarnation. Clare's desire and papal policy were on a collision course.

Some witnesses in the *Acts of the Process of Canonization* and the primary sources that flowed out of the *Process* report that Ugolino as Pope Gregory IX was concerned about the lack of supporting property at San Damiano Monastery and tried to convince Clare to accept some possessions. Clare steadfastly resisted this pressure and fought back by asking Pope Gregory himself to assure her right to live with her Poor Sisters at San Damiano Monastery in absolute poverty. With great reluctance, Gregory granted Clare the *Privilege of Poverty*. This occurred only a month after Cardinal Rainaldo listed San Damiano Monastery as a member of the Order of St. Damian (*Matribus sororibus* on August 18, 1228).

Note that the *Privilege* did not remove Clare from observance of the *Rule of St. Benedict* or Ugolino's *Form of Life*. Instead, it established that the Poor Sisters of San Damiano Monastery could not be forced to own property. In other words, it assured that the *right* to own property in the *Rule of St. Benedict* and Ugolino's *Form of Life* could not be turned into a *requirement* to take on possessions. The *Privilege* became the defining characteristic of Clare and the Poor Sisters at San Damiano Monastery. It enshrined what was unique about them, compared to most other nuns in the region.

The struggle over poverty continued after Gregory granted San Damiano Monastery this privilege. Soon Agnes of Prague would struggle with the papacy over the same issue. This ongoing struggle is visible in the four letters of Clare to Agnes, which encouraged her and her sisters at Saint Francis Monastery in Prague to remain steadfast in their desire to live in absolute poverty. The pressure from others, including from Rome, is visible in Clare's admonition that Agnes listen to no one who might try to turn her from this strict observance of poverty.

Starter questions and suggestions

If you have never heard of an oxymoron, this is an example: the Privilege of Poverty. An oxymoron is a term that appears self-contradictory. Do you consider poverty a privileged condition? Clare did. However, we also need to realize that in canon law, a privilege is an exemption from an existing law or regulation, in this case, pressure to own property. Try to explain how Clare understood this as a privilege.

Absolute poverty was Clare's way to follow Christ and share in his mission. It and a close association with the Friars Minor were core elements of her vocational identity. Explain how she understood that. How might her chosen way to imitate Christ relate to modern attempts to imitate Christ? How might we be able to appropriate poverty as a value in our own day?

Reading the four letters of Clare to Agnes of Prague is an excellent way to understand the ongoing importance of the *Privilege of Poverty*. The second letter especially addresses issues of absolute and radical personal and corporate poverty important to both women. Joan Mueller does an excellent job of fleshing out the meaning of the "privilege" by examining the four letters. In *Clare's Letters to Agnes: Texts and Sources,* Mueller explains how various papal bulls, especially those from Gregory IX, elicited a reaction from Clare and Agnes visible in the letters (207-237).

Cited sources and suggested reading

- Alberzoni, Maria Pia. *Clare of Assisi and the Poor Sisters in the Thirteenth Century.* St. Bonaventure NY: Franciscan Institute Publications, 2004.

- Mueller, Joan. *Clare's Letters to Agnes: Texts and Sources.* St. Bonaventure NY: Franciscan Institute Publications, 2001. See pages 207-237.

- —. *The Privilege of Poverty: Clare of Assisi, Agnes of Prague, and the Struggle for a Franciscan Rule for Women.* University Park PA: The Pennsylvania State University Press, 2006.

The Forms of Life given to Clare

The Form of Life Given by Pope Innocent IV
1247
(CA:ED 89-105)

Sources

FLInn

Authorship and dating

The author of this form of life is certainly Pope Innocent IV who issued it on August 6, 1247 in the papal bull *Cum omnis vera religio.*

Commentary

When Pope Innocent IV became pope in 1243, he continued the policies of Gregory IX regarding the Order of St. Damian. On November 13, 1243, he wrote *In divini timore nominis* to Agnes of Prague who asked to be relieved of observing the *Rule of St. Benedict.* Innocent replied that the *Rule of St. Benedict* was among the greatest of rules and asked Agnes to stop petitioning for her own form of life. Innocent's bull did not calm the sisters, and more petitions were forthcoming. On November 13, 1245, he issued *Solet annuere* which reaffirmed that all monasteries in the Order of St. Damian were to follow Ugolino's *Form of Life* in conjunction with the *Rule of St. Benedict.*

Two years later, with the bull *Cum omnis vera religio* (August 6, 1247), Innocent IV issued his own *Form of Life* for the Order of St. Damian, which was a revision of Ugolino's *Form of Life.* We imagine that the many requests for exemptions convinced him that a total rewrite was necessary. For members of the Order of St. Damian that followed the radical poverty of San Damiano Monastery in Assisi, this revised *Form of Life* was an important step forward in at least one regard. It no longer referred to the *Rule of St. Benedict* explicitly, though it continued a monastic mindset in many ways. For the first time, the Order of St. Damian was conceived as a Franciscan Order. This point was underscored by Innocent's policy to address many issues of female religious by placing them under the jurisdiction of the men from the same movement. For the

Order of St. Damian, this officially acknowledged relationship is visible in links to Francis's own *Later Rule* of 1223.

Still, Innocent's *Form of Life* disappointed Clare and others like Agnes of Prague because it continued to allow property and ignore the *Privilege of Poverty*. It allowed for procurators to administer the properties of the Poor Sisters and furthered the monastification of the Poor Ladies by requiring strict monastic dress, conduct, and enclosure that reflected the ever-stricter requirements of papal policy (see Makowski 9-42). On the other hand, it mitigated some of the strict fasting requirements of the former form of life.

For those following Clare's particular way of life, Innocent's *Form of Life* failed to address their most fundamental concern: absolute corporate poverty in imitation of Christ. Innocent IV obviously intended his new *Form of Life* for the entire Order of St. Damian, which meant it had to apply to even those not following the strict observance of San Damiano Monastery. However, the lack of acceptance must have been widespread. It seemed to please no one. On June 6, 1250, with the bull *Inter personas*, he declared that no sister could be forced to accept his *Form of Life*. Perhaps the most important result of Innocent's *Form of Life* was the birth of final resolve within Clare to write her own form of life. It seemed that was the only way to ensure the safety of her *Privilege of Poverty*.

Catherine Mooney in *Clare of Assisi and the Thirteenth-Century Church* argues that Cardinal Rainaldo had a more important role in the failure of Innocent IV's *Form of Life* than Clare's opposition to it (135-160). It's an interesting theory that has much commending it but needing review by more scholars before embracing it.

Starter suggestions and questions

The edition of Innocent IV's *Form of Life* in CA:ED (89-105) helpfully shows how Innocent revised Ugolino's *Form of Life* by highlighting his changes in bold type. Read through FLInn, focusing on the bold type. List how Innocent's changes made his document more or less Franciscan and to the liking of Clare and other sisters like Agnes of Prague. Also list those elements that continued to disappoint Clare and Agnes.

Cited sources and suggested reading

- Makowski, Elizabeth. *Canon Law and Cloistered Women:* Periculo-so *and Its Commentators, 1298-1545*. Studies in Medieval and Early

Modern Canon Law 5. Washington DC: The Catholic University of America Press, 1997.

- Mooney, Catherine. *Clare of Assisi and the Thirteenth-Century Church: Religious Women, Rules, and Resistance.* Philadelphia: University of Pennsylvania Press, 2016. An excellent summary of current research on the history of the "Order of St. Clare" through the 1260s. Mooney breaks new ground in suggesting that the commonly discounted *Privilege of Poverty* once thought to be issued by Innocent III may actually have been issued by Innocent IV (161-167); that Cardinal Rainaldo (later Alexander IV) was the main force behind the failure of Innocent IV's *Form of Life* and not Clare of Assisi's resistance (135-160); and that Cardinal Rainaldo may have had a more substantial and definitive role in the final redaction of Clare's own *Form of Life* than previously thought (161-196).

The Form of Life of Saint Clare
1252
(CA:ED 108-126)

Sources

1LF
2LF
RH
ER
LR
Last Will
Test
2C 185, 204
FLFr
The Rule of St. Benedict
FLHug
PrPov
FLInn
FLCl

Dating and authorship

Clare's own *Form of Life* is reliably dated 1252. Cardinal Rainaldo first approved it on September 16, 1252 in his letter *Quia vos*. However, Clare successfully sought papal approval so that no one could later renege on the Privilege of Poverty which she enshrined in her *Form of Life*. Pope Innocent IV approved Clare's *Form of Life* in his bull *Solet annuere* dated August 9, 1253, two days before Clare's death.

The authorship of this document requires explanation. First, Clare's *Form of Life* itself includes two other documents written by Francis: an abbreviated version of Francis's *Form of Life* given to Clare (FLCl VI 3-4) and his *Last Will* for the sisters (FLCl VI 7-9). These, obviously, were written by Francis. In addition, Clare's own *Form of Life* utilized many references to and quotations from *The Earlier* and *Later Rules* of Francis.

Second, Clare's *Form of Life* borrowed many ideas from the forms of life previously given by Cardinal Ugolino and Pope Innocent IV. Certainly, without including provisions for the enclosure and fasting, Clare would not have received approval for her own *Form of Life*. A comparison among those documents and Clare's *Form of Life* shows that Clare's ideas on these and other topics come from those previous documents. Pope Gregory IX's *Privilege of Poverty* also was a source. Going back even further in time, ideas from the *Rule of St. Benedict* are found throughout Clare's *Form of Life*.

Third, the Latin used in Clare's *Form of Life* is quite good, and many believe that Bro. Leo of Assisi was acting as a secretary for Clare, as he had for Francis and possibly some of Clare's letters to Agnes of Prague. Related to that idea, Catherine Mooney in *Clare of Assisi and the Thirteenth-Century* argues that Cardinal Rainaldo or his assistant is a likely person to have redacted a final version of this *Form of Life* from all the various sources listed above. Mooney would also add the living community at San Damiano Monastery as an author, since many parts of the *Form of Life* speak in the first person plural (we) or refer to the community (161-196).

It is clear that Clare did not sit at a table and write this *Form of Life* by herself. It was a collaborative venture that likely extended over a considerable amount of time. However, we need to remember that this was not an uncommon occurrence in the Middle Ages.

Finally, the text, especially chapter six on poverty, contains personal testimonies from Clare. Her voice is clearly present and dominant among the variety of other visible voices.

With all these understandings, scholars reliably attribute authorship to Clare of Assisi.

Commentary

It's clear that Clare's *Form of Life* uses Francis's *Later Rule* as an organizational reference point. Perhaps this shouldn't surprise us since scholars increasingly thing Leo of Assisi had a role in writing both. Chapters six and ten of the *Later Rule* appear in their entirety in Clare's document. Parts of most other chapters in the *Later Rule* are incorporated into Clare's as well. The exception is chapter nine of the *Later Rule* on preaching, a topic not applicable to the Poor Sisters who could not preach publicly.

As noted above, Clare borrowed many themes and words from other sources. However, when she did so, she often liberalized the text by which we mean she made it less specific, open to exceptions and less legalistic. Still, she covered all the themes important to please the papacy from which she needed approval, including enclosure, fasting, talking, silence, and invisibility.

While the document is obviously trying to imitate some of the organization of Francis's *Later Rule* and include ideas important to the papacy, it inserts a very strong proclamation of radical and complete personal and corporate poverty in chapter six. That makes Clare's focus on poverty very evident in her *Form of Life*. Joan Mueller quantifies this emphasis by observing that Clare's writing in her *Form of Life* about the visitor, chaplain and cardinal protector is about one-third the length of that in the forms of life given by Ugolino and Innocent IV. On the other hand, her writing about poverty is about two-thirds longer than in those same documents or even that found in Francis's *Later Rule* (*A Companion* 211). For Clare, absolute individual and communal poverty was *the* important principle to definitively establish in her *Form of Life*.

Just before dying, Clare of Assisi received papal approval of her *Form of Life* that would ensure absolute poverty in imitation of Christ at the center of her life. Clare also made history in that this was the first ecclesiastically approved rule or form of life written by a woman. Finally, Clare's new *Form of Life* was approved in contradiction to the Fourth Lateran Council that prohibited new religious rules. What led up to the change in papal policy that previously resisted giving Clare what she wanted?

Frankly, we know more about what happened than *why* it happened. There is no reason to believe that Roman officials changed their opinion that female religious needed a more stable financial foundation to keep their monasteries viable. In fact, the papal bull approving Clare's *Form of Life* did that only for Clare's community at San Damiano Monastery. Other monasteries that claimed the heritage of Clare were not given this new rule when Clare received it. It seems most likely that the Holy See, in one way or another, was worn down by Clare's constant petitions for exemptions from the various forms of life forced upon her. Also, perhaps her fame made it politically difficult to refuse her.

The papal bull *Solet annuere* containing her own *Form of Life* was hand delivered to Clare on August 10th, 1253. She is reputed to have kissed it frequently. Clare died the next day. It should be noted that Honorius III approved Francis's *Later Rule* in 1223 with a bull by the same name. The two should not be confused.

Students of Clare's *Form of Life* need to pay special attention to chapter six in which Clare reported parts of a *Form of Life* that Francis of Assisi gave to her and the other Poor Sisters at San Damiano Monastery. The same chapter contains a *Last Will* from Francis of Assisi for the Poor Sisters. In some earlier editions of the primary sources for Clare's life and writings, these texts were lifted out of her *Form of Life* and listed as separate documents authored by Francis. Today, most authors refrain from doing this, being content to note their presence in chapter six of Clare's *Form of Life*.

Clare's *Form of Life* is the only textual evidence of what Francis might have given to the Poor Sisters. Its essential element is the admonition that the sisters live an evangelical life. While this term needs to be understood as Francis understood it, it should be noted that absolute poverty is not explicitly mentioned (see our earlier chapter section on the evangelical movement). The quotation also expresses Francis's promise that the Friars Minor will always have care and solicitude for the Poor Clares. That will be a subsequent source of conflict with the Friars Minor whose later leadership frequently resisted such responsibility.

Note that neither the bull of Clare's canonization (*Clara claris praeclara*), the *Versified Legend* nor the *Prose Legend* mention that Clare achieved approval for her own *Form of Life*. Only the *Acts of the Process of Canonization* and the text of her *Form of Life* itself are early witnesses to its existence.

Starter questions and suggestions

The *Rule* of the Friars Minor is considered to be a single document with multiple glimpses during its development. This allows that *Rule* to be studied as a development, the approach Workbook I took. Clare's situation was quite different. Clare's own *Form of Life* must be considered its own composition, albeit utilizing many sources, including the forms of life provided by Francis, Ugolino and Innocent IV; Francis's *Later Rule*; the *Privilege of Poverty* given by Gregory IX; the *Rule of St. Benedict*; and various Cistercian documents.

We believe two approaches can help a beginner come to appreciate Clare's text. The first is to read Clare's text in tandem with Francis's *Later Rule*. In so doing, a student should be attentive to material that Clare took directly from Francis. Likewise, it is instructive to identify those parts of Clare's *Form of Life* that are uniquely her own. Identify which are unique simply because enclosed women would have different needs and situations to address. Note how Clare embodied Franciscan values in the unique situation of enclosed Franciscan women.

The history of legislation for the Poor Sisters makes it clear that Clare had a vision not shared or appreciated by many church leaders. Thus, a second useful exercise is to read Clare's *Form of Life* while comparing it to those given by Ugolino and Innocent IV. Note what Clare accepts into her own rule. Pay attention to what Clare changes or does not accept. Explain each of Clare's variations from the earlier forms. Describe how each of the three forms does or does not express Clare and Francis's vision of evangelical life.

Joan Mueller's *A Companion* contains a very helpful yet brief primer on each chapter of Clare's *Form of Life*, which can help any reader study the text more beneficially (209-257). Here we offer questions a student can attempt to answer as she or he compares Clare's *Form of Life* with Francis's *Later Rule* or the forms of life given by Ugolino and Innocent IV.

Chapter One
In the Name of the Lord Begins the Form of Life of the Poor Sisters

How does Clare's name for her community vary from those used by others? While others might prefer to use "ladies" or "nuns" to describe individual members, how does Clare refer to the members of her community? Who is the founder of her community? What is the key purpose of Clare's community as found in chapter one? How might Clare consider her obedience to the pope in comparison with her obedience to Francis? In what ways does Clare take elements from the *Later Rule* but change them to express her unique approach to female Franciscan life? While enclosure and dietary regulation are key to the Ugolinian identity of female religious, what value(s) does (do) Clare bring to the forefront?

Chapter Two
Those Who Want to Accept This Life and How They Are to be Received

How does the admission process for the Poor Sisters differ from that of the Friars Minor in the *Later Rule*? What is the interplay between inspiration of the Spirit and legal prescriptions?

Chapter Three
The Divine Office and Fasting, Confession and Communion

How does practical life influence prayer? Note how the brothers attending to the sisters might share in their prayer. Clare's fasting norms were probably more practical than idealistic. Note how the absolute poverty of the Poor Sisters probably made further dietary regulation unnecessary. Describe the relationship between poverty and fasting.

Chapter Four
The Election of the Abbess

Note that an elected abbess who had not yet vowed to the form of the sisters' poverty was not to be obeyed. This likely referred to the inclination of local nobility to impose a family member as abbess on the community. How is egalitarianism visible in the *Form of Life*? How is the abbess, vicaress, and novice director like and different from everyone else? Clare had strong expectations for the local chapter. Francis's *Rule* focused more on the chapter of the entire Order. How does this difference express itself in the experience of the sisters? How is power and influence in the community balanced?

Chapter Five
Silence, the Parlor and the Grille

What was the purpose and role of silence in the monastery? How might Clare's *Form of Life* have differed from other documents regarding silence? How did the grill function within the need for silence?

Chapter Six
The Lack of Possessions

Chapter six is without doubt the most unique and therefore important chapter in Clare's *Form of Life*. It is important to understand how autobiographical this chapter is, containing testimony about promises and documents from Francis that began the gradual development of a life of absolute poverty at San Damiano Monastery. Here, the voice of Clare is more evident than in other chapters. While there is influence from the previous forms of life given to the sisters, it is muted by the clear voice and experience of Clare herself.

Note again that obedience is given to Francis, not to the pope or even the local bishop. Why might that be important in this chapter on poverty? What importance does that give to the text given by Francis?

Because of enclosure or its absence, the lifestyle of the brothers was quite different from that of the sisters. So, what united them? What common bond was expressed differently by the two groups?

Explain the impact of the *Form of Life* that Francis gave to the sisters early in their formation and his *Last Will Written for the Poor Ladies* near his death. Note how chapter six is a "library" of sources.

Chapter Seven
The Manner of Working

Clare's choice of absolute poverty and acceptance of enclosure have poignant consequences. Other nuns who did not embrace corporate poverty relied on the support of their rents and the labor of others. This automatically put them in the higher classes of society. The Poor Sisters at San Damiano Monastery, on the other hand, embraced corporate poverty, meaning they would have to engage in considerable manual labor themselves. Thus, manual work was not so much an ascetical practice as a simple necessity of everyday life for the Poor Sisters.

By not accepting endowments, the Poor Sisters refused to position themselves in the higher ranks of society and did not become overlords of poor people. In fact, these women entered the ranks of the poor themselves. This significantly contributed to the unique identity of Clare's vision of religious life.

Explain how this situation plays out in chapter seven about manual work. Pay attention to the unique role of alms given to the sisters in light of their economic situation.

Chapter Eight
The Sisters Shall Not Acquire Anything as Their Own, the Sick Sisters

Chapter six established Clare's principle of absolute poverty. Chapter seven elaborated on that by discussing the need for manual labor in the absence of others to do this for the sisters. Chapter eight continues this elaboration by describing the dwelling of the sisters and their seeking of alms. The beginning of chapter eight in Clare's *Form of Life* is nearly a direct quotation of chapter six in Francis's *Later Rule*. The later part of Clare's chapter deals with factors more particular to the situation of enclosed women. Note the focus on egalitarianism in these matters and how class stratification is obliterated in the lifestyle of the Poor Sisters.

Once again, the needs of the sick are mentioned for particular attention. Their situation also alerts us to the common-sense practicality that was part of Clare's vision of religious life, despite its high ideals about absolute poverty. As you did while studying other parts of Clare's *Form of Life*, you may want to consider here how rules and regulations do not govern the sisters' lives as much as the principle of poverty in conversation with the everyday needs of the sisters. The principle of promoting sororal relationships, which is related to the egalitarianism of the monastery, is very important here.

Chapter Nine
The Penance to be Imposed on the Sisters Who Sin

Chapter nine deals with disciplining disruptive sisters, by which Clare mostly means a sister not following their form of poverty. More than a list of offenses, this involves a violation of the most prized value of the monastery: absolute poverty in the context of enclosed *sisters*. So, poverty and sisterhood are the principles at stake.

Chapter nine concludes with consideration of serving sisters. Their role is largely undefined. However, it is clear that they made the same profession as the other sisters and lived the same life with the exception that they were allowed to go outside the enclosure for unspecified reasons. Consider how the presence of sisters working outside the cloister might affect the rhythm of life at San Damiano Monastery. Is this practice related in any way to Francis's *Rule for Hermitages* (see Downing *Document on Solitude*)?

Chapter Ten
The Admonition and Correction of the Sisters

This chapter describes the relationship between the abbess and the other sisters, and the behaviors and attitudes that attend it. Note the images and metaphors used to describe this relationship. Write a summary of the relationship in your own words.

Chapter Eleven
The Portress and Those Who Are Allowed to Enter the Monastery

Some of the sources listed below underscore that, while Clare accepted the enclosure, it was not the core of her charismatic identity. Poverty in the context of a sororal community was. Still, Clare obviously had to include comments on the enclosure in her *Form of Life* since it was considered the central aspect of female religious life in the forms of life of Ugolino and Innocent IV. Without doing so, Clare's *Form of Life* would not have been approved by church authorities.

For now, note that Clare reduced Ugolino's comments about the enclosure to about one-fourth and Innocent's to about one-third. This alone indicates the relative importance of enclosure for Clare. Clare's remaining material on this subject comes from the two popes' forms of life. Compare the three sources, striving to understand the kernel that remained important for Clare.

Chapter Twelve
The Visitator, the Chaplain, the Cleric and the Alms

Clare concluded her *Form of Life* with a chapter describing the relationship of the Poor Sisters with the Friars Minor and church officials. These were difficult subjects for Clare. She always insisted that Francis had promised to care for the Poor Sisters in perpetuity, but after his death fewer friars wanted to offer this service, and ministers were increasingly wary of ministry to enclosed nuns.

Note that Clare cuts the comments of Ugolino's *Form of Life* on this subject in half, and those of Innocent IV's *Form of Life* by one-fourth. It can be very useful to read and compare this chapter with three other documents: the *Later Rule* of Francis of Assisi, the *Form of Life* given by Ugolino (1219) and the *Form of Life* given by Innocent IV (1247). Discern how Clare's life-long struggles are visible in the texts.

Cited sources and suggested reading

- Alberzoni, Maria Pia. *Clare of Assisi and the Poor Sisters in the Thirteenth Century.* St. Bonaventure NY: Franciscan Institute Publications, 2004.

- Beha, Marie. "'Go Forth Swiftly.'" *The Cord* 40.7 (1990) 211-221.

- Blastic, Michael W, Jay M Hammond, and J. A. Wayne Hellmann, eds. *The Writings of Clare of Assisi: Letters, Form of Life, Testament and Blessing.* Studies in Early Franciscan Sources 3. St. Bonaventure NY: Franciscan Institute Publications, 2011.

- Downing, Frances Teresa. *Saint Clare of Assisi: The Context of Her Life.* Vol. 2. Phoenix AZ: Tau Publishing, 2012. Pp. 11-14.

- —. *Saint Clare of Assisi: The Original Writings.* Vol 1. Phoenix: Tau, 2012.

- —. "St. Clare and the *Document on Solitude.*" In *Prayer of Franciscan Solitude.* Eds. André Cirino and Josef Raischl. Phoenix AZ: Tau Publishing, 2018. 25-48. Downing argues that the Poor Sisters' early life at San Damiano Monastery and Clare's *Form of Life* were significantly influence by Francis's *Document on Solitude*, also called his *Rule for Hermitages.*

- Federazione S. Chiara di Assisi delle Clarisse di Umbria-Sardegna: Sinossi Cromatica. *Chiara de Assisi e le Sue Fonti Legislative.* Vol. 1. Padova: Edizioni Messaggero, 2003. Frances Teresa Downing uses this source as the critical edition of Clare's *Form of Life* for her translation, *Saint Clare of Assisi: The Original Writings.* Vol 1. Phoenix: Tau, 2012.

- Godet-Calogeras, Jean-François. "Clare the Woman, as Seen in Her Writings." Trans. Paul Barrett. *Greyfriars Review* 4.3 (1990) 7-30.

- ——. "From Brother Francis to the Poor Sisters of San Damiano: What Is Left of Their Correspondence?" In *Her Bright Merits: Essays Honoring Ingrid J. Peterson, OSF."* Eds. Mary Walsh Meany and Felicity Dorsett. Spirit and Life 17. St. Bonaventure NY: Franciscan Institute Publications, 2012. 61-81. Godet-Calogeras writes about the *Form of Life* given by Francis of Assisi on pages 65-70. Clare inserted it into chapter six of her own *Form of Life.*

- ——. "Structure of The Form of Life of Clare." In *An Unencumbered Heart: A Tribute to Clare of Assisi 1253-2003.* Eds. Jean-François Godet-Calogeras and Roberta McKelvie. Spirit and Life 11. St. Bonaventure NY: Franciscan Institute Publications, 2004. 1-9. A short and easy to read work including a summary of the contents of Clare's *Form of Life*, its transformation from a continuously running manuscript to a document with 12 chapters, and its manuscript tradition.

- Grau, Engelbert. "Saint Clare's *Privilegium Paupertatis*: Its History and Significance." Trans. M. Jane Frances. *Greyfriars Review* 6.3 (1992) 327-336.

- Ingham, Mary Beth. "The Logic of the Gift: Clare of Assisi and Franciscan Evangelical Life." *The Cord* 60.3 (2010) 243-256. This short article is a wonderful synopsis of the history of Clare's *Form of Life*, the importance of poverty, and the evangelical nature of Clare's life.

- Iriarte, Lazaro. "Clare of Assisi: Her Place in Female Hagiography." Trans. Ignatius McCormick. Greyfriars *Review* 3.2 (1989) 173-206.

- Leslie Knox. "The Form of Life of the Poor Ladies." In *The Writings of Clare of Assisi: Letters, Form of Life, Testament and Blessing.* Eds. Michael W. Blastic, Jay M. Hammond, and J. A. Wayne Hellmann. St. Bonaventure NY: Franciscan Institute Publications, 2011.

61-107. Probably the best thumbnail introduction to the technical study of Clare's *Form of Life.*

- —. "One and the Same Spirit: Clare of Assisi's *Form of Life* in the Later Middle Ages." *Franciscan Studies* 64 (2006) 235-254.

- Lainati, Chiara A. "The Enclosure of St. Clare and the First Poor Clares in Canonical Legislation and in Practice." *The Cord* 28 (1978) 4-15, 47-60.

- Lynn, Beth. "The Body and the Text: The Community at San Damiano That Produced the Text Known as *The Form of Life of the Poor Sisters.*" In *Her Bright Merits: Essays Honoring Ingrid J. Peterson, OSF.*" Eds. Mary Walsh Meany and Felicity Dorsett. Spirit and Life 17. St. Bonaventure NY: Franciscan Institute Publications, 2012. Lynn argues that the title of what is commonly called the *Form of Life of Saint Clare* should instead be called the *Form of Life of the Poor Sisters*, and that the entire community at San Damiano Monastery should be considered the author.

- Makowski, Elizabeth. *Canon Law and Cloistered Women: Periculoso and Its Commentators, 1298-1545.* Studies in Medieval and Early Modern Canon Law 5. Washington DC: The Catholic University of America Press, 1997.

- McGrane, Colleen Maura. "The Rule of Virgins: The Evolution of Enclosure." *The American Benedictine Review* 59 (2008) 396-418.

- McKelvie, Roberta. "Clare's Rule: Weaving Together Law and Life." In *Clare of Assisi: Investigations.* Ed. Mary Francis Hone. Clare Centenary Series 7. St. Bonaventure NY: Franciscan Institute Publications, 1993. 1-20. An easy-to-read description of how Clare weaved together the emerging canon law of her day with her evangelical vision and a helpful comparison of the early forms of life under which she lived. However, because it predates subsequent research, this article incorrectly attributes the *Privilege of Poverty* to Innocent III in 1216 rather than to Gregory IX in 1228. Because of the incorrect dating, McKelvie also erroneously asserts that Clare requested a rule from Innocent III between 1215-1216 (pages 5-6).

- Mooney, Catherine. *Clare of Assisi and the Thirteenth-Century Church: Religious Women, Rules, and Resistance.* Philadelphia: University of Pennsylvania Press, 2016. An excellent summary of current research on the history of the "Order of St. Clare" through the 1260s. Mooney breaks new ground in suggesting that the commonly discounted *Privilege of Poverty* once thought to be issued by Innocent III may actually have been issued by Innocent IV (161-167); that Cardinal Rainaldo (later Alexander IV) was the main force behind the failure of Innocent IV's *Form of Life* (1247) and not Clare of Assisi's resistance (135-160); and that Cardinal Rainaldo may have had a more substantial and definitive role in the final redaction of Clare's *Form of Life* than previously thought (161-196).

- Mueller, Joan. *A Companion to Clare of Assisi: Life, Writings, and Spirituality.* Leiden: Brill, 2010. Pp. 209-257. An excellent study of Clare's *Form of Life* chapter by chapter.

- Papa, Diana. *The Poor Sisters of Saint Clare: Their Form of Life and Identity.* Trans. Frances Teresa Downing. Phoenix AZ: Tau, 2010. Papa provides a chapter-by-chapter commentary on Clare's *Form of Life*, comparing it to the *Rule* of Pope Urban (1263) and *The General Constitutions of the Poor Clares.*

- Petroff, Elizabeth. "A Medieval Woman's Utopian Vision: The Rule of Clare of Assisi." In *Body and Soul: Essays on Medieval Women and Mysticism.* Oxford: Oxford University Press, 1994. 66-79.

- Rofe, Sandra and Agnes van Baer. "St. Clare's Expression of the Spirit and Rule of St. Francis." *Greyfriars Review* 2.2 (1988) 101-111.

- Sainte-Marie, Henri de. "Presence of the Benedictine Rule in the Rule of Saint Clare." Trans. Sergius Wroblewski. *Greyfriars Review* 6.1 (1992) 49-65.

- Sr. Mary Clare. "The Finding of the Body of Saint Clare." *The Cord* 35.September (1985) 247-253.

- Van den Goorbergh, Edith. *As Pilgrims and Strangers. Clare of Assisi's Form of Life of the Poor Sisters: A Spiritual Model of Transformation.* Delhi: Media House, 2012.

- Van Leeuwen, Peter. "Clare's Rule." Trans. Joseph Oudeman. *Greyfriars Review* 1.1(1987) 65-76. This is a very cogent and concise summary of the development of Clare's *Form of Life* over the decades of the 1200's. However, much of its content about the *Privilege of Poverty* doubtfully attributed to Pope Innocent III predates more recent research placing its existence in doubt.

Clare's Expression of Governance

Commentary

Clare's *Form of Life* and her own lived experience at San Damiano Monastery provide an interesting study of her leadership within the monastery. It is best understood and appreciated when juxtaposed to developments in her day. In previous centuries, various monastic rules prevailed in the West, notably St. Benedict's and St. Augustine's. These envisioned a monastic form of life that predated the penitential, evangelical and apostolic life movements with their attendant spiritual aspirations (See our chapter entitled "Pre-Francsican Movements"). Their idea of leadership involved an abbess who pretty much possessed and exercised dictatorial powers, although, through the Cistercian reform, the monastery chapter meeting became an important new structure allowing the entire community to be involved in decision making.

It is clear that, shortly after Clare founded San Damiano Monastery, the papacy sought to control female religious life by forcing women to follow the *Rule of St. Benedict* first as supplemented by Cardinal Ugolino's *Form of Life* and later by Pope Innocent IV's *Form of Life*. Structures in these documents were from the monastic model. Clare resisted them for reasons described in our chapter, "Who Founded the Order of St. Clare?" What is important for this study is to realize that Clare's desires also affected the way she governed San Damiano Monastery. In written form, we see Clare's desires in her own *Form of Life*. However, we also see them in the way she lived at and led the community at San Damiano Monastery. Your study of her style of governance will be most fruitful if you can compare her pattern to those that preceded her or that she resisted.

Starter suggestions and questions

Throughout your study, pay attention to the difference in the quality and quantity of information received from Clare's own *Form of Life* compared to the other sources.

What were Clare and Francis's attitudes toward calling Clare and her successors "abbess"? Was accepting this title a political accommodation or a genuine acquiescence? How did Clare's service to the community act as an antidote to any concern she had about taking the title "abbess"? How might you describe her *style* of leadership in modern categories?

How did Clare describe the role of abbess? What images did she use to do so? What personal qualities must an abbess have exhibited? How should suitable candidates for abbess have been discerned? What was the relationship between the choice of abbess and families in the area of the monastery trying to exert influence? What was the relationship between the abbess and the formation of new sisters, the sacramental practice of the sisters, and the sick? What kind of general needs of sisters should the abbess have addressed? How do Clare's expectations for an abbess compare to Thomas of Celano's description of the ideal leader of the Friars Minor found in 2C 185?

What was the abbess's role in correcting other sisters, and the relationship of conscience to correction? How did weekly chapters figure into that practice, and community consultation and organization? Medieval female monasteries were typically filled with noble nuns and lower-class servants. How was San Damiano different? How were resources received from the wealthy families of sisters distributed? How were chapters used to teach the sisters? Who elected or appointed abbesses and other sisters to positions in the monastery? If the *Forms of Life* of Ugolino and Innocent IV are part of your study, check to see if they include the same provisions about chapters and leadership found in Clare's own *Form of Life*.

The Visitator was a key component of Ugolino's plan for governing monasteries in his Order of St. Damian. What was the role of the visitator in Clare's *Form of Life*? How was her vision different from that presented in the forms of life by Ugolino and Innocent IV? In these various documents, what was the visitor most concerned about? What was the difference between a chaplain and a visitator? What was the role of the Friars Minor in providing either? What do Clare's writings disclose about her ideas for the relationship between the Poor Sisters and the Friars Minor?

What purposes for authority can you see in Clare's example? What was she trying to do through authority?

Read the forms of life given by Ugolino and Innocent IV and answer the same questions regarding them. Compare the answers to those you discovered when considering Clare's *Form of Life*.

Cited sources and suggested reading

- Carney, Margaret. *The First Franciscan Woman: Clare of Assisi and Her Form of Life*. Quincy IL: Franciscan Press, 1993. Chapter 5 extensively discusses government, enclosure and visitators (173-215).

- Gennaro, Clara. "Clare, Agnes and the First Sisters: from the "Pauperes Dominae" of San Damiano to the Poor Clares." Trans. Lori Pieper. *Greyfriars Review* 9.3 (1995) 259-276.

- Godet-Calogeras, Jean-François. "Clare as Administrator: Changing the Paradigm." *Franciscan Connections* 6.3 (2016) 9-10.

- Mueller, Joan. "Poverty Legislation and Mutual Relations in the Early Franciscan Movement." *Collectanea Franciscana* 71 (2001) 389-419.

Clare's *Testament*
(CA:ED 60-65)

Sources

TestCl

Authorship and authenticity

Most scholars today accept Clare as the author of this *Testament*. However, many consider it a compilation of Clare's sayings and thoughts, possibly collected after she died. This further implies that someone else or a group of people collected those sayings and thoughts. Leo of Assisi is high on the list of possible redactors, in part because we suspect he acted as Clare's secretary at other times and because the oldest known manuscript containing this *Testament* is in his handwriting. With all these caveats, most scholars consider Clare the author and the document authentic.

However, there is a complicated history to the scholarship about this *Testament*. We relate it here as briefly as possible for those interested. Those who are not interested can move on to our suggestions and starter questions below.

Frances Teresa Downing simply and clearly summarizes four main reasons why various scholars through the years have doubted the authenticity of Clare's *Testament* (*Saint Clare of Assisi: The Original Writings* 237-239):

1. The absence of an early manuscript tradition;

2. No mention of Clare's *Testament* until the Observant Reform of the Poor Clares (the Messina Manuscript of 1445);

3. The mention of a *Privilege of Poverty* by Innocent III (supposedly given in 1216) in that earliest manuscript, which was of doubtful origin, thus casting every work in the manuscript into suspicion, including Clare's *Testament;*

4. A writing style different from Clare's letters to Agnes of Prague and *Form of Life*.

Through the 20th century, belief in the authenticity of *The Testament* was growing until 1995 when Werner Maleczek completed a detailed analysis of the *Privilege of Poverty* attributed to Innocent III and first contained in the Latin manuscript called the Messina Manuscript. The manuscript was found in the Poor Clare Monastery in Montevergine in Messina, Sicily and supposedly miraculously discovered by Eustochia Calafato (1434-1485). That means this first witness to a *Privilege of Poverty* from Innocent III in 1216 and Clare's *Testament* surfaced about 200 years after Clare's death.

Maleczek judged the *Privilege of Poverty* attributed to Innocent III in 1216 within this manuscript a hoax because it lacked the style and norms for writing during Innocent III's papacy. He further argued that the Poor Sisters at San Damiano Monastery had no need for such a privilege or exemption in 1216 since they didn't yet live under a rule or form of life at odds with their desired lifestyle. Maleczek concluded that this 15th-century forgery likely emanated from the Observant Reform that sought the return of the Poor Clares to the early traditions of Clare. He concluded that the plot started at the Poor Clare Monastery at Monteluce in Perugia, which he believed produced other suspicious manuscripts.

Maleczek further concluded that, if Innocent III did not give such a privilege, Clare's *Testament,* which is first found in the same Messina Manuscript, must also be a forgery. His objection wasn't just that the manuscript was not reliable, but that the text of the *Testament* assumed the existence of Innocent III's privilege, which Maleczek proved was not authentic. In her "supposed" *Testament*, Clare wrote: "Moreover, for greater security, I took care to have our profession of the most holy poverty that we promised our father strengthened with privileges by the Lord Pope Innocent, in whose time we had our beginning, and by his other successors, that we would never in any way turn away from her" (TestCl 42-43). The scholarly world was largely convinced by these and other arguments by Maleczek. Clare's *Testament* was included in the hoax.

At the moment when Maleczek's argument seemed to be winning the day among scholars, Bartoli Langeli conducted a handwriting study concluding that the Messina Manuscript was actually dated in the late 13th century. Langeli argued that Leo of Assisi likely handwrote the Messina Manuscript toward the end of his life (d. c. 1270).

Maleczek's concerns about the style of the *Testament* were further undermined in 2003 when Leonhard Lehmann argued that all the letters of Clare to Agnes displayed a style consistent with that of the Roman Curia, suggesting she had help writing all her documents. He then studied the themes and expressions of the letters and the *Testament* and concluded they were similar, suggesting the authenticity of the *Testament* and Leo's role as scribe.

Leo of Assisi is increasingly accepted as a key player in all these activities. Bartoli Langeli determined that the Messina Manuscript was written in his hand. We know Leo was present at Clare's death and when testimony was taken for the *Acts of the Process of Canonization.* This suggests he was frequently around San Damiano Monastery and Clare. Further, all of Clare's writings, like those of so many other medieval authors, show the hand of secretaries who took dictations, filled in and polished the texts, and included other recalled sayings by the same person. Thus, increasingly, Leo is seen as a compiler of thoughts and texts preserved at San Damiano. This may be as true for the *Assisi Compilation* that Leo helped write about Francis of Assisi as it is for Clare's *Testament* and other writings.

Finally, scholars began to take greater note that Clare's *Testament* does not specifically identify Innocent III as the author of the *Privilege of Poverty.* It more accurately testifies that Innocent and his successors issued an undetermined number of privileges. Clare could easily have been referencing Gregory IX as the author of her *Privilege of Poverty.*

Alessandra Bartolomei Romagnoli (Il testamento 245) describes Clare's *Testament* as a "composite" document that weaves together numerous things, including various actual sayings of Clare, other early Franciscan documents like Francis's own *Testament*, the text of Francis prophesying that the Poor Ladies would live at San Damiano, and aspects of Clare's own *Form of Life*. Thus, it may actually have been "composed" (i.e., the various parts brought together) after Clare died, even though the various parts all predated her death. In this view, Clare's *Testament* represents the memory of those who survived her, picking out what they remembered to be of importance, and gathering the parts together so nothing would be forgotten. From their perspective, these memories are Clare's *Testament,* and Romagnoli finds no difficulty considering it an "authentic" text, given this understanding.

While many of Maleczek's arguments definitively proved that Innocent III could not have written a *Privilege of Poverty,* his arguments that the entire Messina Manuscript is a forgery, including Clare's *Testament* and *Blessing* which it contains, is increasingly discounted. Bartoli Langeli's study is convincing more and more scholars that these writings are authentic, even if they show the presence of collaborators, which was not uncommon in the Middle Ages.

Those who want to delve into the manuscript tradition around the *Testament* should read Blastic's chapter on "Clare's Testament" in *The Writings of Saint Clare* 109-123. It is an excellent summary of this entire saga. An English translation of Maleczek's article is included in the bibliography below.

Starter questions and suggestions

Last testaments are typically emotional and look back to the beginning of lifelong projects. Clare's is no different. We count her referencing Francis 28 times in her *Testament*. Many refer to Francis's early interaction with Clare. Locate as many of these references as you can. Sometimes they are not so obvious, so read carefully. Locate and study the note that Francis wrote a form of life for Clare. Examine a similar note in her own *Form of Life* (FLCl VI 3-4). Explain how the two notes are related. What else did Francis write to the Poor Sisters according to Clare's *Testament*? The building of San Damiano was important to both Francis and Clare. Discover and explain references to the building in Clare's *Testament*.

To help you understand how Clare's *Testament* described Francis's relationship to Clare and the early Poor Sisters, answer the following questions:

- What was his role in the founding of the Poor Sisters?
- How did Clare envision her relationship with Francis?
- How did Francis influence Clare's vocation?
- What was the canonical relationship between Francis and Clare?
- How did Francis influence Clare's practice of poverty?
- What was the relationship between Francis's writings and Clare's *Form of Life*?
- What was Francis's role vis-á-vis the Poor Sisters after his death?

Clare's *Testament* devotes considerable space to the Poor Sisters' poverty, and the relationship between them and their abbess. Within this description, how does the *Testament* invoke the poor and humble Christ? Describe the characteristics of poverty that Clare promotes for her Poor Sisters.

Why might Clare's *Testament* spend so much time on the leadership of the abbess and the obedience of the other sisters? What are the leadership qualities espoused by the *Testament*? Why is the obedience of the other sisters so important to Clare?

Cited sources and suggested reading

- Bartoli Langeli, Attilio. *Gli Autografi di Frate Francesco e di Frate Leone.* Turnhout: Brepols, 2000. Bartoli Langeli's work matched the handwriting in the Messina manuscript with Leo of Assisi, thus changing the date of the manuscript containing Clare's *Testament* to before Leo's death in c. 1270.

- Blastic, Michael. "The Testament of Clare." In *The Writings of Clare of Assisi: Letters, Form of Life, Testament and Blessing.* Eds. Michael W. Blastic, Jay M. Hammond, and J. A. Wayne Hellmann. St. Bonaventure NY: Franciscan Institute Publications, 2011. 109-133. Blastic's description of the roller coaster debate over the authenticity of Clare's *Testament* is superb. In a very readable manner, he lays out the chronology of the debate, the central arguments in general and at each stage of the debate, and the current state of scholarly opinion. While the history of this debate may not be of interest to all beginners, it is the best place to begin for those who want to understand the debate. Those happy to simply accept the current state of opinion will find that within this chapter of the Workbook.

- Downing, Frances Teresa. *Saint Clare of Assisi: The Original Writings.* Vol 1. Phoenix: Tau, 2012. The most recent English translation of the writings of Clare based on the most recent critical editions.

- Iriarte, Lazaro. "Clare of Assisi: Her Place in Female Hagiography." Trans. Ignatius McCormick. Greyfriars *Review* 3.2 (1989) 173-206.

- Kuster, Niklaus. "Clare's Testament and Innocent's Privilege of Poverty: Genuine or Clever Forgeries?" *Greyfriars Review* 15.2 (2001) 171-252.

- Maleczek, Werner. "Questions about the Authenticity of the Privilege of Poverty of Innocent III and of the Testament of Clare of Assisi." Trans. Cyprian Rosen and Dawn Nothwehr. *Greyfriars Review* 12.Supplement (1998) 1-80.

- Mooney, Catherine. *Clare of Assisi and the Thirteenth-Century Church: Religious Women, Rules, and Resistance.* Philadelphia: University of Pennsylvania Press, 2016. Mooney's argument that the commonly discounted *Privilege of Poverty* once thought to be issued by Innocent III may actually have been issued by Innocent IV (161-167) is consistent with Bartoli Langeli's findings noted above and further supports the authenticity of Clare's *Testament.*

- Romagnoli, Alessandra Bartolomei. "Il testamento di s. Chiara nella spiritualità femminile medioevale." In *Dialoghi con Chiara de Assisi.* Ed. Luigi Giacometti. Santa Maria degli Angeli: Edizioni Porziuncola, 1995.

- —. "Women's Franciscanism from Its Beginnings Until the Council of Trent." Trans. Edward Hagman. *Greyfriars Review* 19.2 (2005) 91-168. A lengthy article that spectacularly places Clare of Assisi within the larger world of 13th-century women's female life and papal policy.

- Verheij, Sigismund. "Personal Awareness of Vocation and Ecclesiastical Authority as Exemplified in St. Clare of Assisi." Trans. Ignatius McCormick. *Greyfriars Review* 3.1 (1989) 35-42.

The Blessing of Clare
(CA:ED 66-67)

Sources

BlCl
LCl 45
Book of Numbers 6:24-26
BlL

Authorship

Jean-François Godet-Calogeras (Clare's Blessing 135) provides the most up-to-date and easy to understand explanation of scholarship about the authorship of Clare's *Blessing*. He notes that while there are various versions of the *Blessing* sent to different recipients, the most reliable manuscript tradition is that addressed to all the sisters.

The Messina Manuscript in the Poor Clare Monastery of Montevergine (Sicily) has already been discussed in our chapter on Clare's *Testament*. A brief review here is valuable but reading the worksheet on Clare's *Testament* might be interesting to the reader.

Clare's *Blessing* was increasingly considered authentic through most of the 20th century. That changed in 1995 when Werner Maleczek conducted a study of the Messina Manuscript that first contained Innocent III's supposed *Privilege of Poverty* and Clare's *Testament*. Maleczek noted that the *Privilege of Poverty* attributed to Innocent III did not follow the writing norms for papal documents at the time of Innocent. Further, there was no need for such a privilege or exemption in 1216 when Clare and the Poor Sisters were not yet living under a form of life opposed to their desired lifestyle. He deemed her *Testament* inauthentic because he judged that it included a reference to the discredited *Privilege of Poverty*. Both documents were contained in the Messina Manuscript. Since the *Blessing* was contained in the same manuscript, some deemed it inauthentic by association.

In 2000, Attilio Bartoli Langeli compared the handwriting in the Messina manuscript to that of Leo of Assisi in the *Chartula* of Francis of Assisi that contains both the *Praises of God* and a *Blessing* by Francis of Assisi given to Leo. Leo famously made comments in red around the document. Bartoli Langeli also compared the handwriting to that of

294

the *Breviary of Saint Francis* known to contain handwriting by Leo. He concluded that Leo of Assisi handwrote the Messina manuscript himself. That dates the manuscript not in the 1400s as Maleczek claimed, but before Leo's death c. 1270. While other arguments sustain Maleczek's conclusion that the *Privilege of Poverty* attributed to Innocent III in 1216 is inauthentic, his conclusions that the *Testament* and *Blessing* of Clare of Assisi were also inauthentic were undermined.

We also need to remember that Leo was close to both Francis and Clare. His association with Clare seemed to intensify after Francis's death, perhaps mutually preserving the more primitive remembrance of Francis and observance of Franciscan life. We know he was present at Clare's death (LCl 45).

There also is an important tradition holding that San Damiano Monastery preserved many writings of early companions, particularly of Leo, many of which entered the hagiographic tradition through the *Assisi Compilation* in its original simple form. Note that we do not have that version because the *Assisi Compilation* went through numerous developments and additions until 1311, the date of the oldest manuscript we have (see Workbook I, 77-82).

As with the *Testament*, this twist of research shifts the probability in favor of Clare as the author of the *Blessing*. Its likely date would be 1253, the year of Clare's death.

Starter questions and suggestions

This text yields little biographical information about Clare. However, begin by determining what biographical information can be ascertained. How does it portray Francis's relationship with Clare and the early sisters at San Damiano? Is this information consistent with other information about that relationship from earlier worksheets?

If Clare's deathbed was the origin of the *Blessing*, Clare clearly could not have written it down herself. Would the "transcriber" have had parchment and quill in hand to record Clare's words as spoken? Could her long blessing have been perfectly remembered for later transcription? Could a later author have polished a preexisting beautiful document she or he deemed worthy of the dying Clare?

The text clearly harkens back to Francis's own blessing for Leo of Assisi. Both use Aaron's famous blessing found in the *Book of Numbers*. Can you draw any conclusions from these observations?

The text displays a wide appeal to both men and women. Does this cause you to draw any conclusions?

Carefully reading the text can underscore spiritual themes that were important to Clare. What values surface as the most important?

Cited sources and suggested reading

- Bartoli Langeli, Attilio. *Gli Autografi di Frate Francesco e di Frate Leone.* Turnhout: Brepols, 2000. Bartoli Langeli's work matched the handwriting in the Messina manuscript with Leo of Assisi, thus changing the date of the manuscript containing the *Blessing* to before his death in c. 1270.

- Downing, Frances Teresa. *Saint Clare of Assisi: The Context of Her Life.* Vol. 2. Phoenix AZ: Tau Publishing, 2012. Pp. 17-18.

- Godet-Calogeras, Jean-François. "Clare's Blessing." In *The Writings of Clare of Assisi: Letters, Form of Life, Testament and Blessing.* Eds. Michael W. Blastic, Jay M. Hammond, and J. A. Wayne Hellmann. St. Bonaventure NY: Franciscan Institute Publications, 2011. 136-147. For more information about the controversy surrounding the Messina Manuscript, also see Michael Blastic's chapter in the same volume: "The Testament of Clare," 109-133.

- Kuster, Niklaus. "Clare's Testament and Innocent III's Privilege of Poverty: Genuine or Clever Forgeries?" *Greyfriars Review* 15.2 (2001) 171-252. Kuster was in quick disagreement with Maleczek's conclusion that the *Blessing* and other works associated with the Messina manuscript were hoaxes.

- Maleczek, Werner. "Questions About the Authenticity of the Privilege of Poverty of Innocent III and of the Testament of Clare of Assisi." *Greyfriars Review* 12.Supplement (1998) 1-80. Maleczek turned Clare studies upside-down when he seemed to prove that the Messina manuscript, thought to have originated in the Monteluce Monastery near Perugia under the influence of the Observant Reform of Poor Clares, was a hoax. This led many to believe the *Blessing of Clare* was inauthentic.

- Mooney, Catherine. *Clare of Assisi and the Thirteenth-Century Church: Religious Women, Rules, and Resistance.* Philadelphia: University of Pennsylvania Press, 2016. Mooney's argument that the commonly discounted *Privilege of Poverty* once thought to be issued by Innocent III may actually have been issued by Innocent IV (161-167) is consistent with Bartoli Langeli's findings noted above and further supports the authenticity of *The Blessing of Clare*.

Clare's Death and Funeral

Sources

VL XXXI—XXXIII
LCl XXVII—XXX

Starter questions and suggestions

The stories about Clare's final illness, death and funeral are quite straightforward. If you are preparing a presentation to a study group, we recommend that you focus on telling the story of these final days in narrative form. Your group will want to know the details.

After summarizing the events, discuss how various elements of Clare's spirituality continue to be expressed through the stories of her death. This technique in the hagiography heightens the sense that Clare was faithful to the end, just as she encouraged Agnes of Prague to do in her various letters.

Medieval hagiography is always interested in portraying miraculous events because it helps to achieve its goal, i.e. prove that the subject was indeed a saint. How does the miraculous figure into these final stories about Clare?

Notice that the *Acts of the Process of Canonization* does not talk about Clare's death. That makes sense since the testimony was taken just months after her death. All would likely assume that everyone was familiar with those events.

Suggested reading

- Downing, Frances Teresa. *Saint Clare of Assisi: The Context of Her Life*. Vol. 2. Phoenix AZ: Tau Publishing, 2012. Pp. 77-79 discusses Clare's Burial at San Giorgio.

The Notification of Clare's Death

Sources

The Notification of Clare's Death (CA:ED 135-138)

Starter questions and suggestions

Our treatment of the *Notification of Clare's Death* in the Tools section of this workbook already alerts us to the little historical information we can obtain from this document. See that chapter before working on this worksheet.

The dearth of scholarly studies about the document could cause us to question its reliability. However, there can be merit for a student of Clare to examine the meaning of Clare's life and spirituality that is presented in the notification. We offer you the following questions as you study the text and prepare a presentation for your study group.

Finally, if your study group is composed of few members, you may want to consider assigning the worksheets on the papal bull of Clare's canonization (*Clara claris praeclara*) and *The Notification of Clare's Death* to the same person. In that case, the presenter may want to compare the two documents, showing how the disorganized notification reached incredible literary height in the papal bull.

- Where does the document allude to historical facts about Clare?

- Examine how the document plays on themes of light, darkness and vision as so many other documents about Clare do. Obviously, these themes play on her name, *Chiara*, which can be translated in various ways associated with light, clearness, etc.

- How does the notification use mirror spirituality compared to Clare's four known letters to Agnes of Prague? In the notification, what images does the mirror reflect?

- What names and images are used to describe Jesus?

- What names and images are used to describe Clare? Note that there are many more images for Clare than for Jesus. What might that mean? What aspect of the historical Clare might each image reflect? What is the spirituality associated with each image?

- What is the role of prayer and contemplation as found in this document? How does it compare to Clare's own description of prayer in her second and fourth letters to Agnes of Prague?

- In your own modern language, tell your group what you think the sisters at San Damiano Monastery were trying to say about Clare.

Clara claris praeclara:
Alexander IV's Bull Canonizing Clare of Assisi

Sources

BC
1C 18-20
Acts of the Process of Canonization (references are almost everywhere)

Starter questions and suggestions

Clare was canonized by Pope Alexander IV at Anagni on August 15, 1255, though the papal bull of canonization, *Clara claris praeclara,* was not promulgated for another month or two.

We refer above to Thomas of Celano's *The Life of St. Francis* (1C 18-20) simply because it provides the imagery for Alexander's bull. Recall that *The Life of St. Francis* was completed about 27 years earlier. 1C 18 states: "She was steadfast in purpose and most eager in her desire for divine love; endowed with wisdom and excelling in humility; bright by name, brilliant by life, and most brilliant by character." *Clara claris praeclara* expands on this simple sentence for nine pages in CA:ED 263-271.

Our treatment of *Clara claris praeclara* in the Tools section of this workbook already alerts us to the little historical information we can obtain from this document. However, there can be merit for a student of Clare to examine the meaning of her life and spirituality presented in the bull. We offer you the following questions to consider as you study the text and prepare a presentation for your study group.

Finally, if your study group is composed of few members, you may want to consider assigning the worksheets on both this papal bull and *The Notification of Clare's Death* to the same person. In that case, the presenter may want to compare the two documents, showing how the disorganized notification reached incredible literary height in the papal bull.

- Where does the document allude to historical facts about Clare?

- Examine how the document plays on themes of light, darkness and vision as so many other documents about Clare do. Obviously, these themes play on her name, *Chiara*, which can be translated in various ways associated with light, clearness, etc.

- How does the document use mirror spirituality compared to Clare's four known letters to Agnes of Prague? In *Clara claris, praeclara*, what images does the mirror reflect?

- How does the document juxtapose Clare's life in the enclosure with her "brilliance"? What effects are asserted?

- What names and images are used to describe Jesus?

- What names and images are used to describe Clare? Note that there are many more images for Clare than for Jesus. What might that mean? What aspect of the historical Clare might each image reflect? What is the spirituality associated with each image?

- Among the images of Clare are numerous paradoxes of seeming opposites. List and explain them.

- What is the role of prayer and contemplation as found in this document? How does it compare to Clare's own description of prayer in her second and fourth letters to Agnes of Prague?

- How does the document characterize Clare's way of life? How might those characterizations serve the political goals of the papacy regarding female religious life? Refer to our chapter, "Who Founded the Poor Clares?" for more information. How might those characterizations have been accurate or not? What political struggles between Clare and various popes are visible in the document? How are they represented?

- How does this papal bull characterize Clare's distinctive style of leadership? Relate that to how Clare describes leadership in chapter four of her *Form of Life*. See our worksheet on Clare's own *Form of Life* for assistance.

- In your own modern language, tell your group what you think Pope Alexander was trying to say about Clare.

Suggested reading

- Pattenden, Miles. "The Canonization of Clare of Assisi and Early Franciscan History." *Journal of Ecclesiastical History* 59 (2008) 208-226.

Additional Bibliography

Accrocca, Felice. "Some Knotty Problems in the Franciscan Sources: Two Recent Editions." Trans. Edward Hagman. *Greyfriars Review* 11.2 (1997) 143-183. This is a very technical article that deals with questions about the dating, authenticity and importance of many sources for the life and writings of Francis and Clare of Assisi.

—. "The Unlettered One and His Witness: Footnotes to a Recent Volume on the Autographs of Brother Francis and Brother Leo." *Greyfriars Review* 16 (2002) 265-282.

Baker, Derek, ed. *Medieval Women*. Oxford: Blackwell, 1978.

Becker, Marie-France. *15 Days of Prayer with Saint Clare of Assisi*. Trans. Pacelli Millane. New York: New City Press, 2011.

—. "Praying with Clare of Assisi." *The Cord* 57.4 (1997) 185-93.

Bezunartea, Jesús María. "Clare of Assisi and the Discernment of Spirits." Trans. Paul Barrett. *Greyfriars Review* 8.Supplement (1994) 3-110.

Bigaroni, Marino. "The Church of San Giorgio in Assisi and the First Expansion of the Medieval Walls." Trans. Lori Pieper. *Greyfriars Review* 8.1 (1994) 57-101.

—. "San Damiano – Assisi: The First Church of St. Francis." Trans. Lori Pieper. *Franciscan Studies* 47 (1987) 45-97.

Blastic, Michael. "Clare of Assisi, the Eucharist and John 13." In *Clare of Assisi: A Medieval and Modern Woman: Clarefest Selected Papers*. Ed. Ingrid Peterson. Clare Centenary Series 8. St. Bonaventure NY: Franciscan Institute Publications, 1996. 21-45.

Boswell, John. *The Kindness of Strangers*. New York: Vintage Press, 1988. Discusses admission practices of medieval monasteries of women.

Brooke, Rosalind, and Christopher N. L. Brooke. "St. Clare." In *Medieval Women*. Ed. Derek Baker. Studies in Church History, Subsidia 1. Oxford: Basil Blackwell, 1978. 275-287.

Bruzelius, Caroline. "Hearing Is Believing: Clarissan Architecture, ca. 1213-1314." *Gesta: The International Center of Medieval Art* 31.2 (1992) 83-91.

Budzik, Helen B. and Roberta A. McKelvie. *Guidelines for the Study of Clare of Assisi.* Washington DC: Franciscan Federation Third Order Regular, 1992. At the time of publication, this was the preferred English guide for a critical study of St. Clare's life and writings. Because of the enormous amount of research since 1992, much of this study is now dated. However, it remains a good source for locating primary sources about the life of St. Clare.

Bullough, Vern and James Brundage. *Sexual Practices and the Medieval Church.* New York: Prometheus Books, 1994.

Clara Claris Praeclara. Atti del Convegno Internazionale: L'esperienza Cristiana e la memoria di Chiara d'Assisi in occasione del 750° anniversario della morte. Assisi 20-22 novembre 2003. Santa Maria degli Angeli: Edizioni Porziuncola, 2004.

Clare Centenary Series. Ed. Mary Francis Hone. 8 vols. St. Bonaventure NY: Franciscan Institute Publications, 1992-1996. A collection of eight publications celebrating the 800th anniversary of Clare of Assisi's birth. The first four are compendiums of primary source material with bearing on various aspects of Clare's life, the manner of life at San Damiano, values, and aspects of spirituality. Regis Armstrong and Pacelli Millane edited those first four volumes.

Coughlin, F. Edward. "Clare of Assisi: A Paradigm for Building Partnership." *New Theology Review* 9 (1996) 58-70.

Dhont, René-Charles. *Clare among Her Sisters.* Franciscan Pathways. St. Bonaventure NY: The Franciscan Institute, 1987.

Downing, Frances Teresa. *Living the Incarnation: Praying with Francis and Clare of Assisi.* Quincy IL: Franciscan Press, 1993.

—. *Saint Clare of Assisi: Her Charism.* Vol. 3. Phoenix AZ: Tau Publishing, 2012.

—. *This Living Mirror: Reflections on Clare of Assisi.* Maryknoll NY: Orbis, 1995.

Fonck, Benet A. *To Cling With All Her Heart to Him: The Spirituality of St. Clare of Assisi.* Quincy IL: Franciscan Press, 1996.

Godet-Calogeras, Jean-François. *Clare of Assisi, A Woman's Life.* Phoenix: Tau Publishing, 2013.

Godet-Calogeras, Jean-François, and Roberta McKelvie, Eds. *An Unencumbered Heart: A Tribute to Clare of Assisi 1253-2003.* Spirit and Life 11. St. Bonaventure NY: Franciscan Institute Publications, 2004.

Hubaut, Michael. "Christ, Our Joy: Learning to Pray with St. Francis and St. Clare." Trans. Paul Barrett. *Greyfriars Review* 9.Supplement (1995) 1-136.

Iriarte, Lazaro. "Saint Clare's Vocation in Faith and in Hope." Trans. Madonna Balestrieri. *Greyfriars Review* 6.3 (1992) 319-325.

Knox, Lezlie. "Clare of Assisi and Learning: A Foundation for Intellectual Life within the Franciscan Second Order." *The Cord* 46 (1996) 171-179.

Lainati, Chiara A. "Saint Clare of Assisi, A Beautiful Woman." Trans. Jayme Lee Mathias. *Greyfriars Review* 7.2 (1993) 151-166.

McNamara, Jo Ann. *Sisters in Arms: Catholic Nuns through Two Millennia.* Cambridge MA & London: Harvard University Press, 1996.

Miller, Ramona. *In the Footsteps of Saint Clare: A Pilgrim's Guide Book.* St. Bonaventure NY: Franciscan Institute Publications, 1993.

Miller, Ramona, and Ingrid Peterson. *Praying with Clare of Assisi.* Companions for the Journey Series. Winnona MN: Saint Mary's Press, 1994.

Mooney, Catherine. *Imitatio Christi* or *Imitatio Mariae?* Clare of Assisi and her Interpreters." In *Gendered Voices: Medieval Saints and their Interpreters.* Ed. Catherine Mooney. Philadelphia: University of Pennsylvania Press, 1999. 52-77.

Nugent, Madeline Pecora. *Clare and Her Sisters: Lovers of the Poor Christ.* Boston: Pauline Books and Media, 2003.

Pellegrini, Luigi. "Female Religious Experience and Society in Thirteenth-Century Italy." In *Monks and Nuns, Saints and Outcasts: Religion in Medieval Society.* Eds. Sharon Farmer and Barbara Rosenwein. Ithaca NY: Cornell University Press, 2000. 97-122.

Peterson, Ingrid. *Clare of Assisi: A Biographical Study.* Quincy IL: Franciscan Press, 1993.

Poor Clares of the Holy Name Federation and the Mother Bentivoglio Federation. *Doing What is Ours to Do: A Clarian Theology of Life.* St. Bonaventure NY: Franciscan Institute Publications, 2000.

Prini, Pietro. "St. Francis and St. Clare in the Medieval Mysticism of Love." Trans. Edward Hagman. *Greyfriars Review* 11.3 (1997) 301-309.

Ranft, Patricia. "An Overturned Victory: Clare of Assisi and the Thirteenth Church." *Journal of Medieval History* 17.2 (1991) 123-134.

Roest, Bert. "Education and Religious Formation in the Medieval Order of Poor Clares: Some Preliminary Observations." *Collectanea Franciscana* 73 (2003) 47-73.

Rubin, Miri. *Corpus Christi: The Eucharist in Late Medieval Culture.* Cambridge: The University of Cambridge Press, 1991.

Schatzlein, Joanne. "The Implications of Fasting and Illness in the Death of Clare of Assisi." In *Clare of Assisi: A Medieval and Modern Woman.* Ed Ingrid Peterson. Clare Centenary Series 8. St. Bonaventure NY: Franciscan Institute Publications, 1996. 75-84.

Schulenburg, Jane Tibbets. "Women's Monastic Communities, 500-1100: Patterns of Expansion and Decline." In *Sisters and Workers in the Middle Ages.* Eds. Judith M. Bennett, Elizabeth A. Clark, Jean F. O'Barr, B. Anne Vilen, and Sarah Wespahl-Wihl. Chicago: Chicago University Press, 1989.

Shahar, Shulamith. *The Fourth Estate: A History of Women in the Middles Ages.* London: Methuen, 1983.

Sister Christina. "Some Reflections on the Personality of St. Clare." Trans. Patrick Colbourne. *Greyfriars Review* 2.3 (1988) 57-62.

Sister Marie Aimée of Christ. "The Charism of St. Clare: A Prophecy for Women in Every Age." Trans. Charles Serignat. Greyfriars Review 1.1 (1987) 77-91.

Van Asseldonk, Optatus. "The Holy Spirit in the Writings and Life of St. Clare." Trans. Charles Serignat. *Greyfriars Review* 1.1 (1987) 93-104.

Van Dijk, Stephen. "The Breviary of St. Clare." *Franciscan Studies* 8 (1948) 25-46.

Vauchez, André. *Sainthood in the Later Middle Ages.* Trans. Jean Birrell. New York: Cambridge University Press, 1997.

Wood, Jeryldene. *Women, Art, and Spirituality: The Poor Clares of Early Modern Italy.* Cambridge: Cambridge University Press, 1996.

Wood, Susan. *The Proprietary Church in the Medieval West.* Oxford: Oxford University Press, 2006.

Index

Also Available from New City Press:

Studying the Life of Saint Francis of Assisi
A Beginner's Workbook

978-1-56548-397-2
paper, 247 pages
$19.95

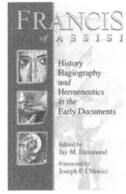

Francis of Assisi
History, Hagiography and Hermeneutics in the Early Documents

978-1-56548-199-2
paper, 280 pages
$19.95

The Lady
978-1-56548-221-0
paper, 461 pages
$39.95

The Saint
978-1-56548-1
paper, 640 pages

The Founder
978-1-56548-112-1
paper, 880 pages

The Prophet
978-1-56548-114-5
paper, 880 pages

Index
978-156548-1
paper, 240 pages

For more information visit: www.newcitypress.com

New City Press

New City Press is one of more than 20 publishing houses sponsored by the Focolare, a movement founded by Chiara Lubich to help bring about the realization of Jesus' prayer: "That all may be one" (John 17:21). In view of that goal, New City Press publishes books and resources that enrich the lives of people and help all to strive toward the unity of the entire human family. We are a member of the Association of Catholic Publishers.

www.newcitypress.com
202 Comforter Blvd.
Hyde Park, New York

Periodicals
Living City Magazine
www.livingcitymagazine.com

Scan to join our mailing list
for discounts and promotions
or go to www.newcitypress.com
and click on "join our email list."